Suspect Citizens

Suspect Citizens

Women, Virtue, and Vice in Backlash Politics

Jocelyn M. Boryczka

TEMPLE UNIVERSITY PRESS
PHILADELPHIA

TEMPLE UNIVERSITY PRESS
Philadelphia, Pennsylvania 19122
www.temple.edu/tempress

Library of Congress Cataloging-in-Publication Data

Boryczka, Jocelyn M.
    Suspect citizens : women, virtue, and vice in backlash politics /
Jocelyn M. Boryczka.
        p. cm.
    Includes bibliographical references and index.
    ISBN 978-1-4399-0893-8 (cloth : alk. paper) —
ISBN 978-1-4399-0894-5 (pbk. : alk. paper) —
ISBN 978-1-4399-0895-2 (e-book)   1. Women—Political
activity—United States.   2. Feminist ethics—United
States.   3. Political participation—United States.   I. Title.
    HQ1236.5.U6B67 2012
    320.082—dc23

                                                                    2012003232

Printed in the United States of America

2 4 6 8 9 7 5 3 1

For Tony—always

Contents

Acknowledgments

Projects such as this one result from the support and engagement of so many that acknowledging them all is a nearly impossible task. Here I recognize some of the people and institutions that factored significantly in the process of bringing this project to completion.

Many people contributed to the thinking behind this book. Joan Tronto, in particular, encouraged me to exercise curiosity by letting it lead me into unexpected spaces and to imagine alternative possibilities. Her thoughtful and analytic input has informed this project since its inception. Mary Hawkesworth, Wendy Sarvasy, Claire Snyder-Hall, Traci Levy, Dan Engster, Jill Locke, Edwina Barvosa, Katie Young, Bill Niemi, and Sara Brill, at different stages, offered critique, input, advice, and intellectual engagement that strengthened the book and propelled it forward.

Fairfield University provided institutional support through a pre-tenure leave and summer research grant. The Sophia Smith Collection at Smith College awarded me a travel-to-collections research grant. The Sexuality Information and Education Council of the United States (SIECUS) allowed me access to its extensive archival collection of sex education manuals. Alex Holzman and the team at Temple University Press offered critical support for the book as well as editorial and production assistance that greatly benefitted the final product. Reviewers of the manuscript also provided constructive and insightful commentary that strengthened this work.

Many friends and colleagues have been important to sustaining me while this project took shape. Sara Brill and Susanna Jones have thought through moments of this book with me, made me laugh, and shared the ups and downs of the journey. The WKWAs—Ronni Michelle

Greenwood; Dorinda Tetens; Tracy Steffy; Effie MacLachlan; Susanna Jones; Benz, my erstwhile dissertation writing partner; and Jennifer Leigh Disney, who worked to find this book a good home at a crucial point in its journey—remained integral to this project from the beginning. Stephen Pimpare always encouraged me to keep going, and Neal and Susan Kennedy have sustained me through many years of friendship.

The Fairfield University community has been very supportive of this endeavor. Members of the Politics Department—Marcie Patton, Eunsook Jung, Gwen Alphonso, David Downie, Janie Leatherman, and Kevin Cassidy—provide a collegial, convivial environment in which to work, a key factor in doing intellectual labor. Jerelyn Johnson, Emily Orlando, Ryan Drake, Nels Pearson, Liz Langran, Paul Lakeland, Elizabeth Petrino, Melissa Quan, Kris Sealey, Gisela Gil-Egui, Robbin Crabtree, Renée White, and Jim Bowler, to name only a few, all offered their professional input and personal friendship in ways that nurture a scholar's spirit. My students at Fairfield University, who inspire and challenge me, collectively have made an indelible mark on this book.

Family members also play an important part in the support necessary to complete such a project. My mom, Patricia Michaels, has shared stories from the front lines of feminism that shaped her life and, as a result, this book. The boys (Big and Little Fella) always make me smile. And this project simply would not have been possible without my partner in life, Tony Acevedo, whose belief in me is unrelenting and whose emotional and material support, which grants me the space to do this work, is invaluable. This book is dedicated to him. While this community of family, friends, and colleagues has shaped this project, any flaws or limitations remain my sole responsibility.

Suspect Citizens

Introduction

Moral Guardians but Suspect Citizens:
Women, Virtue, and Vice in the Western
Political Imaginary

F ive thousand women formed the Jeannette Rankin Brigade Protest on January 15, 1968, when they descended on Washington, D.C., to petition Congress to end the Vietnam War. Protest organizers encouraged participants to use as leverage their traditional roles as mothers and wives to gain a sympathetic hearing from legislators. The New York Radical Feminists (NYRF) rejected this conventional strategy and, carrying picket signs in gloved hands, marched amid thousands to stage a protest within a protest.[1] This small band of thirty women dressed all in black walked behind a huge blow-up doll wearing a blank face, blonde curls, and feminine garb. The doll floated above a coffin draped with the trappings of womanhood—curlers, garters, hairspray cans, and S&H Green Stamps. A funeral dirge lamenting women's traditional roles played in the background. Streamers waved in the air proclaiming, "DON'T CRY! RESIST!" and "TRADITIONAL WOMANHOOD IS DEAD!" Dramatizing this point further, the NYRF held a mock burial for Traditional Womanhood later that night at Arlington Cemetery. These events mark how second wave feminism came to identify and challenge Traditional Womanhood as a cultural icon of femininity and morality that obstructs women's access to equal rights and liberation.

Traditional Womanhood also points to a paradox in the ideological construction of American women's relationship to the political sphere. Kathie Sarachild (formerly Kathie Amatniek) conveys this paradox in her "Funeral Oration for the Burial of Traditional Womanhood," which she delivered to the five hundred women who gathered for the mock burial at Arlington Cemetery following the Jeanette Rankin Brigade Protest. Her oration urges women to abandon their traditional sex roles as wives and mothers. Any power derived from these roles, Sarachild declares, "is only a substitute for power. . . . [T]hat it really amounts to nothing politically, is the reason why all of us attending this funeral must bury traditional womanhood tonight" right alongside icons of traditional manhood at the national monument to war.[2] This absence of real political power derives from the female submissiveness required of Traditional Womanhood. Despite this politically disempowering sex role, women, however, remain integral to the nation's political future. Sarachild indicates this incongruity by linking "the woman problem" to other problems confronting American democracy such as the Vietnam War, stating that, "we cannot hope to move toward a better world or even a truly democratic society at home until we begin to solve our own problems."[3] The paradox, then, is that women play a critical part in determining American democracy's fate, while at the same time, they lack the political power to participate fully in the processes that actually chart the nation's course.

Understanding this paradox and its political implications for women involves unpacking how gendered traits such as female submissiveness animate symbols of women's political role. Traditional Womanhood's virtues, such as piety, chastity, and modesty, and vices, such as promiscuity and infidelity, become essential factors in charting the moral dynamics that shape American women's citizenship. Virtue and vice, as their omission from Sarachild's oration suggests, however, generally remain marginal to studies of women's political identity. This book moves virtue *and* vice to the center of analysis in order to spotlight how morality frames women's paradoxical relationship to political power.

Female virtue, in particular, facilitates the mobilization of backlash politics against women's progress toward equality and freedom.[4] Second wave feminism's challenge to Traditional Womanhood struck such a deep moral chord within the American polity that nearly three decades of backlash politics have ensued. The Right and family values advocates use female virtue as a tool to attempt to preserve the family and women's traditional role in it. The New Right formed in response to congressional approval of the Equal Rights Amendment (ERA) in 1972 and the United States Supreme Court's legalization of abortion in *Roe v. Wade* in 1973. The New Right joined ranks behind leaders such as Reverend Jerry Falwell, who formed the Moral Majority, and Phyllis Schlafly, who organized the Eagle Forum. The ERA and abortion rights represented the force of the 1960s Sexual Revolution, a historical marker used by religious and social conservatives to reference a decline in morality, the rise of social problems, and the general decay of the American way of life. To resolve this national crisis, the Right campaigned to reestablish the moral belief system and traditional institutions of heterosexual marriage and the family supposedly abandoned by women who exercised sexual freedom and entered the workplace. Women's return to Traditional Womanhood as the symbolic standard of female virtue would, the Right hoped, reset the nation's moral compass to where it was before the Sexual Revolution.

"Family values" debates subsequently gained momentum throughout the 1990s and brought virtue back into the public eye when social conservatives, communitarians, and some liberals advocated that traditional morality could cure the social ills spread by the Sexual Revolution. Social conservative William Bennett's *The Book of Virtues*, a primer designed to help parents teach their children the proper moral character for citizenship, climbed to the top of the *New York Times* best-seller list, an indicator of how returning to virtues such as responsibility, self-discipline, and faith spoke to many Americans. Other social conservatives such as Gertrude Himmelfarb argued that the social revolutions of the 1960s started a tectonic shift from virtues to values that generated a much more significant moral revolution by ushering in the subjectivity and relativism capable of undoing the social order.[5] Communitarians such as Mary Ann Glendon pointed to how, in the wake of the 1960s, liberalism gave rise to "rights talk" and a rampant individualism that caused Americans to lose the virtue necessary to bond citizens together in a community through a set of shared moral beliefs.[6] Liberals, including Stephen Macedo, William Galston, and Peter Berkowitz, took issue with this particular communitarian claim. Liberal democracy, they assert, inherently possesses virtues that emanate from voluntary associations and the family, granting the liberal tradition the moral vitality necessary to revive community.[7] Despite different ideological orientations, these thinkers share the view that democratic citizenship demands a particular moral character and that saving American democracy from moral and, thus, political disorder requires cultivating virtue.

The family, these social conservatives, communitarians, and liberals further agree, acts as a "seedbed of virtue" from which grows flourishing citizens who acquire a solid moral education and the strong familial roots that allow democracy to thrive. Glendon conveys the essence of this position when she asserts that "the state of the nation's child-raising families is also importantly linked to the fate of the American experiment in liberal democracy."[8] Women, who do most of the child rearing, play a key part in determining this experiment's success or failure given their traditional role in the family, one that changed dramatically starting in the 1960s. Female virtue, then, helps advocates for family values illustrate how important women's traditional roles as wives and mothers are to the nation's future.

This "back to virtue" position took a decidedly sharp turn to the Right after President George W. Bush took office in 2000. Calls in the 1990s by commentators such as Wendy Shallitt for American women to embrace "a return to modesty" to relieve the stress and anxiety caused by the Sexual Revolution became the moral grounds for certain social policies advanced by the Christian Right.[9] The abstinence movement, led by organizations such as the Christian-based group that developed True Love Waits, a campaign best known for devising the virginity pledge (which, it claims, 2.4 million American teens have signed), rejects sexual liberation and advocates for chastity. This moral position translated into national public policy.

Beginning in the mid-1990s, forty-eight states received nearly $1 billion in federal funding to support abstinence-only programs over the next decade, and 86 percent of America's public school districts mandated that sex education curricula promote abstinence.[10] The expansion of these programs resulted from the Bush administration's dramatic increase in federal support for them. The Community-Based Abstinence Education program, the most lucrative federal funding stream for abstinence-only sex education programs, distributed grants to state and local organizations totaling $100 million in 2005 alone.[11] These programs use a character-based curriculum designed to promote, particularly for young women, the traditional virtues of chastity and modesty. The pendulum swung back toward comprehensive sex education when the Obama administration dropped all abstinence-until-marriage funds from its 2010 federal budget. This shift, nonetheless, still anchors sex education policy in abstinence, exemplifying how the "back to virtue" position translates into this and other federal social policies designed to enforce female virtues and return Americans to their traditional moral foundation.

"Back to virtue" advocates and second wave feminists such as Kathie Sarachild, though with quite different political goals in mind, similarly recognize the paradoxical link between women's political role and democracy's fate. To understand the implications of this paradox for women's citizenship, this study focuses on aspects of second wave feminism and the ongoing backlash against it, along with comparable junctures earlier in American political history, when those who fight for women's citizenship, rights, and liberation have been and continue to be portrayed as threats to democracy's future in a way that resonates powerfully with many Americans. The question driving this analysis then remains: What elements of the American political script allow such backlashes to be triggered against women's struggle for full citizenship?

Female virtue and vice, working in tandem as a dualism, I argue, can trigger backlash politics because these concepts represent a set of gendered moral beliefs embedded in the American political script that define women's political role in terms of what I call suspect citizenship. At its most basic level, citizenship signifies membership in a political community and entails obligations that reflect certain societal values. Suspect citizenship here refers to women's tenuous membership in the political community that derives from the paradox of their moral responsibility for either democracy's success or its failure despite their lack of formal political power relative to male citizens. Turning explicit attention to female virtue and, most importantly, vice reveals the precarious nature of American women's political position.

Female virtue—basically defined as the standards of excellence established for women by the political community—often plays a part in explaining how American women gained political status as protectors of the family. The private sphere of tradition, religion, and morality grants women the virtue to anchor the nation against the political and economic cycles of change inherent to liberal democracy and market capitalism. Feminist historians capture this dimension of women's political role in various ways reflecting different historical contexts that range from the Republican Mother and Wife to the Victorian era's Traditional Woman and the New Woman of the 1950s. Here I use the term "moral guardianship" to capture a shared dimension underlying these historical symbols of women that conveys a theme running throughout the American political script: female moral virtue, regardless of changing political contexts, entails a double burden of moral responsibility that extends from the private sphere to the common good and becomes a civic obligation that neither women nor any other class of citizens could fulfill. This double burden places such a heavy political weight on women as moral guardians that flaws in female moral character can rise to the level of jeopardizing American democracy's future. Moral guardianship, furthermore, intersects with race and class since it references those belonging to the white upper and middle class, who serve as the standard of moral excellence for all American women. Female virtue and moral guardianship, however, only explain one part of this story.

Female vice acts as the crucial, though often overlooked, negative moral counterpart to virtue. This default moral category encompasses any deviation by women from the standards of virtue and can entail social and legal penalties. Female vice, then, poses an ever-present threat to political order and stability that puts the political community's trust in women's ability to uphold their moral and, thus, civic obligation to liberal democracy in question. It is this interplay between female virtue and vice that, given the possibility that women may at any time deviate from the virtuous path, creates the conditions of mistrust necessary to place their citizenship under suspicion. Suspect citizenship captures how women's morality undermines their legitimacy and, thereby, their capacity to be full members of the political community. This book's central argument is that identifying the gendered dynamics of virtue and vice exposes a paradox in the ideological construction of American women's political role that casts them as suspect citizens, a precarious political position that makes women vulnerable targets in backlash politics and seriously impedes the possibility of their full citizenship.

To make this argument, I develop a conceptual history of virtue and vice limited to key points in the American political script when women push against the preconceived conditions of their political membership, which sets backlash politics into motion. This study adds to a growing body of work in feminist political theory on citizenship by revealing how women's morality shapes their political role as suspect citizens. Its primary focus, however, is on creating a conceptual history of virtue and vice that contributes to the revisioning of political concepts in feminist political theory and addresses issues central to feminist ethics and democratic theory. A feminist perspective turns particular attention to how these concepts operate in relationship to women and reveals certain internal and external gendered dynamics of virtue and vice. These concepts, I argue throughout this book, anchor a moral belief system that erects four key barriers to women's full citizenship: inequality, constraint, exclusion, and suspicion. This conceptual history suggests that it may be necessary for feminist political theory to go beyond virtue and vice in order to continue developing an ethics more consistent with democratic values and goals. This study concludes by outlining collective responsibility as a starting point for considering an alternative to the virtue-vice paradigm that may overcome its barriers and move toward a more democratic feminist ethics.

Defining Virtue and Vice

The etymology of virtue and vice introduces the way in which sex, gender, and sexuality determine the contours of these two moral categories. Virtue, according to the *Oxford English Dictionary* (*OED*), originates in the Latin root *vir*, meaning "man." Its etymology splits into two gendered branches. The masculine branch relates to the physical strength arising from male sexual potency conveyed by terms such as "virile," a characteristic of male strength or force, and "virility," the masculine quality of sexual maturity and vigor marked by the ability to procreate. The feminine branch stems from *virago*, a man-like, heroic woman or female warrior, indicating how women must adopt masculine qualities in order to acquire moral worth. The *OED* then jumps to the Judeo-Christian tradition, which focuses on the "virgin," an unmarried, chaste woman devoted to God, in a manner similar to the Virgin Mary, and underscores the religious dimension of virtue's historical development. Chastity, in contrast to the value placed on active male sexual activity, becomes the primary female virtue consistently assigned to women. Male and female sexuality, whether in terms of virility or virginity, mold virtue's meaning in gendered and sexual ways that foreshadow how assumptions about masculinity, femininity, and heterosexuality will determine moral standards of excellence. Men and women who adhere to their sex's assigned virtues receive the social and political rewards of status and recognition within their political community.

Vice operates as an enforcement mechanism that carries social and, at times, legal penalties for those who deviate from virtuous behaviors, particularly those related to sex and sexuality. The *OED* defines vice as "depravity/corruption of morals; evil, immoral, or wicked habits of conduct; indulgence in degrading pleasures/practices; a habit or practice of an immoral, degrading or wicked character." This moral category encompasses a wide range of behaviors extending from ordinary moral flaws such as hypocrisy and snobbery to evil habits and even legally punishable offenses. The way in which society attributes vice to men and women indicates a sexual double standard illustrative of sex and sexuality's centrality to this moral category. Vice, according to the *OED*, for example, originates in the United States to reference certain crimes such as prostitution, drinking, and gambling. Women who engage in such vices, unlike men whose same actions society usually deems as less harmful and part of "being a man," often encounter stiff social and legal penalties, a situation reflective of the sexual double standard.

Men and women, however, similarly endure harsh consequences for breaking with certain sexual standards of virtue that uphold patriarchy. Prostitution, for instance, represents the epitome of female vice as the antithesis of the female virtues of modesty, chastity, and fidelity, and triggers legal punishment because it threatens to undermine the bonds of monogamous marriage. Homosexuality, in a similar vein, challenges traditional conceptions of virtue rooted in male sexual virility exercised in relation to women. Men who sexually identify with other men also abandon the heterosexual norms that uphold men's sexual domination over women, a power dynamic critical to patriarchy. These sets of behaviors can result in criminal charges ranging from public indecency to disorderly conduct and prostitution, which suggests the political importance of regulating heterosexual sex and sexuality. Vice overall serves both as a default moral category for all nonvirtuous behaviors and as a marker for deviance from normative standards that support patriarchy and heterosexuality and morally justify social and legal consequences for men and women.

Underscoring how virtue and vice function as a dualism, defined as two oppositional categories that never overlap, marks an important contribution to a feminist understanding of these political concepts. An inherent duality appears in the *OED*'s definition of virtue as "conformity of life and conduct with the principles of morality; voluntary observance of the recognized moral laws and standards of right conduct; abstention on moral grounds from any form of wrong-doing or vice." Virtue's meaning, then, derives from its oppositional relationship to vice.

Feminist political theorists and philosophers have long recognized how dualisms such as public-private, man-woman, culture-nature, and reason-emotion shape a way of knowing the world in terms of gendered either/or categories. Indeed the male-public and female-private spheres lay the groundwork for women's inequality and exclusion from political participation. Carole Pateman's *The Sexual Contract*, for instance, shows how a man and woman enter into a sexual contract grounded in procreation, which, although the basis for political community, remained invisible to social contract theorists such as John Locke, who erected a high barrier between public and private life. This male public–female private dualism perpetuates women's oppression and subordination by exempting them from the contract's promise of political equality and freedom. Virtue and vice, I argue in a similar vein, belong to the series of dualisms identified by feminist political theorists that work against feminist and democratic values by maintaining women's inequality, constraint, exclusion, and suspicion.

Defining virtue and vice as a dualism that functions within historical contexts further exposes how it sustains oppressive ways of knowing the world over time. "Even the ancient forms [of dualisms] do not necessarily fade away," Val Plumwood explains, "because their original context has changed; they are often preserved in our conceptual framework as residues, layers of sediment deposited by past oppressions. So old oppressions stored as dualisms facilitate and break the path for new ones."[12] The virtue-vice dualism acts as a conduit for channeling "old oppressions" into new historical contexts by translating ancient Judeo-Christian, Puritan, and Victorian conceptions, among others, about women's morality into the twenty-first century. This perspective grants insight into how the virtue-vice dualism conveys traditional moral beliefs about women, which fuel backlash politics, from one time period to the next and spreads within the broader community to marginalized or "suspect" communities.

The specific virtues and vices attributed to women in the American political script reveal a previously unseen dynamic internal to these two concepts, identified here as the infinite and finite. These two dimensions of virtue and vice link women's individual moral behavior—the finite—to an expansive responsibility for the common good—the infinite—which uncovers how these concepts operate in relation to women to create the double burden of moral responsibility. Finite virtue and vice refer to the tangible, physical activities visible to and easily assessed by others that, according to the standards established by the dominant political culture and its traditions, constitute moral or immoral behavior. Society often relies on cues from women's demeanor, dress, and sexual activity to determine whether their actions align with the finite female virtues of cheerfulness, chastity, modesty, and fidelity, or with vices such as promiscuity, immodesty, and infidelity.

Infinite virtue and vice refer to the intangible, unseen internal workings of moral character that transcend the material world and guide women's actions based on a higher, often godly, purpose. Religion serves as a key factor in this infinite capacity for moral purity emanating from a spiritual orientation toward the sacred. Piety and sacrifice, two infinite female virtues, indicate, for instance, how women's affiliation with religious faith enables them to give up the self for family and country. This expansive quality emanates from the spiritual origins of female virtue, which allows women, not men, to encompass something as amorphous as the common good. Infinite female vice derives from Eve's original sin, which allows society to hold women morally culpable for an endless number of vices, including the nation's fall into moral decay.

Together, infinite and finite female virtue and vice illustrate how the internal dynamics of these concepts establish women's double burden of moral responsibility. The observable finite behaviors link to the infinite, extending moral responsibility from the individual to the entire society and its future. In this way, women's adherence to finite virtues such as modesty and chastity relate to the viability of the American family and the success of the democratic experiment. Such an expansive responsibility for the nation's future extends beyond the capacity of any one class of citizens, much less an economically, socially, and politically vulnerable one.

Here I define these two concepts based on their gendered etymology, dualistic relationship, and infinite and finite dimension: virtue and vice are a dualism characterized by infinite and finite mechanisms that operate in tandem to enforce the internal and external moral standards established by the dominant political class and its traditions.[13] This definition locates these concepts in a contextual reality where political power is critical to determining what constitutes virtue and vice and for whom. Framing virtue and vice as a dualism facilitates tracking these relationships of power since it clarifies the moral boundary between them, which shifts according to changing political contexts. This political aspect becomes visible by examining these moral concepts through a feminist lens that spotlights the gendered dynamics of virtue and vice. To do so, I focus primarily on sex and gender and take the variables of race, class, religion, and sexuality into account as they relate to these two factors. A gendered perspective helps to explain the paradox in women's political identity by revealing the precarious nature of women's morality, which results in suspect citizenship and perpetuates backlash politics. This approach further sheds light on dynamics internal to virtue and vice that include an etymology rooted in masculine and feminine traits and the inequality inherent to dualisms. Renaming specific virtues and vices, reframing virtue and vice, or separating their moral from their civic dimension may not resolve particular problems with these concepts, making more evident the need to move beyond them in order to achieve a democratic feminist ethics.

Virtue and Vice in Contemporary Political Theory: Displacing Women and Politics

Virtue has recaptured political theorists' attention. The gendered operations of virtue and particularly vice remain relatively marginal to this resurgent interest, however, as indicated by the absence of an article on virtue or vice in *The Blackwell's Encyclopedia of Political Thought*. Works central to the study of political concepts such as James Farr and colleagues' *Political Innovation and Conceptual Change*, which examines political concepts including constitution, patriotism, and corruption, also omit virtue and vice. The growing body of literature in feminist political theory that revisions political concepts ranging from freedom and equality to justice and care also does not include work that explicitly analyzes virtue and vice. Such a gap in contemporary and feminist political theory reflects how virtue and vice function in the American political script to displace women and politics.

Two general ways of thinking, reflective of this point, shape the debate about the relationship between morality and politics in contemporary political theory. John Rawls in *A Theory of Justice* claims that "justice is the first virtue of social institutions, as truth is of systems of thought."[14] This liberal perspective favors moral neutrality and pushes other virtues to the margins of the political sphere. In *After Virtue*, Alasdair MacIntyre criticizes Rawls for radically circumscribing morality in political life by attending only to the external goods distributed by social institutions and, thus, failing to account for the internal goods that make up each citizen's moral character. MacIntyre offers an alternative position inclusive of multiple virtues designed to address his deep concern about the disorder of contemporary morality arising from the 1960s. Identity politics, he asserts, disconnected the people from their human *telos*, or understanding of their end as determined by human existence, and a unified conception of political community. A vibrant polity requires many virtues in addition to justice, MacIntyre contends, in order to establish the moral standards that emanate from human *telos* and will reconnect citizens to their community and moral tradition. MacIntyre's criticism of Rawls sparked the liberal-communitarian debate that left behind a dualistic legacy locking political theorists, particularly communitarians and feminists, into a monolithic approach based on binary oppositions. Thinking about morality and politics, as a result, narrowed into either/or categories that delimit the complexity required of democratic politics and attention to the status of women.[15]

In a vein similar to MacIntyre, communitarians hope to reconnect people with traditions primarily through virtues in order to secure a moral consensus that will bind them closer to their political communities.

Amatai Etzioni proposes a "sociology of virtue" that, by returning to the moral standards of the 1950s, blends the order of a virtue tradition with the freedom of modernity to enable Americans to escape the moral relativism ushered in during the 1960s.[16] William Galston, sharing this concern about moral relativism, turns to the liberal democratic tradition. He argues that liberalism requires certain virtues such as tolerance, independence, honor, and self-restraint, which can generate moral consensus around a common good. Communitarians, importantly, locate people within community, a position that contributes to a fuller understanding of the moral subject than liberalism's individualism. They, however, ultimately circumscribe the fullness of this understanding by displacing both women and politics.

Invoking tradition, whether that of the 1950s or liberalism, displaces serious political concerns, particularly for women as the keepers of virtue and morality in marriage and family. Communitarians portray these two social institutions as essential to cultivating the virtue needed for a stable political community. Yet they fail to consider how political power determines women's role in the private sphere. Further shifting attention away from public life, communitarians also focus on voluntary associations such as religious and civic organizations as critical to mending America's tattered moral fabric. A relatively vacuous sense of political community removed from social contexts and the diverse identities of the people who live in them results. Communitarians sidestep political issues related to women, power, and inclusion, which, I find, undermines their efforts to reinvigorate democratic community and leads them to ignore important questions about the virtues on which they rely and the vices that they avoid. Are these concepts consistent with the democratic values of freedom, equality, and inclusion? How do virtue and vice affect different classes of citizens such as women?

Contemporary feminist political theorists, in contrast, do include women. Yet they too struggle with women's relationship to the dominant ways of thinking about morality and politics, a framework that displaces certain aspects of politics. Many feminist theorists, recognizing the limits of Rawls, agree with MacIntyre that justice simply is not enough because it results in a thin conception of the moral subject and political life. Care, a trait traditionally associated with women in the private sphere, some feminist theorists argue, offers an alternative on which to base a feminist ethic. Grounded in the practices and emotions definitive of all human life, which requires giving and receiving care, a feminist ethic of care, then, contributes to a fuller understanding of what constitutes the moral subject as well as the practices and relationships necessary to sustain political community.

Whether care is a virtue, however, remains an open question. Some care theorists such as Virginia Held define care as a virtue, while others such as Joan Tronto remain less convinced. Other feminist political theorists who turn to specific, well-known virtues further indicate how unsettled the issue of virtue remains. Sarah Hoagland's *Lesbian Ethics: Toward New Values*, for instance, illustrates the debilitating effects of feminine virtues such as self-sacrifice and altruism on feminist, especially lesbian, ethics. She argues for abolishing these particular virtues and replacing them with others. Holloway Sparks turns to the traditionally masculine virtue of courage and makes a compelling argument for revisioning it from a feminist perspective in order to develop courage into a tool for women's political resistance.[17] These feminist political theorists and communitarians, though from different vantage points, greatly contribute to a fuller understanding of the moral subject and, thus, a political life inclusive of multiple virtues that could allow room for care, justice, and others in the public sphere.

The theoretical, historical, and political traditions and functions of virtue and vice, particularly as they relate to women, I contend, need further consideration before moving in this direction toward multiple virtues. Instead of asking if care, courage, self-sacrifice, or altruism should be considered virtues, we should ask if virtue is a concept consistent with the political circumstances and goals of contemporary feminism. Answering this question will facilitate addressing certain political dynamics displaced by focusing on women's relationship to specific virtues.

Feminist political theorists who directly examine virtue and vice illustrate how both concepts function to displace attention to politics. Bonnie Honig, though aware of virtue's etymology, establishes the theoretical framework of *Political Theory and the Displacement of Politics* on the categories of virtue and *virtù*. She does so without considering their gendered dynamics, qualities, or political usages. Contrary to her overall purpose then, Honig displaces a major political issue pertaining to gendered difference by dismissing its importance to how virtue functions.[18]

Selma Sevenhuijsen, in her work on citizenship and care, does identify how virtue negatively affects women.[19] She then uses virtue interchangeably with terms such as "values" and "perspectives." This creates a "slippage problem," meaning that virtue, seemingly synonymous with these other terms, appears as a gender-neutral concept equivalent to them. The way in which gender operations determine the power dynamics within and between virtue and vice are displaced or moved outside the immediate area of focus.

Vice, despite its dualistic relationship to virtue, usually is analyzed independently of virtue. Feminist political theorists such as Claudia Card and Sarah Hoagland who address the implications of negative morality for women frame the issue in terms of evil, not vice.[20] Judith Shklar's *Ordinary Vices*, though not a feminist work, directly examines the vices of liberalism such as snobbery, hypocrisy, and cruelty. She argues that such ordinary vices are necessary to liberal democracy in order to show that the moral perfectionism promoted by a virtue-based position such as MacIntyre's actually undermines democracy. A diverse and tolerant society, Shklar contends, requires moral ambiguity if citizens hope to navigate its often conflictual, complex terrain and to accept a range of differences in identities, interests, and opinions. Shklar, who avoids the gendered dynamics of vice or virtue, implies that ignoring, dismissing, or failing to recognize the importance of how such concepts operate closes off spaces for political engagement. The ambiguous status of virtue and vice in feminist political theory, taking a cue from Shklar, should provide a space rich with potential for political exploration.

Women's long association with virtue in the private sphere and the use of vice to keep them there raises a further question. Why have virtue and vice eluded conceptual analysis despite the attention of feminist political theorists to so many other political concepts and critical ethical issues? One explanation may relate to virtue's acceptance as a standard of moral excellence that has enabled American women to translate moral superiority into political power. Feminist historians such as Linda Kerber and Mary Beth Norton helped to establish this important perspective on virtue by contending that republican mothers of America's founding era stabilized the new nation by transmitting virtue to their husbands and children.[21] Claire Snyder looks to nineteenth-century

American women's civic activism to argue for a radical civic virtue as necessary for providing a sense of public-spiritedness in democratic republics that generates social reform on behalf of the common good.[22] Virtue and moral superiority, I agree, benefit women by granting them political power and advancing a sense of the common good important to social reform. Yet virtue, synonymous with moral excellence, appears to be a positive good, or what Nancy Hirschmann and Christine Di Stefano call an "innocent" concept, that does not require interrogation or revisioning.[23] This positive value inherent to virtue, I contend, can deflect attention away from its negative implications for women and the importance of vice.

Another explanation arises from the dualistic function of virtue and vice that closes off avenues for exploring other ways of thinking about how morality relates to politics. Vice, as such, remains generally absent from feminist considerations of virtue. Also, feminist political theorists who challenge virtue, according to the either/or logic of this moral framework, find themselves in the uncomfortable and politically dangerous position of advocating for vice. The virtue-vice dualism, then, can limit how we imagine the moral universe, which displaces difficult questions about whether and how to revision these two political concepts.

The ambiguous status of virtue and vice in contemporary and feminist political theory illustrates how these concepts displace either women, politics, or both while simultaneously making them, though in different ways, as the feminist and communitarian approaches suggest, central to it—the paradox of primary interest in this book. This conceptual history, alternatively, locates women and politics at the center of analysis in order to achieve two goals. First, examining virtue and vice from a gendered perspective begins to fill a gap in feminist and contemporary political theory by developing a conceptual history that challenges positive and negative assumptions about both concepts and examines how they operate in tandem as a dualism. The American political context provides the historical framework for identifying strengths and weaknesses of virtue and vice in order to determine their conceptual compatibility with a democratic feminist ethics. Doing so facilitates achieving the second goal, to offer a feminist response to communitarians and social conservatives who dominate the political discourse on virtue. A direct response to them on this point, I believe, will benefit feminists in the ongoing fight against the backlash and for women's full citizenship.

Methodological Matters

The conceptual histories approach used here to examine virtue and vice frames political concepts as "essentially contested," or key elements in understanding how people create political change.[24] Feminist political theorists generally accept this view of political concepts, and those who engage in revisioning them, according to Hirschmann and Di Stefano, do so by using one of three approaches. First, they politicize concepts such as care and the family associated with the "nonpolitical" private sphere. Second, feminist political theorists rethink the gendered dimensions of essentially political concepts such as power and authority. Third, they challenge the "value-neutral" or uncontested nature of concepts essential to democracy such as freedom and justice.[25] This conceptual history employs all three approaches by politicizing virtue and vice by tracking their interconnected role in the private and public spheres and identifying their gendered implications. This project also challenges the value-neutral appearance of virtue as necessarily a positive moral good associated with human flourishing and vice as an assumed negative moral badness aligned solely with human degeneration. As moral standards of good and bad, right and wrong, virtue and vice often seem to be uncontested concepts inherited from tradition as opposed to deriving from ongoing political contestation. These generally uncontested normative assumptions, I argue, fall away in a feminist analysis that sheds light on their gendered and political dynamics and the way in which both concepts relate to women in the American political script, revealing their "essentially contested" nature.

The conceptual histories approach also engages concepts with normative value such as virtue and vice as important sites of political contestation. Normative concepts represent moral belief systems embedded in social and political traditions often emanating from religion that, when challenged, can trigger battles over political power. Virtue and vice's normative orientation deflects attention away from their political function since they serve as moral standards of "good" and "bad" for political action rather than as constitutive of that action. It is exactly the framing of virtue and vice in normative terms, I maintain, that makes these concepts essentially contested when groups such as second wave feminists and social conservatives fight over the opinions, interests, beliefs, and values involved in political change.

Contradictions between actions and ideas or beliefs are further spotlighted in this approach, which locates concepts in relation to political actors and historical contexts that here centralize virtue and vice in the struggle over how women's citizenship links to American democracy's fate. Language from this methodological perspective *constitutes* the political world to the same degree as observable actions such as a voter pulling the lever on election day or soldiers marching into battle. James Farr refers to this as "the linguistic constitution of politics."[26] This conveys how political actors use specific concepts to influence, negotiate, and alter the course of events given changing historical circumstances that determine different directions of language usage. Specific concepts correspond with a particular vocabulary that creates a shared set of meanings and a constellation of beliefs. Concepts, then, track change when a political context stretches the human imagination to the point that current frameworks, beliefs, actions, and practices no longer meet the current belief system's demands. Contradictions between political actions and beliefs often arise at these points and become evident in the ways that political actors struggle over specific concepts related to the set of beliefs being contested. These historical junctures offer the opportunity to identify how concepts contribute to political change.

Second wave feminism and the backlash against it represent such a juncture as political actors ranging from Kathie Sarachild to Reverend Jerry Falwell and Phyllis Schlafly fought to resolve a contradiction between women's role in American democracy and its belief system based on freedom, inclusion, and equality. On one level, this political context illustrates the contradiction between second wave feminists, who challenged women's traditional role as moral guardians, and advocates of backlash politics, who believe that preserving women's traditional role and female virtue would best protect American democracy. On another level, this battle reflects a much broader ideological war over a moral belief system built on the virtue-vice dualism that perpetuates inequality, constraint, and exclusion, thereby contradicting the feminist and democratic goals of full citizenship. Both levels of contradiction inform this conceptual history of virtue and vice. They reveal how the dualistic logic of these essentially contested political concepts act as pillars supporting a moral belief system that places women in the precarious political position antithetical to democratic values as suspect citizens.

The Plan of the Book

This study aims to determine how virtue and vice operate in the American political script when women struggle for full citizenship with the ultimate goal of identifying the strengths and weaknesses of these concepts in terms of further developing a democratic feminist ethics. Conceptual histories facilitate this type of analysis since, as Farr explains, they "tell the tales of conceptual change and political innovation. They narrate some stretch of human imagination—in belief, action, or practice— by tracing the emergence, transformation, and sometimes the demise of political concepts."[27] To do so, conceptual histories include three components that shape the plan of this book: the concept's point of emergence or prehistory and genesis, its location in theoretical constellations related to other concepts and political arguments, and its usage by political actors to achieve their political ends. These three elements guide this project in tracking the broader theoretical shifts necessary to understand how virtue and vice relate to developing a democratic feminist ethics. This book does not aim to offer a comprehensive history of the second wave, backlash politics, the other debates covered in its chapters, or virtue and vice in Western political thought. Key turning points in women's role in the American political script combine in each chapter with the purpose of understanding how virtue and vice operate in the political discourse accompanying certain struggles for women's freedom, inclusion, and equality. A significant contradiction between virtue and vice, and values consistent with democracy and feminism, as a result, becomes apparent, raising serious concerns about the compatibility of these two concepts with a democratic feminist ethics.

Chapter 1, "Conceptual Locations: Where Virtue, Vice, and Citizenship Intersect," outlines key conceptual locations or historical moments critical to changes in the gendered dynamics of virtue and vice in ancient and medieval Western political theory and in the modern political thought of Mary Wollstonecraft and Alexis de Tocqueville. While the long history of virtue and vice in Western political theory is well beyond the scope of this study, this chapter establishes the background for how these concepts operate in the American political script. Citizenship intersects with male and female virtue and vice, which change in relationship to the shifting boundary between public and private life. Chapter 1 tracks these shifts by focusing on two dimensions of virtue and vice—the moral, which typically aligns with the private sphere of the family and religion, and the civic, which generally connotes a broader awareness of the common good and public sphere. Conceptual movements of virtue and vice across moral and political boundaries, as we shall see, shape male and female citizenship differently at different historical junctures. The additional aspects of infinite and finite virtue and vice developed in this book pinpoint how an ever-shifting moral terrain determines the tenuous nature of women's citizenship. Uncertainty about women's commitment to the nation results, placing their legitimate membership in the political community in question. This suspicion fuels backlash politics, which gains momentum when women actively make a claim to their fuller inclusion in the American democratic community.

Chapter 2, "The Religious Roots of Moral Guardianship: American Women as the Daughters of Eve and Zion," examines second wave radical feminist Mary Daly's work in *Gyn/Ecology* and *Pure Lust* against the backdrop of Puritan discourse represented by Cotton Mather's writings and sermons. The Puritan context serves as a point of conceptual emergence for virtue and vice in the American political script. The apocalyptic biblical nature of early American Puritanism, which framed the New World as humanity's last hope for salvation, makes apparent the infinite aspect of virtue and vice as sacred, otherworldly, and beyond humanity's grasp, and the finite, its worldly, painfully human, counterpart. Cotton Mather's work captures the expansion of Puritan women's moral identity from the vice-ridden daughters of Eve to include the possibility of achieving virtue as the daughters of Zion. This shift roots American women's political identity in the borderlands between virtuous moral guardianship and vice-ridden suspect citizenship. Mary Daly's radical feminist theology challenges such patriarchal religious traditions in part by attempting to retrieve virtue and vice from Christianity's patriarchal tradition and redefine them in her metaethical project to advance women's liberation.

Two intertwined problems with virtue and vice become evident by reading Daly's work against Puritan discourse. The first is that of reversals, an internal moral dynamic inherent in dualisms such as virtue and vice that maintain hierarchy and inequality. Transcendence, the second problem, represents the spiritual realm associated with the infinite, which turns moral attention away from the material reality that feminists identify as critical to ethical decision making. Reversals and transcendence represent two intransigent problems inherent to the virtue-vice dualism that make it incommensurable with a democratic feminist ethics defined by its commitments to equality and freedom and its grounding in the material contexts and human relationships of everyday life. This dualistic moral logic, this chapter argues more broadly, remains a deeply embedded feature of the American political script that facilitates ongoing cycles of backlash politics.

Chapter 3, "'Back to Virtue' Backlash Politics: Privileging Irresponsibility," focuses on the backlash politics characterizing two national debates over education that illustrate how the virtue-vice dualism channels old forms of oppression into the contemporary context. Juxtaposing the republican era debates over expanding women's education and their access to it with the contemporary debates regarding abstinence-only versus comprehensive sex education illustrates how the dualistic logic of virtue and vice perpetuates a democratic politics held hostage by purity, chastity, and modesty. A paradox embedded in American women's political identity becomes evident when examining these debates over women's moral capacity to engage in the decision making necessary for legitimate citizenship: the nation entrusts women as moral guardians with the common good while mistrusting their ability to make decisions about their bodies and intimate relationships. Alternatively, male citizens retain the trust to protect women while they pose the greatest threat to them, in terms of violence and political oppression, and fail to possess the infinite capacity for virtue to ensure the nation's future. These two backlash discourses speak to a broader societal mistrust of the average man's and woman's ability to fulfill the responsibilities and obligations required of democratic citizenship. Privileging irresponsibility results to deflect average citizens' attention away from structural solutions to political problems and from interrogating standing moral assumptions that makes questioning certain virtues and vices dangerous. A nation's moral compass polarized by male and female virtue and vice may ultimately point in the direction of all American citizens being suspect.

Chapter 4, "Suspect Citizenship: From Lowell Mill Girls to Lesbian Feminists and Sadomasochism," brings together two seemingly disparate debates between nineteenth-century loyalist and rebellious Lowell mill girls and twentieth-century anti- and pro-sadomasochism (S/M) lesbian feminists to illustrate how embedded the virtue-vice dualism is in the American political script, where the moral logic of backlash politics operates even within marginalized political groups. These debates turn the spotlight on how vice functions in political discourse to locate those women who deviate from norms of moral behavior outside the protections of virtue and moral guardianship, making them suspect citizens. Participants in these two sets of debates internal to their communities, whether by working in a factory or loving other women, became suspect citizens as women associated with vice who challenged the dominant moral standards aligned with the patriarchal status quo. Despite this shared political vulnerability as suspect citizens who broke with traditional sex roles and sexuality, the moral dynamics of the virtue-vice dualism provided an effective means for the loyalists and anti-S/M lesbian feminists to leverage power against their opposition by redeploying the very moral logic used against them in the dominant political culture. Charged by their female counterparts with vice and, thereby, suspect citizenship, the rebels and pro-S/M lesbian feminists' writings reveal a libatory space in which these women function outside the dominant moral paradigm. This space enabled them to question the virtue-vice moral framework, consider other ethical possibilities, and effectively organize political action against the status quo. Such suspect citizens, from their position on the margins, this chapter contends, gain a particular theoretical vantage point from which "to see," or to have vision beyond an immediate reality in order to imagine the horizon of possible futures and ways to attain them.

Chapter 5, "'Ozzie and Harriet' Morality: Resetting Liberal Democracy's Moral Compass," revisits Alexis de Tocqueville's *Democracy in America* to determine how his separate spheres ideology informs contemporary backlash politics. Communitarians, in particular, often redeploy Tocqueville's view of the American family in their efforts to reset

America's moral compass back to the 1950s and what I call "Ozzie and Harriet" morality. This references the popular 1950s television show featuring the separate spheres for Ozzie Nelson and his wife, Harriet, who stays home while sending her husband and two sons, Ricky and David, off to face the world. "Ozzie and Harriet" morality here captures how the virtue-vice dualism channels Tocqueville's separate spheres ideology into contemporary debates over the family that frame American women's mass exodus from the kitchen to the workplace as an indicator of the nation's moral demise. Positioning the multiple virtues argument as put forward by Amatai Etzioni, William Galston, and Alasdair MacIntyre in relationship to Tocqueville's depiction of male and female virtue and vice in *Democracy in America* creates an analytic space for considering how moral assumptions about men's and women's roles in public and private life shift attention away from democratic politics. "Habitual inattention," Tocqueville states, "must be reckoned the great vice of the democratic spirit."[28] This chapter examines how the gendered moral logic of the virtue-vice dualism functions to perpetuate a vision of democratic politics predicated on a suspicion of men's and women's active and sustained engagement in it. The "Ozzie and Harriet" morality promoted in contemporary backlash politics holds broader implications for American liberal democracy by deflecting attention toward the family and civil society and away from public life as the space to address structural political problems. Habitual attention to politics becomes devalued and a marker of suspect citizens.

Chapter 6, "The Legacy of Virtue and Vice: Mary Wollstonecraft and Contemporary Feminist Care Ethics," brings Mary Wollstonecraft's *A Vindication of the Rights of Woman* into dialogue with feminist care ethics to address the question of whether care *should* be defined as a virtue. Reading contemporary feminist care ethics against Wollstonecraft's political thought on female virtue exposes how the legacy of virtue and vice perpetuates three problems for theorizing a feminist ethics that advances women's full citizenship: moral perfectionism, parochialism, and inequality. Structuring this analysis around these issues illustrates two central ways in which the legacy of virtue and vice subverts the purpose of feminist ethics. First, Wollstonecraft's work advances moral perfectionism, achieved by adhering to the virtuous standard of excellence, as the goal for men and women. This position, inherent to a virtue-based ethics, contradicts feminist ethics' grounding in the material realities of everyday life. Second, and surprisingly given her Victorian moral context, Wollstonecraft accounts for sex and sexuality, which starkly contrasts with their marginality in feminist care ethics despite its focus on relationships, emotions, contexts, and basic human needs. The moral logic of the virtue-vice dualism operates in feminist care ethics to deflect attention from sex and sexuality as two central aspects of human life generally aligned with female vice. This dualistic moral logic imports certain moral assumptions from one historical context to another, which, through the concepts of virtue and vice, as this analysis of feminist care ethics reveals, seriously inhibits freedom, equality, and inclusion. Care, understood as a political concept revisioned to advance democratic citizenship inclusive of women's ethical perspective, I argue as a result, should not be understood as a virtue.

The conclusion considers how to move beyond virtue and vice toward a democratic feminist ethics. This process, among other things, involves changing a dualistic epistemological perspective in order to shift our orientation from boundaries and borders to the frontiers of morality and politics. Collective responsibility acts as a point of departure for developing a feminist ethics that aligns more closely with its democratic goals of freedom, equality, and inclusion. Normative judgment, while remaining important to political decision making, becomes part of a negotiation process aimed at rethinking morality in terms of deliberation rather than inherited tradition. The democratic element of a feminist ethics centralizes politics in terms of participation and engagement as crucial aspects of democratic life deflected by the virtue-vice framework. The feminist dimension focuses attention on the role of responsibility in constructing women's political identity and how equalizing the double burden of responsibility is a necessary part of full citizenship for women. Thinking beyond virtue and vice, however, invites a consideration of moving beyond citizenship. The moral dynamics of the virtue-vice dualism tracked throughout this conceptual history specify how its inherent logic functions to include some in the political community while excluding others, leaving some such as women to exist on the borderlands as suspect citizens. Membership in a community requires boundaries and identities shaped in opposition to others, a vision of citizenship antithetical to a global understanding of politics that may be better conveyed through alternative concepts such as belonging.

Ignoring morality in politics shifts attention away from a critical aspect of democratic life that also generates cycles of backlash politics. Yet the question remains: How can the relationship between morality and politics be addressed without promoting the unity and certainty about certain moral standards associated with moralism? Going beyond virtue and vice to reimagine normative judgments as outcomes of continued negotiations carried out through deliberative processes, I argue, represents a key step in establishing a moral reference for society freed from a static tradition designed to remain unresponsive to changing political demands. This approach aims to put politics into morality and to recognize morality in politics as critical to resolving the paradox of women's suspect citizenship that perpetuates backlash politics.

1 | Conceptual Locations

*Where Virtue, Vice, and
Citizenship Intersect*

Virtue, vice, and citizenship belong to the tradition of Western political theory that, while beyond the scope of this study in its entirety, provides the background necessary for exploring how these concepts operate in the American political script. Key conceptual locations in ancient and medieval Western political theory and in the modern political thought of Mary Wollstonecraft and Alexis de Tocqueville capture how male and female virtue and vice change in relation to public and private life, which results in changes to citizenship. The infinite and finite aspects of virtue and vice intersect with their moral and civic dimensions to identify how the political community distributes moral responsibility unequally between men and women.

The moral and civic dimensions of virtue, which I extend to vice, specify how these movements shape changing ideas about citizenship at different historical junctures. *Moral* virtue and vice, broadly speaking, refer here to a belief system that emanates from tradition, social institutions, and often, though not necessarily, religious doctrine to provide individuals with the means to make normative judgments about right and wrong. Comparatively, *civic* virtue and vice, respectively, relate to a public-spiritedness or value attributed to an active commitment to the collective good and to behaviors associated with harming, damaging, and even destroying it. Oriented toward moral private and civic public life, these two dimensions of virtue and vice track how shifting and permeable boundaries determine the ways in which men and women engage in political life.

Exploring these conceptual locations in Western political theory prepares the groundwork for understanding how American women's citizenship remains rooted in morality compared with the civic nature of men's political membership. This moral grounding establishes women's infinite capacity for virtue or vice that holds them responsible for the common good to the point that it becomes their civic obligation. This precarious political position places their legitimate membership in the community in question. Trust, the necessary requirement for establishing the bond between government and its citizens, becomes attenuated for women, which generates uncertainty about their commitment to the nation despite their moral responsibility for it. Societal distrust and doubt manifest in a sustained suspicion that enables the polity to cast women as potential traitors to democracy. Backlash politics builds on such suspicion to mobilize particularly when women actively assert their claim to freedom, equality, and full inclusion as citizens in American democracy. This chapter introduces suspect citizenship as the framework developed throughout this book to help understand the moral triggers for American backlash politics.

Virtue and Vice in Ancient and Medieval Western Political Thought

The ancient Greek political thought of Plato and Aristotle establishes a deep connection between what is now identified as moral and civic virtue and vice and their gendered dynamics in Western political theory. The term for virtue—*arete*, a heroic excellence that humans should strive for in politics and on the battlefield—conveys how an individual's moral worth emanates from civic duty. Plato and Aristotle, using different means, link the political realm (*polis*) with virtue as the source of the good life or happiness (*eudaimonia*). This teleological view of virtue works from a fixed conception that virtue or the good exists and can be achieved through specific practices related to that ultimate good.

Reason (*logos*) and speech combine as human capacities that intersect with virtue and vice to establish the gendered nature of citizenship in Western political theory. Only male citizens in ancient Athens were perceived as possessing the capacity for reason and, thereby, the moral and civic virtue required of political participation. Women possessed the ability to speak; however, Athenian society viewed them as lacking the reason required for public deliberation, a necessity for political participation. Women's emotional nature and physical ability for childbearing, it was believed, rendered them too close to nature and less able to reason, which, for Plato and Aristotle, made women better suited for domestic life in the household (*oikos*).[1] Exclusion from the *polis* denied women access to the level of moral and civic virtue demanded of male citizens.

Given the dualistic nature of these concepts, women, by default, acquire an association with vice, or *kakia*, a term meaning "bad" or "ugly" in the sense of aesthetically displeasing and morally wrong.[2] Politically, this translates into women's civic vice. Aristotle and Plato identified women as sources of fear and corruption whose lesser capacity for reason threatened stability in Athens. Women's containment in the *oikos* served to control them by cordoning them off from the *polis* in the private sphere.[3] Thus, for the ancient Greeks, women's alignment with nature, a force well beyond human control, along with their diminished ability to reason and thus to exercise the moral virtue required of civic life, makes them suspect and establishes a central moral justification for denying them political citizenship in Western political theory.

Niccolò Machiavelli's medieval political thought sustains this suspicion of women through the interplay of male *virtù* and female *Fortuna*, in which men's and women's virtue and vice assume a political capacity that extends well beyond the ability of any group of people. *Virtù*, for Machiavelli, differs from the specific individual moral dispositions or virtue that men exhibit in the political arena. A civic commitment to the common good characterizes *virtù* that only men can exercise through active political participation and military service. Citizenship, then, demands that men cultivate a moral belief system strong enough to stall the republic's inevitable decline. Machiavelli enlists male citizens in a losing battle to protect the common good against the natural process of decay by exercising their moral strength.

Fortuna, embodied by women in Machiavelli's sexual politics, represents the greatest threat against which men must protect the republic.[4] A disruptive force of necessity and nature, women evoke desire and temptation in men, who must exercise the male virtues of self-discipline, fortitude, and courage to preserve the common good for as long as possible. Male *virtù* ultimately depends on men's ability to control their sexual nature. Excluding women from the political sphere limits their seductive influence on men. Women, unlike men, lack the ability to control their sexual nature, which makes them morally responsible for the republic's decline as a natural force of moral decay. Machiavelli's *Fortuna* captures how female vice acquires a civic dimension as a force of nature capable of destroying a political community.

Solidifying a monotheistic religious tradition during the medieval period, Christianity maintains women's primary association with vice as the daughters of Eve, who is held morally responsible for original sin and the Fall of humankind. Female and male vice acquire such a heavy moral weight in this context that individual character flaws easily transform into mortal sins, making vice difficult to discern from sin. The vices of vainglory, covetousness, lust/sexual desire, envy, gluttony, anger, and sloth in St. Thomas Aquinas's *Summa Theologica* transform into the seven deadly sins capable of condemning one's soul to eternal damnation. While the struggle against sin and evil characterized men's and women's moral lives, women still represented the primary moral threat to the political and religious community, which manifested in the witch trials and executions carried out by the church in its efforts to centralize power throughout the Middle Ages.[5] The infinite dimension of vice further becomes evident as an individual's behaviors acquire the capacity to determine his or her eternal fate, which, for women, remains inherently linked to the future of humankind.

Despite their responsibility for original sin, women gain access to moral virtue through Christianity's belief in the Virgin Mary, who symbolizes female chastity and purity, the antithesis of female moral vice characterized by uncontrollable sexual desire and temptation. As Christianity built its moral foundations on the cornerstones of virtue and vice during the medieval period, and faith in God eclipsed faith in the common good, this access to redemption for women gained further significance. Plato's four virtues—justice, courage, wisdom, and temperance—became codified as the cardinal virtues in the Christian tradition, while the Roman Catholic Church specified faith, hope, and charity as its core virtues. As the church assumed divine power within Europe's developing monarchies, exhibiting faith in God and loyalty to the monarch eclipsed active civic engagement as a marker of civic duty, essentially collapsing civic into moral virtue. Christine de Pizan's *The Book of the City of the Ladies* captures the moral and civic significance of women's acquisition of virtue. Her utopian City of the Ladies emanates from female moral virtues such as chastity, purity, and beauty, which allow this all-female society to achieve perfect peace and harmony. Attributing moral virtue to women encompasses a civic dimension linking them to, rather than excluding them from, political life.

Whereas Plato and Aristotle emphasize reason and Machiavelli *virtù*, Christianity locates religious faith as the factor determining moral and civic virtue and grants women access to this standard of excellence that assumes an infinite dimension beyond material reality or human capacity. Religion, the quest for the common good, and the ancient concept of reason combine in the American political script to construct women as suspect citizens. Their affiliation with religion in private life allows women to sustain moral virtue amid American democracy's civic vices and possess enough ability to reason to assume responsibility for the nation's common good while remaining the greatest threat to the nation's future. The suspect nature of American women's citizenship derives from their sustained association with political instability as it relates to their close connection with nature, emotion, and original sin. Suspicion of women's commitment to the nation, however, arises even more from their location between moral and civic, infinite and finite virtue and vice, which enables dominant forces in society to shift them back and forth across moral boundaries according to its particular political needs.

Modern Theoretical Groundings: Alexis de Tocqueville and Mary Wollstonecraft in America

Alexis de Tocqueville's *Democracy in America* and Mary Wollstonecraft's *A Vindication of the Rights of Woman* respond to a major shift in modern political thought that, while granting all humans reason to establish their capacity to consent to legitimate political authority, denies women citizenship on the basis of their moral virtue. Modern political theorists such as Jean-Jacques Rousseau construct women as sentimental wives elevated on a pedestal of moral virtue above the vice-ridden political world, belonging in the protected realm of the family, where they remain excluded from political life and civic virtue.[6] Tocqueville and Wollstonecraft, from differing perspectives, challenge this construction of the sentimental wife. Their work shows how cultivating women's reason through education and religion grants them moral *and* civic virtue and assigns women the double burden of moral responsibility that makes them suspect citizens.

Tocqueville's and Wollstonecraft's works receive detailed treatment here and in Chapters 5 and 6 because of their influence on Americans' understanding of women's morality and citizenship. *Democracy in America* captures America's democratic spirit in a way that still resonates with its citizens almost two hundred years after Tocqueville arrived on the nation's shores in 1830. His work remains integral to Americans' view of themselves as democratic citizens and even to the national imaginary.[7] Though less celebrated in mainstream American political thought, Wollstonecraft advances controversial claims for women's equality that locate her at the forefront of the European Enlightenment. Across the Atlantic her thinking influenced advocates for women's rights such as Susan B. Anthony, Elizabeth Cady Stanton, and Lucretia Mott.[8] Wollstonecraft today is considered perhaps the most famous protofeminist who transformed debates on women's morality, education, and citizenship in Europe and the United States. Tocqueville drew on Wollstonecraft to compare European and American women, creating a link between these thinkers who left an indelible imprint on the American political script that extends beyond its democratic founding into the contemporary context.[9]

Wollstonecraft's *A Vindication of the Rights of Woman* identifies male and female moral and civic vice as functioning just beneath the veneer of virtue in Victorian society, which upheld the image of the sentimental family by mistaking manners for morals. Instead of acquiring the moral virtue of honor, Wollstonecraft observed, men exhibit chivalrous and modest behavior in public while engaging in immodest and pleasure-seeking acts in private. European women behave according to the female virtues of chastity and modesty by dressing conservatively and following strict codes of politeness, which give them a reputation for virtue without necessarily reflecting a truly moral character. "I am afraid that morality is very insidiously undermined, in the female world," Wollstonecraft laments, "by the attention being turned to the shew [*sic*] instead of the substance."[10] Women's dependence on men further deforms their moral character by denying them the freedom and independence to navigate decision making about right and wrong. It leads women to engage in female vices ranging from gossiping to manipulating men and seeking pleasure over love. Confined to the private sphere, Wollstonecraft's women focus on the petty concerns of immediate family and friends instead of broader public issues. Without access to formal education, women lack the resources to cultivate enough reason to achieve "true" moral virtue. Victorian men and women essentially play their respective parts in a romantic portrayal of the sentimental family by appearing to adhere to strict moral codes without actually believing in them.

This gap between the appearance and reality of moral virtue illustrates an important dimension of suspect citizenship related to societal doubt about women's ability to fulfill their civic duty as moral guardians of the family. While it diminishes men's moral standing, male vice fails to negate their access to reason or public life, which enables them to retain economic and political citizenship independent of their moral virtue. Alternatively, women's primary link to the public arena depends on their moral and civic virtue. Failure to attain "true" morality, for Wollstonecraft, prevents women from carrying out their critical role in European society as wives and mothers committed to their husbands and children in families anchored less in emotion and more in reason. Societal doubt about the authenticity of female virtue generates enough suspicion, even in societies that confine women to the sentimental family, to sever women's already tenuous ties of legitimacy to the political community.

Escape from behind the façade of morality erected by female manners requires that governments based on the social contract uphold the promise of equality by allowing women to attain an education equal to that of men. "To render also the social compact truly equitable, and in order to spread those enlightening principles, which alone can meliorate the fate of man," Wollstonecraft explains, "women must be allowed to found their virtue on knowledge, which is scarcely possible unless they be educated by the same pursuits as men."[11] Cultivating reason would enable women the opportunity to acquire "true" moral virtue. Independence and freedom would then follow.

Shifting the moral groundwork of the family from sentiment to reason allows Wollstonecraft to argue for a more equal distribution of moral responsibility between men and women. "The two sexes mutually corrupt and improve each other," Wollstonecraft asserts. "This I believe to be an indisputable truth, extending it to every virtue. . . . Public spirit must be nurtured by private virtue, or it will resemble the factitious sentiment which makes women careful to preserve their reputation and men their honour."[12] Men and women both assume responsibility for grounding private virtue in reason and working together to develop their true moral characters. "Make women rational creatures, and free citizens, and they will quickly become good wives, and mothers," declares Wollstonecraft, who then stipulates, "that is—if men do not neglect the duties of husbands and fathers."[13] "True" virtue enables women to comprehend how their responsibility as mothers who cultivate moral and civic duty in future generations of citizens, and as wives who act as friends to their husbands, keeps the public spirit alive, granting them a vital role in the political community as citizens. Men's and women's shared efforts in the family as parents and spouses extend to the "public spirit" or common good, thus linking a moral conception of virtue to a civic one that extends to the entire society.

Nothing less than the future of the political community is at stake. Society's fate requires that men and women share moral responsibility for cultivating true virtue in order to replace their political community's vacuous Victorian manners with substantive morals rooted in reason. Yet, Wollstonecraft explains, "I have dwelt most on such as are particularly relative to the female world, because I think that the female world oppressed; yet the gangrene, which the vices engendered by oppression have produced, is not confined to the morbid part, but pervades the society at large."[14] Women's constraint, dependence on men, and lack of access to reason undermine the true virtue necessary for the liberty and equality for all that is promised by the social contract, generating moral decay throughout the entire political community.

Despite access to equal education and even citizenship, Wollstone-craft's women still carry the double burden of moral responsibility that maintains their political identity as moral guardians but suspect citizens. The weight of the nation's fate rests on women's ability to acquire reason and to cultivate "true" virtue, which will enable them to overcome the oppression that steadily injects vice and corruption into the mainstream of society. Women's subordination, as opposed to men's domination, represents the primary source of social decay for which women must assume responsibility even though they remain unequal, constrained, and confined to the private sphere. Reason replaces sentiment in Woll-stonecraft's moral equation for attributing to women the "true" virtue that would enable them to assume their civic duty as moral guardians, supporting their husbands and nurturing future citizens. Men, alter-natively, lack "true" virtue, despite their access to education, and still possess full citizenship. Women's dependence on their husbands limits men's freedom and draws men into Victorian society's petty concerns instead of allowing them to focus their attention on broader public is-sues. Curing the disease of moral vice infecting the public spirit falls to Wollstonecraft's women, who must attain enough reason to cultivate the moral virtue to overcome their oppression and achieve the freedom and equality necessary to revive the public's spirit. Failure to do so equates women's morality with the demise of the common good, leav-ing them, despite Wollstonecraft's valiant attempt, moral guardians but suspect citizens trapped in the gendered moral logic of the virtue-vice dualism. Women's double burden of moral responsibility became the primary means for linking wives and mothers to public life as nations transitioned toward liberal democracies built on the social contract that promised freedom and equality for all.

Chaos characterized the fledgling democracy that Tocqueville en-countered as Jacksonian America engaged in unbridled nation building that altered men's and women's relationship to public life. Rapid po-litical, social, and economic change accompanied the nation's transition from a republic to a liberal democracy as moral *and* civic virtue shifted from an increasingly identifiable male public arena to a female private sphere.[15] Tocqueville advances a "separate but equal" argument to ex-plain how Americans justify segregating men and women into separate spheres despite the nation's democratic commitment to equality. The moral aspect of this process begins with a republican conception of virtue in which a person's moral commitment to the common good determines his or her citizenship and becomes what Tocqueville calls self-interest properly understood. This doctrine combines a person's "own advantage with that of [his] fellow citizens" and "does not inspire great sacrifices, but every day, prompts small ones; by itself it cannot make a man virtuous, but its discipline shapes a lot of . . . self-controlled citizens."[16] Individualism, then, supersedes the common good, as democratic civic virtue requires only that American men constrain their self-interest enough to protect the political community.

Political participation comes to represent an instrumental means to economic ends as the market begins to trump politics as the driving force in American public life.[17] Male citizens increasingly leave the job of politics to politicians, who they generally view as morally corrupt, indicating the decreased value of public service. Moral vices such as wealth, greed, ambition, and self-interest acquire a certain civic value as traits necessary for economic success. Tocqueville's views on the United States resonate with those Bernard Mandeville expressed about England. In *The Fable of the Bees*, Mandeville writes, "Without great Vices, is a vain / EUTOPIA seated in the Brain. / Fraud, Luxury and Pride must live, / While we the Benefits receive" to capture how liberal market-driven societies require vices such as fraud, luxury, and pride for the people to thrive.[18] These views echo Mary Wollstonecraft's concern that the moral and civic vices "engendered" by women's oppression had spread like "gangrene" throughout the entire body politic. Public life during the modern period became increasingly associated with civic vices that, left unchecked, could contaminate entire nations.

Tocqueville's American men cultivate the civic virtues of hard work and discipline that contain the free market's necessary vices and enable them to withstand its volatile economic cycles. Character traits necessary for economic survival develop into standards of excellence as politicians, not citizens, perform the daily business of politics and the common good moves to the margins of male public life. The good citizen no longer needs to be a good man as the moral disconnects from these new civic male virtues that align more with economic success than with political commitment and participation. Representative democracy in the United States transforms republican civic virtues by shifting a male citizen's measure of value from politics to the market.

Filling the moral gap in politics falls to Tocqueville's American women, who assume a crucial, yet paradoxical, role in protecting liberal democracy that contradicts European conceptions of the sentimental wife. As "I come near the end of this book in which I have recorded so many considerable achievements of the Americans," Tocqueville declares, "if anyone asks me what I think the chief cause of the extraordinary prosperity and growing power of this nation, I should answer that it is due to the superiority of their women."[19] This superiority derives from women's close affiliation with religion in an increasingly secularized democracy that intensifies female moral virtue by imbuing it with the infinite dimension of faith in God. The American woman then channels morality in the diluted form of mores to her husband, who "derives from his home that love of order which he carries into affairs of state."[20] Conveying these mores, or *moeurs*, defined as "the habits of the heart . . . the sum of ideas that shape mental habits . . . the whole moral and intellectual state of the people," makes women moral guardians assigned the expansive responsibility for preserving the nation's political future.[21]

Moral guardianship, though a term never used explicitly by Tocqueville, captures how his American women assume a political posture predicated on protecting the moral standards necessary to ensure some stability through shared traditions and beliefs.[22] Religion combines with education to grant the American woman the reason also needed to fulfill the demands of moral guardianship. Educated alongside young men and allowed to move freely in the public sphere, American girls, unlike the European women described by Wollstonecraft, enjoy the independence and freedom of youth and learn about the vice and corruption from which they will protect their families when they agree to assume "the yoke of marriage." American women exercise their reason when voluntarily consenting to exchange their youthful freedoms for the constraints of private life in the family. Women then rationally comprehend their role in contributing to democratic society as different from men's. "The Americans," Tocqueville asserts, "do not think that man and woman have the duty or the right to do the same things, but they show an equal regard for the part played by both and think of them as beings of equal worth, though their fates are different."[23] This "separate but equal" argument, similar to the sentimental wife position, maintains women's exclusion from public life while differently justifying it on the basis of women's reason instead of on the basis of emotion. American women learn that their separate but equal fates in the private sphere allow them as moral guardians to assume a responsibility for themselves, their husbands, and their families that extends to the entire nation.

This double burden of responsibility for moral *and* civic virtue assigned to American women encompasses the common good essential to binding the people together as a nation amid tumultuous social, economic, and political change. "Therefore, everything which has a bearing on the status of women, their habits and their thoughts is, in my view, of great political importance," Tocqueville concludes.[24] American men escape responsibility for *moeurs*, or the "moral and intellectual state of the people," as the market displaces politics in public life, shifting civic virtue into the private sphere where woman's moral capacity, granted to them by their affiliation with religion, allows their moral virtue to assume an infinite civic responsibility for the entire nation's common good. This burden of moral responsibility becomes a political obligation that puts women in a double bind, since their ability to carry out this duty is premised on their exclusion from the formal political arena.

Tocqueville's American women also assume the double burden of responsibility for moral and civic *vice*. Virtue operates in tandem with vice as its default oppositional category. Its gendered dualistic logic dictates in this context that any real or imagined departure by women as moral guardians from the path of virtue can rise to the level of infinite moral and civic vice to threaten the nation's future. An individual woman's failure to fulfill finite moral virtues generally related to her self-sacrifice for her family carries an infinite moral weight with vast political implications that transform moral indiscretion into civic vice. As a potential threat to the nation, American women's moral and civic vice allows them to acquire political power despite their exclusion from full citizenship. Assigned the double burden of moral responsibility for the nation's success or failure, however, women are placed in a politically precarious and paradoxical position that undermines their legitimacy as citizens. Any indication of abandoning their assigned political duty as moral guardians jeopardizes the nation, perpetually casting American women as suspect citizens.

Tocqueville and Wollstonecraft challenge the idea of the sentimental wife by framing women's moral and civic virtue in terms of reason, illustrating how the gendered moral logic of the virtue-vice dualism becomes lodged in liberal democratic conceptions of women's citizenship. Reason and virtue should secure women's political membership in the stable foundation of normative standards of right and wrong determined through rational decision making. Women, as moral guardians, should then possess the means necessary to protect moral and civic virtue in the private sphere against the vice and corruption disrupting public life. Their double burden of moral responsibility, however, sets women up for failure by basing their moral and civic virtue on exclusion from the very public sphere that the nation obligates them to preserve. Societal suspicion of women's ability to fulfill their double burden characterizes moral guardianship.

Vice in all its forms undermines women's ability to meet the demands of this double burden and achieve legitimacy as full citizens, the point of origin for women's political identity. Tocqueville gestures toward women's infinite capacity for vice, which lingers in the shadows of virtue as an unspoken threat to America's prosperity. Wollstonecraft directly engages with female moral vices deriving from women's lack of education and dependence on men, which also jeopardize a nation's well-being. Reading Tocqueville alongside Wollstonecraft reveals that, for both writers, despite their emphasis on reason and virtue, because female moral vice retains the infinite capacity to destabilize and even destroy civic and political life, civic vice is attributed to women located in private life. Any real or perceived departure from the standards of virtue aligns women with a moral vice that carries with it such a heavy weight of civic responsibility that it is capable of damaging the common good. This gendered moral logic enables democratic society to doubt women's legitimacy as citizens on the basis of moral assumptions requiring no evidence or proof of wrongdoing. The shaky scaffolding of doubt supporting the seemingly stable façade of the certainty of women's moral guardianship always threatens to collapse into suspect citizenship under the weight of the virtue-vice dualism.

Suspect Citizenship: At the Intersection of Morality and Politics

Suspect citizenship, the conceptualization developed throughout this book, becomes visible by looking through the conceptual lens of the gendered virtue-vice dualism. Its moral logic locates women, regardless of whether they actively dissent from the state, in the precarious borderlands between good and bad, legal and illegal, citizen and alien, guardian of and traitor to the nation. This dynamic helps explain why cycles of backlash politics intensify when women battle for their freedom, inclusion, and equality. Such times of political struggle put into stark relief the suspicion clouding the legitimacy of women's claim to full democratic citizenship that derives from their location at the edge of this moral precipice.

Citizenship represents a highly contested concept. Some feminist political theorists reject citizenship as an inherently masculine and exclusionary concept. The concepts of the "public sphere" and "belonging" serve as some alternatives put forward to capture feminist conceptions of inclusionary participation, engagement, and deliberation in contemporary democracies and transnational contexts.[25] Others who take citizenship's conceptual limitations seriously still see it as an effective and available means for women to leverage political power against inequality, constraint, and exclusion. "For all its exclusionary and disciplinary tendencies," Ruth Lister argues, "citizenship, I believe, provides an invaluable strategic theoretical concept for the analysis of women's subordination and a potentially powerful political weapon in the struggle against it."[26] Exposing how the boundary between public and private life has determined women's historical exclusion from and struggle for inclusion in the political characterizes feminist analysis of citizenship, whether the approach involves transcending, transforming, or traversing this barrier. Citizenship in this study functions as a conceptual tool for tracking how the power dynamics of the virtue-vice dualism determine the status of women's membership in the political community. However, citizenship, virtue, and vice remain suspect in this analysis. Examining this constellation of concepts from a gendered perspective, while critical to interrogating what triggers backlash politics, raises serious doubts about its effectiveness in advancing democratic feminist ethics.

Morality, as a mechanism of political power, informs the definition of citizenship developed here. T. H. Marshall provides the classic liberal definition of citizenship as "a status bestowed on those who are full members of a community. All who possess the status are equal with respect to the rights and duties with which the status is bestowed."[27] "Status," while referring to merit, involves the process of assigning value to rank particular positions in a society on the basis of a standard of moral excellence codified as virtues. Identifying a set of ideals, values, and beliefs, for Marshall, plays a significant role in determining membership in the political community. "There is no universal principle that determines what those rights and duties shall be," Marshall states, "but societies in which citizenship is a developing institution create an image of an ideal citizenship against which achievement can be measured and towards which aspiration can be directed."[28] The "image of an ideal citizenship," against which citizens measure themselves and others, equates with virtue, a standard of moral and civic excellence that determines a person's membership, level of inclusion, and ultimately his or her status within a political community.

Citizenship, as defined here, builds on this moral dimension to reference membership in a political community as entailing certain responsibilities and obligations necessary to fulfill the duties required by that community and to meet its people's basic needs. These responsibilities include the demands usually placed on women in the private sphere that fall outside the formal public arena of obligations. The often overlooked responsibilities to care for the self, others, and our world in order to meet basic human needs and to live well become integral to this formulation of citizenship.[29] This perspective, in contrast to that of traditional liberalism, which focuses on individual rights, objectivity, and obligations, integrates relationships, material contexts, and responsibilities into an understanding of citizenship as premised on complex interrelationships between public and private life.

Modifying citizenship with the term "suspect" adds to the list of descriptors, ranging from "sexual," "social," and "subordinate" to "dissident" and "resistant," assigned to this concept by feminist political theorists in their effort to identify different dimensions of women's tenuous and complex relationship to the political community.[30] The conceptual location where morality, or the virtue-vice dualism, intersects with politics, characterized as citizenship, illuminates how virtue and vice determine the degrees of women's inclusion in and exclusion from the political arena. The shifting responsibility for moral and civic virtue and vice charts women's movement across the public-private boundary, which creates the unstable nature of their political membership. Bringing the moral dynamics of women's citizenship into focus involves relying on what I call blurred vision to determine the value of women's role in public life that makes them moral guardians *but* suspect citizens.

This blurred vision references a capacity to see while in motion across conceptual boundaries. Tocqueville captures this type of vision when metaphorically describing his theoretical standpoint in *Democracy in America*:

> What I am going to say will be less detailed but more certain. Each object will stand out less distinctly, but the general lines will be clearer. I will be like a traveler who has gone beyond the walls of some vast city and gone up a neighboring hill; as he goes farther off, he loses sight of the men he has just left behind; the houses merge and the public squares cannot be seen; the roads are hard to distinguish, but the city's outline is easier to see and for the time he grasps its shape.[31]

Traveling from one location to the next puts vision into motion that, in this study, constantly moves our sight lines between the more finitely defined city streets and public squares and their more abstract contours in order to provide a broader view of America's moral and political terrain without losing its particularities. Such vision also facilitates seeing the fluid movements between infinite and finite female virtue and vice. The sight lines of this moral landscape necessarily remain blurry. "The details of this huge picture are in shadow," Tocqueville explains of his ability to see the future of America, "but I can see the whole and form a clear idea of it."[32] Charting America's moral geography requires identifying the amorphous category of vice and how it locates women outside the city walls, where they acquire the ability to see the whole picture of the political community's moral framework from its shadows. Blurred vision transforms a lack of clarity into a capacity to see the complexities and dynamics of political communities set into motion by its members.

Suspect citizenship conceptualizes this blurriness in terms of serious doubt about women's legitimacy as members of the political community who, because of their moral and civic capacity for infinite virtue and vice, always represent potential threats to the polity. The term "suspect" captures the fluid dynamic between the categories of virtue and vice that makes it particularly difficult to see the deeply embedded gendered morality shaping women's citizenship. From a legal perspective, "suspect" refers to a person under suspicion of breaking the law or engaging in illegal activity but who has not been proven guilty. A suspect stands as a citizen whose legitimacy comes into question at the intersection where politics meets morality, since even alleged illegal activity aligns him or her with vice-ridden behavior that signals a break with the community's normative standards. Doubt generates this suspicion, which operates on a set of moral assumptions arising from circumstances, past behaviors, and even an indefinable sense that a person acted outside predetermined moral and legal bounds. This type of societal doubt extends to an entire category of people whose capacity to act according to a community's moral standards remains permanently in question and classifies them politically as suspects: women.

Women fall into this category because of the construction of their primary political identity as moral guardians who, at any time, can be perceived as failing to uphold their civic obligation to carry the double burden of moral responsibility for preserving the nation's common good. Beneath moral guardianship's virtuous veneer, finite and infinite vice intensify societal doubt about women's capacity to fulfill this civic duty, since their original moral position casts them as potential disruptors of behaviors, norms, and even laws merely by their political presence. The virtue-vice dynamic exposes this suspicion surrounding women's citizenship. Such societal doubt undermines the trust necessary in a liberal democracy to bind the citizen to the state, which jeopardizes the legitimacy of women's membership in the political community. Mistrust confers a level of illegitimacy that places women's citizenship under suspicion, making them vulnerable to societal blame for events such as political decay well beyond their control and even to charges that they are traitors, outlaws, and, on occasion, terrorists.

This suspicion creates a paradox that becomes evident when women actively fight for the freedom, equality, and inclusion granted to full citizens in a liberal democracy that propels backlash politics. Women's political activism and engagement triggers suspicions that their full citizenship weakens, instead of strengthens, the nation by causing its moral decay. Abandoning the confines of moral guardianship disturbs the gendered status quo and threatens instability. Backlash forces use the double burden of moral responsibility to deflect national attention away from structural social, economic, and political issues to blame women's immoral behavior for the nation's real or perceived decline.

Liberal democracy's normative standard of passivity toward a political life left largely to politicians is further disrupted when women claim their place as active, engaged participants in the public arena. As Michael Walzer notes in his conceptual history of citizenship, movements such as second wave feminism in the United States remind democrats that something "vital has been lost" with the passive enjoyment of rights and liberties eclipsing active engagement.[33] Women's claim to participation serves as a call to action for the entire democratic polity to remember citizenship as actively belonging in a community. This call to action intensifies suspicion of women's citizenship by breaking with the normative standard of passivity and threatening to change how many Americans understand their relationship to politics. Backlashes then move beyond opposing particular movements to defending a particular way of democratic life.

2 | The Religious Roots of Moral Guardianship

American Women as the Daughters of Eve and Zion

S tanding aboard the *Arbella* as it sailed to Salem in 1629, governor of the Massachusetts Bay Colony John Winthrop made a proclamation to his fledgling Puritan community that made an indelible impact on the American political script. "We must Consider that we shall be as a City upon a Hill," he stated. "[T]he Eyes of all people are upon us; so that if we shall deal falsely with our god in this work we have undertaken and so cause him to withdraw his present help from us."[1] Winthrop's words, taken from Matthew 5:14, capture the essence of biblical thought in the American political tradition. This biblical tradition positions the nation as always confronting the moral choice either to follow the path of righteousness and earn God's favor or to fail to do so and fall into the decay experienced by most nations.[2] The idea of the "City upon a Hill" eventually evolves into American exceptionalism, a central feature of the political script that frames the United States as a nation granted by God and, as such, elevated above all others as a beacon of virtue and goodness. Women, according to this biblical storyline, represent either an explicit or implicit threat to the nation's ideal moral and political status, since, as the daughters of Eve, they remain responsible for the Fall of humankind.

This chapter brings the Puritan discourse that used women's original sin to justify their subordination to men into analytic contact with second wave radical feminist Mary Daly's work in *Gyn/Ecology* and *Pure Lust*, which aims to rename and reclaim virtue and vice for a feminist metaethics designed to liberate women from such patriarchal religious traditions. Placing what at first glance appear to be incommensurable perspectives into spatial relationship with each other intentionally disrupts the conventional biblical narrative in the American political script. This disruption opens a space for seeing how such religious discourses, which focus on the spiritual realm of human existence, reveal virtue and vice's infinite dimension. The infinite in this context accounts for transcendence beyond material reality as part of a previously unseen dynamic operating in tandem with the finite to determine this dualism's internal logic.

The infinite becomes evident in American women's construction as moral guardians beginning with the Puritan women who, as the daughters of Eve, initially stood in the shadows of Winthrop's "City upon a Hill." Their original sin granted them a capacity for evil and infinite vice that posed a permanent threat to the Puritan's mission to establish heaven on earth and to preserve the possibility of good in the world. Women from various backgrounds, including servants, African slaves, and Native Americans, lived in and near Puritan towns, villages, and settlements. Ministers and magistrates, however, focused on the moral and spiritual well-being of upper-, middle-, and lower-class white Puritan women, who, they felt, possessed the capacity for godliness and virtue.[3] Male Puritan settlers established patriarchal and theocratic rule in the villages dotting New England's coastline where God's elect ruled over the masses, and men ruled over women on the basis of their belief that God made women to be their helpmeets. Internal and external challenges to Puritan authority in the 1690s led to a major moral shift for women. A few select Puritan women who performed their duties and adhered to strict moral and legal codes acquired social status as the daughters of Zion, or as brides of Christ in New Testament terms.[4] As the daughters of Zion, their infinite virtue could help protect the Puritan's sacred mission in the New World.

This move out from the shadows of political importance in Puritan society marks an initial stage in the formation of American women's political identity as moral guardians. Women embodied the potential for disorder that threatened these settlers' precarious existence. Virtuous Puritan women became protectors against their own predisposition toward vice and that of other women. Female vice took on apocalyptic proportions in this context, where women were accused of witchcraft, working as Satan's partners in destroying the community. Witchcraft trials, while relatively common, intensified in the late seventeenth century as Puritans waged a battle against Satan on the New World's shores. Ministers and magistrates enlisted virtuous women in this fight and, in doing so, made them moral guardians over a community that simultaneously regarded them with suspicion for being women.

Puritan women assumed a morally and politically precarious position as the daughters of Eve and Zion, responsible for infinite vice yet capable of infinite virtue. This moral dynamic still anchors American women's political identity. Puritan recognition of women as members of the community at this early juncture in American political history indicates the deeply embedded nature of the societal doubt arising from women's unstable moral location between virtue and vice. Such doubt cements the foundation of American women's citizenship in a morality based on a level of suspicion that continues to undermine their political legitimacy.

Nearly three hundred years later, second wave feminists challenged institutionalized religion broadly and the church specifically because of its patriarchal nature, which was represented in an extreme form by Puritanism. Radical feminist theologian Mary Daly's *The Church and the Second Sex* (1968) exposed Christianity and particularly the Roman Catholic Church as misogynistic. Her subsequent philosophical and theological work develops a feminist ontology built on a woman-centered spirituality and metaethics as an alternative to religion's misogynistic way of knowing the world.[5] Daly's work in *Gyn/Ecology* (1978) and *Pure Lust* (1984) assumes an important role in this analysis since, unlike other feminist theorists, she interrogates the virtue-vice dualism from a feminist perspective. Specifically, Daly attempts to retrieve virtue and vice from Christianity's patriarchal tradition and redefine them in a metaethical project designed to advance women's liberation. Daly's efforts to rename and reclaim virtue and vice demand consideration here as a counterpoint to this book's main argument against revisioning virtue and vice for a democratic feminist ethics.

Mary Daly and Cotton Mather, an influential Puritan minister, here represent two different aspects of America's biblical storyline that help identify how women's morality assumes an apocalyptic weight. The Puritan discourse puts into stark relief the dynamic between the spiritual and earthly arenas that shape how religious morality intersects with women's political identity formation. The typology of infinite and finite virtue and vice emerges from this analysis. Mather's writings and sermons capture the relationship between religiously oriented virtues and vices, which constitute the infinite dimension of these political concepts, and the finite, earthbound virtues and vices exhibited through material behaviors observed by others. Exploring Daly's work against the backdrop of Puritan discourse spotlights how this infinite dimension represents a problem inherent to revisioning virtue and vice for a feminist ethics grounded in material contexts and egalitarian human relationships.

The dualistic logic of virtue and vice facilitates an ongoing cycle of reversals that entails transcendence as one category of people elevates itself above the other to claim moral excellence, a process that informs our understanding of contemporary backlash politics. This process of transcendence derives from the abstract realm associated with the infinite, which exists outside of, though linked to, material reality and deflects attention away from it. Identifying the infinite-finite dynamic within the virtue-vice dualism clarifies the heavy moral weight placed on women—a responsibility that assumes a central role in backlash politics. This internal dynamic, in which the biblical tradition plays an integral part, I argue, is necessary to understanding why American women remain in a precarious political position as moral guardians but suspect citizens and targets for backlash politics centuries later. Champions of backlash politics, many of whom make claims based on religion, tap into the sacred construction of women as moral guardians. Any departure from female virtues, then, can align women with the profane, which enables society to assign them blame that can reach apocalyptic proportions when they are accused of destroying the common good and even jeopardizing the fate of humanity. This deeply problematic moral location, however, also underscores the necessary aspect of ethical decision making that entails thinking beyond given contexts, structures, and material realities in order to engage the political imagination needed to overcome the debilitating cycle of backlashes against women.

The Puritan Point of Emergence:
Infinite and Finite Virtue and Vice

The Puritan discourse about female virtue and vice serves as the historical point of departure for this conceptual history. This political moment, in part, meets James Farr's criteria that "for a conceptual history to be a genuine history, the concept's genesis must be told; and this requires an understanding of its pre-history. . . . How concepts (and words) emerge—sometimes explosively, usually rather more glacially—out of earlier conceptual material is itself an essential part of the story."[6] This prehistory occurs between 1620, when the Mayflower Compact was signed, and 1730, when the Puritan's religious and political authority significantly declined in the northern colonies, marking a critical period in British colonization that influences America's moral and political founding. The gendered moral logic of the virtue-vice dualism in this discourse, more importantly, reveals how Puritan women, despite their political, social, and economic invisibility, acquired the double burden of moral responsibility that establishes the initial conditions for American women's relationship to political life as moral guardians but suspect citizens.

Puritan ministers' sermons provide the primary materials for investigating female virtue and vice in this political discourse. Women generally lacked a verbal or written voice in the Puritan context. Cotton Mather's extensive writings on female virtue and vice reflect his pivotal part as a minister and magistrate in a broader political debate over women's role in Puritan communities that, while focusing on their vices, granted them the capacity for virtue. This critical shift occurred amid internal and external threats to Puritan control in the New England colonies. A rising mercantilist class challenged the landed agrarian Puritan elite. The French and Indian Wars destabilized Puritan communities as Indian raids frequently decimated their frontier villages and inspired fear throughout the entire region. This fear manifested in the witch trials, in which women personified the unknown evil lingering in the wilderness.[7] Women's increased church attendance during this time captured ministers' attention. The ministers feared the decay of Puritan society—and with it heaven on earth—and made a strategic decision to grant women virtue in order to enlist them in the earthly battle for their utopia. Puritan authorities reformulated the moral calculus, previously based solely on women's embodiment of original sin, to meet the changing demands of their political landscape. Cotton Mather takes a relatively innovative approach to these circumstances by addressing the limitations of a moral discourse that denied women virtue despite their evident part in building the Puritan community, putting them in a complex and contradictory moral location as the daughters of both Eve and Zion.

Vice for Puritans represents humans' original moral condition, a sinful nature that caused the Fall. Thus, vice stands between humankind and God's love, and its potential to cause further decay in society derives from its infinite dimension. "We have in our own *Corrupt Nature*, a Disposition of Sin," Cotton Mather declares. "We brought into the world with us, a *Corrupt Nature*, a *Carnal Mind*, an *Evil Heart*, which is always Disposed to *Sin*. In this *Corrupt* Nature we have a continual *Temptation*."[8] Carnal temptation, which often leads to adultery, fornication, and immodesty, posed such a serious danger to the essential social institutions of marriage and the family that sexual desire or lust became the most significant of the Seven Deadly Sins for the Puritans. Women, as child bearers, men's helpmeets, *and* the original sinners, represented the greatest threat to these institutions.

The Puritan view of women derives from the biblical story in which Eve physically comes from Adam's rib and then, after eating from the Tree of Knowledge of good and evil, is punished by God, who makes Eve into Adam's servant and subjects her to pain and suffering in childbirth. Genesis 3:16 conveys God's commandment: "Unto the woman . . . I will greatly multiply thy sorrow and thy conception; in sorrow thou shalt bring forth children; and thy desire shall be to thy husband, and he shall rule over thee." The Fall translates into the etymology of virtue and its relationship to vice, as illustrated by the *Oxford English Dictionary*'s definition of "virago": "name given by Adam to Eve—called 'virago' or taken from man. 1576, Gascoigne: 'Before she sinned, Eva was called Virago, and after she sinned she deserved to be called Eva.'" Eve encompasses the infinite vice of women, whose very nature embodies original sin and, for the Puritans, the Devil. This innate connection to evil empowered Puritan women with the ability to take humanity down the path to hell, which set in place a narrative of female morality that continues to shape American women's political identity.

This intense biblical identification with vice and sin underscores the significance of the fact that Puritans attributed virtue to some women. Cotton Mather begins this moral recalculation by interpreting as a blessing God's curse that women endure the pain of childbirth. Women's fear of death in childbirth, Mather argues, powerfully motivates them to find God:

> The *Curse* is turned into a *Blessing* unto them. The *Dubious Hazards* of their Lives in their *Appointed Sorrows*, drive them the more frequently, & the more fervently to commit themselves into the Hands of their Only Savior. They are *Saved thro' Childbearing*; inasmuch as it singularly obliges them to *Continue in Faith, and Charity, and Holiness, with Sobriety*.[9]

Punishment for original sin transforms into women's ability to give birth to humankind's virtue and goodness. Mather then identifies Eve, not Adam, as "the *first Believer* of our Savior" and "the *Mother of all that Live unto God*" and "a *Mother* to her own *Husband*, and the Instrument of bringing him to Believe in the *Great Redeemer*."[10] This interpretation radically transforms Eve from being the source of humanity's destruction into its salvation. Mather even declares that "*Virtue* itself, and the *Names* of all particular *Virtues*, are grammatically of the *Female Gender*."[11] Though well acquainted with Latin, which defines virtue as rooted in *vir*, meaning "man," Mather decides to emphasize the female branch of virtue's etymology, which stems from virgin, virginity, and the Virgin Mary. Reconfiguring the Puritan moral calculus to grant women access to virtue establishes their infinite capacity to guard themselves, other women, their families, the community, and even humankind from moral downfall. Politically, women now could join the few elected by God to enter heaven, the gateway to authority in the Puritan theocracy.

Piety, sacrifice, humility, and modesty act as the four central virtues populating the moral universe of Puritan women. Piety represents the source of all virtue for Puritans. This virtue requires absolute conformity and commitment to God's will, which demands that men and women distance themselves from the physical temptations that distract them from their spiritual focus. Such piety entails the courage to reject the earthly desires that drive most people. "*A Vertuous Woman*, the Word which we render *Vertuous*, carries *Courage* in it," Mather explains. "Some note that it implies a *Piety* Embued [*sic*] with such *Fortitude*, as to do *Good Works*, when one shall be despised, and abused for the doing of them."[12] Puritan women thus acquired the ability to achieve courage, a virtue traditionally reserved only for men, and fortitude, one of the four cardinal virtues, which grants women the moral strength to do God's work even in the face of great hardship. Some Puritan women, then, could join men in their community's struggle to protect heaven on earth.

A highly sexualized language also characterizes Puritan discourse about female piety, which requires women's marriage to God. Cotton Mather, for instance, describes the mating ritual between God and a young woman. She eventually succumbs to her desire for His "Comeliness" and "Beauty." Their marriage culminates when the young woman can "*cleave* to him, with *full purpose of Heart*; a full and fixed Purpose, to be *for him*, and *not for another*. Behold the *Knot* now tied," Mather declares. "*It will not be long* before the *Consummation of the marriage*, thy eternal *Cohabitation* with thy SAVIOUR."[13] "Consummation," of course, refers to the first sexual act that, for the Puritans, establishes a woman's permanent bond to God for life and eternity. Sexual subordination to God represents the act of absolute conformity to His will necessary for a woman's spiritual salvation. The Puritans' grounding of female piety, their highest form of virtue, in sex and sexuality indicates how, even in this rarified discourse directed toward abstract spirituality and faith, women's bond to the broader community remains embedded in a sexual act.

The female virtue of sacrifice links women more directly to the Puritans' political struggles in the New World by attributing to them a responsibility for giving the self, including the will, over to God as an act beneficial to the entire community. Cotton Mather sets out an exceptional model for female sacrifice in a sermon retelling the biblical story in Judges 12 and 13 of Jephtah, who literally sacrifices the life of his only child, a virgin daughter, to God to keep a vow to save his people. His daughter, the paradigm of female sacrifice, willingly accepts this fate on behalf of her community. "The *young Daughter of Jephtah*," Mather explains, "who when she understood that her *Life* must be the

Price of a *Redemption* for the People of GOD, and of their *Victory* over their Enemies, the lovely Creature willingly submitted unto it, and said, *Well then let me be made a Sacrifice! Let my Life go for it, if the Israel of God may but live and flourish!*"[14] Puritan women, while keeping their lives, should willingly sacrifice the self to conform to God's will, which will permit their spiritual salvation and the survival of Puritan beliefs. This Puritan understanding of self-sacrifice shapes female virtue within the American political script, where it retains the expansive character of these spiritual origins that connect women to the common good through religious morality.

Humility and modesty, two virtues also applied to men, work in tandem to assume heightened moral significance for women. For the Puritans, humility refers to lowliness, meekness, and submissiveness, which are part of women's service to God and men. Modesty demands a greater effort because of women's susceptibility to the physical temptations of beauty and vanity. Women's clothing, in particular, can put their moral status in jeopardy. Cotton Mather advises women, "You will have the *Wisdom* to abandon such *Apparel*, as may render your *Virtue* questionable. But you are to be well-advised unto this further *Wisdom*; That your *Apparel* be not a Thing of more Account with you than your *Virtue*."[15] Puritans equate a woman's modest dress and behavior with a humble acceptance of her station. The daughters of Zion, as representations of physical and earthly temptations of the flesh, which turn their attention away from the soul and the embrace of God's spirit, must adopt plain clothing without jewelry, scarves, or other adornments and avoid all dancing.

Piety, sacrifice, humility, and modesty illustrate the infinite dimension of female virtue in the Judeo-Christian religious morality that characterizes the American political script. Female morality's spiritual nature orients women's initial relationship to political community toward an expansive capacity to sacrifice the self for a common good extending well beyond a nation's constructed or geographical boundaries. Women's moral value, accordingly, derives from devoting their physical and spiritual selves to God. The infinite conveys the moral capacity to transcend material reality in order to attain a higher spiritual plane above the entanglements of everyday life. Puritanism's biblical discourse makes the infinite dimension of virtue evident and reveals how female morality acquires a sacred meaning in the American political script, even as this religious aspect shifts further into the background as the nation's storyline unfolds.

The infinite intersects with finite female virtues through the Virgin Mary, Puritan women's model of moral excellence that conveys the sacred nature of their roles as wives and mothers. Finite female virtues dictated how Puritan women acted in the material world where others observed and judged how well their behavior reflected their spiritual commitment to God. Visible behaviors communicated the purity of one's soul. The Virgin Mary symbolizes the precarious space between this world and the next occupied by Puritan women who engaged in the finite act of sex for procreation with their husbands while remaining spiritually married to God.

Purity and fidelity, the two critical finite female virtues, represent the sexualized component of Puritan women's morality. A Puritan woman's "Mystical Marriage" to God, according to Cotton Mather, grants her the piety to embrace the purity associated with the Virgin Mary. Her first marriage is to God and cleanses the woman's soul enough to ensure a finite form of sexual purity that mirrors its infinite counterpart, Mary's Immaculate Conception. Fidelity requires a wife to commit her physical and emotional being completely to her husband, which involves banishing any adulterous thoughts from her mind. A mother's fidelity to her children involves giving birth to them, modeling moral excellence, and educating them to read the Bible, write, and accept her authority. These virtuous acts should, Cotton Mather contends, earn her the right to be esteemed by her sons as Christ esteemed his mother.[16] Purity and fidelity reflect the moral responsibility assigned to a Puritan wife and mother, who, despite her subordinate place in this patriarchal society, protects her husband and children from vice, evil, and sin and ensures their spiritual salvation by utterly committing herself to them.

Passive submission and obedience as helpmeets to their husbands defined Puritan women's finite moral life. Their moral status increased the less visible they became in Puritan society. "The Name for you in the Original of the Bible, signifies, *Hidden ones*," Mather explains to Puritan women. "And be willing to pass thro' the World, without much *Observation*, under much *Obscurity*; to pass *Hidden*, and after a sort *Incognito*, thro' the World, and with very little Notice taken of you."[17]

Puritan women were civilly dead, lacking any independent standing in the eyes of the law, which gave husbands absolute authority over their wives and required wives' complete obedience to their husbands. Mather advises women that "it is the highest *Ignominy*, not of the *Wife*, but of the Man for a *Man* to beat his *Wife*. But if thou haft an Husband that will do so, bear it patiently; and know thou shalt have *Rewards* hereafter for it, as well as *Praises* here."[18] The English common laws of coverture under which Puritan women lived included the "rule of thumb," which granted husbands the legal right to beat their wives with a stick no thicker than their thumbs in order to control and punish them. The three finite female virtues of subordination, passivity, and obedience cemented the moral foundation of Puritan patriarchy.

Despite living in a community based on their political exclusion, Puritan women's morality includes the finite virtues of courage, charity, and industry, which ironically derive from their active engagement in building Puritan communities. Courage, traditionally assigned to men for bravery on the battlefield or independence in politics, is granted to Puritan women as immigrants from England who participated in pioneering the American wilderness. Mather praises the pioneering Puritan women "who cheerfully bore their part, in the terrible Transportation over the huge *Atlantic* Ocean, into this horrid and howling Wilderness, were such Patterns of *Patience* and of *Courage* in going thro' that Glorious Undertaking to take *Possession* of these *Uttermost parts of the Earth*, for our Savior."[19] These forgotten women, Mather continues, should be models of virtue for his congregation. Puritan women labored alongside their fathers, husbands, and brothers, beginning the nation-building process by establishing territory under Puritan authority and creating a kingdom of God on earth.

That Puritans such as Cotton Mather attributed virtue to such contributions indicates how they attempted to resolve a growing contradiction between morally valuing women for their obscurity and honoring their visible role in building a new society. Charity manifests as compassion for the poor and afflicted, shown by giving them alms and volunteering to help the sick. Such acts required women's engagement beyond the family sphere, which, while an extension of their domestic labor, involved some independence to participate as members of their community. Industry references the efficient use of labor and illustrates

how Puritans valued women's work as a necessary factor in a pioneering agrarian society's survival. Identifying how Puritans attributed these
finite virtues to women exposes a moral dynamic operating just beneath
the surface of a Puritan discourse defined by patriarchy. Puritan women
as women, not solely as wives and mothers, acquire positive normative
value for participating in the work required for a fledgling political
community to survive.

Infinite female vice, however, still defined Puritan women's moral
character, measured in terms of its finite dimension or visible, earthly
behaviors. Any departure from the strict moral code represented a threat
to these fragile Puritan communities in which "people who did not accept their place in the social order were the very embodiments of evil."[20]
Discontent captures the essential nature of male and female finite vices
for Puritans. Although political discontent mobilized Puritans to rebel
against their persecution in England, any expression of similar displea-
sure with the status quo in the New World indicated a faltering belief
in God and their sacred mission to establish heaven on earth. Women
posed the greatest threat, since their social, economic, and political
subordination to men was believed to be ordained by God and thus
formed this patriarchy's theological foundation. Their failure to follow
the moral code challenged male domination and, as such, the entire social system. Finite female vices, as a result, took on an infinite quality
with apocalyptic implications, since Puritan society held women, as the
daughters of Eve and Zion, responsible for protecting it and humanity
against another fall.

Disobedience to male authority represented a central female finite
vice. Challenging one's husband went against God's command that
women serve as men's helpmeets. Puritan ministers viewed a wife's inability to please her husband as an act of disobedience equivalent to
rebellion. "Traitors to their Husbands, whose Authority they usurp,"
Reverend John Sprint describes undutiful wives. "Rebels to the great
Monarch of the World, whose Sacred Laws they Impiously violate."[21]
Any exercise of independence, whether intentional or circumstantial,
also broke with the moral code, often invoking serious legal punishment
for women. Mistress Ann Hibbens, for instance, sued carpenters for un-
satisfactory work on her home. At the trial, Governor John Winthrop
disregarded Mistress Hibbens's legal claim against the carpenters and,

instead, accused her of discontent and contentiousness for acting independently and disobeying her husband's counsel, a sin against God's law. The ministers excommunicated Hibbens from the church. Two years after her husband's death, when she became financially independent, the Puritan authorities accused, convicted, and executed Mistress Hibbens for witchcraft.[22] Widows who gained independence from male authority posed serious threats to this patriarchal society.

In another case, Katherine Harrison became one of the wealthiest people in the Connecticut colony after her husband died. Her property immediately came under attack; neighbors slaughtered cows, damaged oxen, and burned crops. Harrison filed grievances against her neighbors, who retaliated by charging her with witchcraft. After losing most of her estate to fines and fees paid to her neighbors and local magistrates, Harrison ultimately left Connecticut for New York.[23] Puritan women such as Hibbens and Harrison who tried to protect their property through legal channels directly challenged male authority by claiming a right to voice grievances publicly. Puritans, who viewed the spoken word as defining the self and even holding magical power, feared female speech.[24] Such acts of women's independence and disobedience transformed from finite to infinite vice because of their implications for patriarchy.

Women's sexuality, which included any actions, real or imagined, that deviated from the chastity and modesty reflecting their marriage to God, represented the penultimate challenge to male authority, making this female finite vice central to charging Puritan women with witchcraft. Eve's seduction of Adam in the Garden of Eden provided the biblical basis on which ministers and magistrates took such legal action against women. "All witchcraft comes from carnal lust, which is in women insatiable," states *The Malleus Maleficarum* (*The Witches' Hammer*), the medieval legal codes used in Puritan witch trials. "Wherefore for this condition the sake of fulfilling their lusts they consort even with devils."[25] Cotton Mather repeatedly describes carnal lust as central to the many infamous Salem witch trials over which he presided. In one account, John Louder testifies in Bridget Bishop's trial that she appeared in his bed, "the likeness of this Woman grievously oppressing him; in which miserable condition she held him, unable to help himself, till near Day."[26] Bernard Peache similarly explains in Susan Martin's trial how she scrambled through his bedroom window in the night, "took hold of this Deponent's Feet, and drawing his Body up into a Heap, she lay upon him near Two Hours."[27] Women, in these cases and many others, are portrayed as sexual predators who sneak into men's bedrooms where they force men to submit to their seductive powers. Men's dreams about such alleged events often served as evidence in these cases, obscuring the lines between fantasy and reality. This obscurity, despite the supposedly clear dualistic moral distinction between God and Satan, heaven and hell, good and evil, indicates the permeable boundary between the finite and infinite, material and abstract, dimensions of Puritan moral logic.

Real or perceived moral infractions acquired apocalyptic meaning as Puritan magistrates and ministers accused women of witchcraft for rebellious behavior, which, they believed, jeopardized their earthly community and God's triumph over Satan. The witchcraft epidemic of the late 1600s represented nothing less than the Devil's renewed battle to stop God's people from conquering the last bastion of evil in the American wilderness. "WITCHCRAFT is a most Monstrous and Horrid *Evil*," Mather asserts. "Indeed there is a vast heap of Bloody Roaring Impieties contained in the *Bowels* of it. . . . There is in *Witchcraft*, a most explicit *Renouncing* of all that is *Holy*, and *Just* and *Good*. . . . *Witchcraft* is a Siding with *Hell* against *Heaven* and *Earth*."[28] Witches, by tipping the spiritual and moral scales in the Devil's favor, brought humanity closer to the brink of destruction by threatening the Puritans' heavenly utopia of the New World. Cotton Mather explains that many great people misunderstood Sir Thomas More's Utopia as a real place in the New World, whereas John Winthrop and the Puritans actually established New England as a "City upon a Hill," or "a true *Utopia*."[29] Puritan women could support this utopian project by exhibiting the finite virtues reflective of their complete commitment to God, which would empower them with the infinite virtues of piety, sacrifice, humility, and modesty necessary to protect themselves and all of humanity from downfall.

Alternatively, women could succumb to finite female vices such as disobedience, independence, and sexuality, which, because of their responsibility for original sin, empowered them with a capacity for infinite vice, linking them directly to Satan. Mather warns his community, "But such is the descent of the Devil at this day upon our selves, that I may truly tell you, *The Walls of the whole World are broken down!*"[30]

Those who diverged from this virtuous path, even in another's dreams, threatened the fragile utopia.

Puritan women, as daughters of Eve and Zion, stood on the precipice, where they could either guard their community or pull it down to hell. This precarious location establishes the origins of women's moral guardianship in the American political script. The apocalyptic Puritan discourse transforms into an inextricable bond between women's morality and the fate of America's exceptional future as the "City upon a Hill." Moral guardianship evolves from this deep suspicion that women's real or perceived failure to adhere to finite virtues holds an infinite capacity to generate religious and political devastation of cosmic proportion. The few Puritan women who acquired the infinite virtue that legitimized their part in establishing, building, and sustaining the community as the daughters of Zion did so in response to the disorder threatening Puritan authority, which took the form of witchcraft.

Even in a polarized moral universe defined by good and evil, heaven and hell, however, Puritan women, as the daughters of Eve, straddled the space in between virtue and vice, the finite and infinite. Society's linking of women's material behavior to a spiritual, eternal realm provides the means by which future generations of American women assume the double burden of advancing America's success or the responsibility for its failure, given their role as moral guardians but suspect citizens. Women's relationship to the political, even in America's Puritan prehistory, emanates from a precarious moral location that grants a few some access to the virtue necessary to help guard the community against evil while still defining them by a capacity for sin that mires them in societal doubt and suspicion.

The Infinite as a Necessary Problem: Mary Daly's *Gyn/Ecology* and *Pure Lust*

Renaming and reclaiming virtue and vice anchors Mary Daly's meta-ethical project in *Gyn/Ecology* and *Pure Lust*, in which she retrieves these moral concepts from a patriarchal religious tradition in order to advance women's liberation. Men, Daly asserts, secure domination over women by assigning them moral value for passively accepting their oppression and penalizing those women who challenge the status quo. "The traditional 'virtues,' as defined and used by the Masters of Morality[,] constitute a veritable arsenal of weapons commonly employed in the perpetual war against the Race of Racy Women," explains Daly.[31] This "phallic ethic" leads women to internalize a patriarchal moral system on a spiritual, emotional, and psychological level to the point that they devalue themselves, their active part in the world, and other women. Women's liberation requires a "feminist ethic" built on revisioning virtue and vice. The dynamic between the infinite and finite made evident in Puritan discourse ultimately undermines Daly's ethical project. Its theological nature emphasizes the abstract spiritual realm of the infinite to reveal two intertwined problems inherent to the virtue-vice dualism: reversals and transcendence.

Reversals refer to cyclical processes inherent in dualisms that involve shifting social value from the dominant to the subordinate category. This process entails renaming and reclaiming concepts such as virtue and vice to retrieve their full meaning, which, for Daly, involves rescuing them from their patriarchal past. "The word *virtue* itself encased in coffins of patriarchal moral ideology seems to have a putrid odor about it," she states. "Indeed the word *virtue*, when Viragos first struggle to exhume it from the graveyards of phallic ethics, reeks of reversals."[32] Men appropriated women's virtues of strength and independence while projecting petty and weak male traits onto women. These "pseudovirtues" contain and paralyze women by valuing their dependence and passivity. Male virtues are actually female, and female vices are actually male. To reverse this reversal, Daly returns to virtue's etymological roots, where *vir*, meaning "man," branches off into the female "virgin," generally associated with sexual purity and, in Christian contexts, the Virgin Mary. Daly reimagines "virgin" to mean "'never captured: UNSUBDUED.'" "Knowing that *virgin* is thought to be derived from the Latin *virga*, meaning green branch," she explains, "we claim the name *Virtue* also as a green branch, a New Name on the tree of words. *Virtue*, used by Virgins to Name our strengths, is a Virgin Word. Our virtues are Virgin Virtues."[33] Returning to this etymological origin of virtue cleanses this concept of male moral hypocrisy in order to capture women's free and independent state before patriarchy.

Reclaiming virtue in this way aims to release the power essential to women's revolt against male domination. "Raging, racing, we take on the task of Pyrognomic Naming of Virtues," Daly explains. "Thus lighting, igniting the Fires of Impassioned Virtues, we sear, scorch, singe, char, burn away the demonic tidy ties that hold us down in the Domesticate State, releasing our own Diamons/Muses/Tidal Forces of Creation."[34] This process empowers women to name themselves and the world in which they live by reclaiming the capacity to determine their social value instead of passively accepting what men grant them. Women, Daly claims, will "name our own good (that is life-affirming) qualities (operative habits). When we choose to call these 'virtues,' we hear this old word in a new way, and it thus becomes a new word."[35] Escaping the feminine ethic of passivity, then, requires redefining virtue to mean "operative habit," which refers to women engaging in behaviors consistent with the Virgin Virtues that value their independence and strength.

Daly's redefinition of virtues as "operative habits" illustrates how the internal infinite-finite dualism sustains the problem of reversals. St. Thomas Aquinas's moral theory in *Summa Theologica* serves as the basis for Daly's redefinition of virtue. Scholastics such as Aquinas viewed virtue and vice in terms of a person's ability to control his or her emotions or passions and act according to the moral principles of good established by God. Daly maintains the connection between emotions and moral principles, adding that "virtues are not identical to the passions, however, for virtues are habits, not movements. They are 'principles of movements.'"[36] Passions, habits, and movements refer to finite dimensions of virtue expressed or experienced in relationship to the material world that, then, translate into virtues as principles that determine these behaviors. People achieve infinite virtue when aligning passions with moral principles becomes a habit effortlessly directing their everyday actions. Women, Daly contends, must change their behaviors in accordance with the finite virtues of independence and strength. Over time, these new habits will operate in their daily lives and enable women to find their way to an infinite virtue untarnished by patriarchy. The infinite retains the preferred moral status within this internal dynamic in which the finite realm serves as a means to something greater—something beyond human control. The very material world in which people live and the one associated with women remains devalued in this dualistic moral logic, which internally operates according to patriarchal rules.

Reversals such as Daly's reclaiming and renaming of virtue serve as a primary strategy for feminist political theorists who revision concepts as part of a broader project committed to liberating subordinate groups from domination. Yet the logic of dualisms dictated by oppositional, either/or categories remains in place in the reversal process, which maintains its structural hierarchy and inequality. Gendered dualisms such as virtue and vice lead to the problem that Val Plumwood identifies as uncritical reversals in which "a new feminine identity comes to be specified *in reaction to* the old."[37] Male definition of valued qualities remains undisturbed in this process, since women claim these traits for themselves without exploring alternatives framed by female experience, which ultimately sustains their position of subordination. Daly engages in an uncritical reversal when reacting against the old female identity characterized as passive by reclaiming the masculine virtues of freedom and independence for women. Virgin Virtues, then, derive from reversing men's original reversal and appropriation of female virtue in order to allow women to establish a new female identity. The male-female dualism undergirding Daly's work confines it to an essentialist claim that obfuscates the complexities of these gendered identifications and their intersection with a range of race, class, religious, and other variables. Applying this gendered dynamic to the virtue-vice dualism leads Daly to claim women's moral superiority over men. The inequality and constraint inherent in the logic of dualisms grounded in hierarchical relationships is left unchallenged. Attributing value to one category of people still occurs at the expense of denying it to another. A patriarchal understanding of the moral world, despite Daly's efforts to the contrary, still determines how virtue and vice function as a gendered dualism in opposition to the feminist goals of equality and freedom.

The second problem, transcendence, becomes evident as Daly attempts to escape the cycle of reversals inherent to dualisms. Daly collapses female virtues and vices into one category in order to dissociate these concepts from their patriarchal past by renaming the Eight Deadly Sins (the eighth is Processions, added by Daly to represent the collective deception of patriarchy). She calls them the "Volcanic Virgin Virtues." "Thus understood *Vice* is a New Word," Daly claims. "It calls to mind the fact that the Virtues/Vices (the Virtuous Vices) of Virgins are like spiral staircases, making possible movement out of the Foreground/

Flatland into Other dimensions. Our spiraling movement, overcoming the dronish dichotomies of virile/viral virtues and vices."[38] Renaming vices as virtues purifies these concepts of their patriarchal meaning. Lust, for example, traditionally one of the Seven Deadly Sins, transforms into a Virgin Cardinal Virtue when Daly classifies it as "pure" to eradicate its association with physical and emotional sexual desire such as genital fixation, fetishism, obsession, and aggression. Purifying lust, instead of valuing its raw sexual power and unbridled desire and relating it to women's sexual freedom, pushes women back into a moral universe where sexual purity, chastity, and modesty prevail. Female vice, as the Puritan discourse illustrates, enables women, even in governing systems premised on their oppression, to leverage power. Collapsing vice into virtue eradicates a source of political power for women and, most importantly, maintains virtue as the standard of moral value achieved by transcending physical, emotional, and material contexts. The capacity to overcome the finite realities of everyday life, conventionally identified with women's biological link to nature, is essential to Daly's ethical project, which ultimately remains unable to transcend a patriarchal moral system built on the gendered virtue-vice dualism.

Identifying transcendence as an aspect of the infinite clarifies the challenges inherent in revisioning virtue and vice from a feminist perspective. Transcendence entails actions to overcome the limits of material life and achieve a higher plane of existence; it functions to deflect attention away from structures and contexts that determine everyday life, which, then, assume a devalued moral status generally associated with women. Daly's feminist ethics focuses on transcending patriarchal virtue and vice to liberate women from an endless cycle of reversals. Such liberation requires women's personal journey to change their finite behaviors in order to reappropriate the virtues of independence and strength. Attention turns away from changing the external structures of oppression to an internal spiritual and emotional plane. And, more pertinent to Daly's objective, the dualistic categories that sustain the hierarchy, inequality, and constraint consistent with patriarchy still define a person's way of knowing the world. Daly's feminist ethics attempts to transcend the virtue-vice dualism without addressing the moral structure of oppositional categories that confines her thinking within its patriarchal logic by assuming the value of virtue and by devaluing vice.

Reversals and transcendence combine to illustrate the inherent challenges that the infinite poses to a democratic feminist ethics grounded in material contexts and human relationships and defined by its commitments to equality and freedom.

Daly's project also makes apparent the necessity of defining the infinite in terms of transcendence in ethical decision-making processes, regardless of whether they include the virtue-vice dualism. Such decision-making processes require that those involved consider the range of possible outcomes given the circumstances. The imagination needed to participate in ethical processes requires thinking beyond certain material realities to envision the means or actions necessary to achieve a particular end. This process involves a certain capacity to transcend or to see beyond a given reality without disconnecting from it. This capacity, I argue, is necessary for further developing a democratic feminist ethics grounded in relationships, everyday life, and contexts that also retains the ethical vision to see beyond them as well.

Martyrs for Democracy: The Sacred, Profane, and Double Burden of Moral Responsibility

The Puritan prehistory outlines how the infinite and finite dimensions of virtue and vice establish American women's political identity as the daughters of Eve and Zion, leaving a patriarchal legacy that Mary Daly attempts to disrupt. Her inability to succeed speaks to the challenges posed by this gendered dualism, which, through reversals and transcendence, maintains inequality and constraint. Placing Daly's work in relation to Cotton Mather's makes evident how deeply the patriarchal logic of virtue and vice is embedded in the American political script. Further, examining these concepts from a biblical perspective clarifies that the infinite aspect of virtue and vice belongs to a constellation of concepts such as good and evil, God and Satan, heaven and hell, which carry apocalyptic weight. Contemporary backlash discourses, often relying on biblical language, tap into the Puritan narrative and assign American women an infinite moral capacity to protect the nation's future. As martyrs for democracy, if they fail, they assume responsibility for its fall.

Infinite virtue and vice encompass the religious aspects of the sacred and profane. "Sacred" comes from the Latin word *sacrum*, which, for the Romans, referred to the temple where religious rites occurred. "Profane" derives from *profanum*, the space adjoining the temple where priests performed sacrifices, including those of virgins. This etymological background underscores the intensity assigned to female infinite virtue and vice within the tradition of Western religious discourse. The sacred translates into a central feature of American women's morality as sacrifice of the self for their families, community, and nation. Women's ability to transcend everyday material reality through finite acts such as modest dress and marital fidelity indicates their moral purity and sacred commitment to godliness. Above all, women must exercise self-restraint regarding their natural desire to tempt men with their sexuality. Holding women responsible for this sacrifice morally cleanses men of responsibility for acting on their desires and wants, which establishes the sexual double bind. Relinquishing material wants and emotional needs marks the restrained female character necessary to focus on the spiritual realm. Any transgression can be interpreted as profane and, as such, trigger harsh punishment, ranging from social ostracism to execution in the Puritan community. Infinite virtue and vice retain the gendered character of the sacred and profane, in which virgin or pure women represent a link between the human and spiritual worlds.

Backlash discourses capitalize on this link between the infinite and the finite. The finite actions of American women hold infinite implications for the nation's success or failure. Teenage pregnancy, unwed motherhood, immodest dress, and working outside instead of inside the home translate into profane behaviors causing the nation's demise. This moral dynamic places such a heavy weight on women as moral guardians that their individual behavior can determine the fate of not only the nation but humanity. Given the possibility of such apocalyptic outcomes, American women's moral guardianship entails an infinite ability for sacrifice that makes them martyrs for democracy. Their capacity for giving up the self for their families, the nation, and the common good becomes the measure of their moral value and commitment to the political community. Any divergence from such sacrifice puts the nation in jeopardy, making women potential suspects with the ability to act as traitors to the common good simply by asserting their finite material interests, needs, and desires. Women's legitimate claim to membership in the political community always hangs in this moral balance.

3 | "Back to Virtue" Backlash Politics

Privileging Irresponsibility

Women's moral character, whether at the turn of the nineteenth or twenty-first century, represents a site of struggle in "family values" debates, a feature of "back to virtue" backlash politics. Following the American Revolution, women's education moved into the national spotlight at the beginning of the nineteenth century as political leaders attempted to hold together the fledgling republic's fragile coalition of independent states. Challenges to the traditional family structure threatened to undermine the nation's patriarchal order.[1] American men increasingly avoided marriage. American women left farms for cities and wage-paying jobs, married later, exercised more choice in their marital decisions, and gave birth to fewer children. Female virtue assumed prominence in the political discourse as a way to mend the nation's fraying moral and civic fabric. "Women became the keepers of the nation's conscience," Mary Beth Norton explains, "the only citizens specifically charged with maintaining the traditional republican commitment to the good of the entire community."[2] Assuming this double burden of moral responsibility, most agreed, required that women gain access to enough formal education to acquire the reason necessary for cultivating a civic counterpart to their moral virtue.

National debate about women's education and its impact on the traditional patriarchal family ensued. Reformers such as Benjamin Rush and Judith Sargent Murray advocated for women's increased access to a broader education that would better enable them to serve the republic as wives and mothers and to raise its future male citizens. Opponents to these measures such as Reverends James Fordyce and John Bennett feared that a more rigorous curriculum would "unsex" women, deprive them of their "softer" nature, and distract them from their domestic duties. This republican era "family values" debate tracks how civic virtue shifts from the male public to female private life and defines women's explicit relationship to politics as moral guardians but suspect citizens.

The ongoing debates over sex education today illustrate how the virtue-vice dualism channels old oppressions from the republican era into contemporary backlash politics. The comprehensive approach to sex education, defended by organizations such as Sexuality Information and Education Council of the United States (SIECUS), Advocates for Youth, and Planned Parenthood, includes information about reproduction and contraceptives while still promoting abstinence as the best choice for young people. Conservative organizations such as the Heritage Foundation, the Medical Institute, and Focus on the Family advocate for abstinence-only-until-marriage programs as the only way to address the fact that U.S. teen birth, abortion, and sexually transmitted disease (STD) rates rank among the highest in the developed world.[3] Curricula for these abstinence-only programs teach young men and women to stand against the vice-ridden dominant culture of sexual promiscuity by exhibiting courage to embrace the virtues of sexual purity, modesty, and chastity. The *Heritage Keepers: Abstinence Education* curriculum links these moral virtues with the civic ideals on which Americans founded an exceptional nation. Early Americans "built a land full of opportunity with ideals that would eventually inspire the world," the *Heritage Keepers* manual reads. "Today, we have the privilege of living in America. . . . A Heritage Keeper understands this privilege—they strive to preserve what they have been given and build upon it."[4] The message of abstinence, drawing on the nation's Puritan moral legacy and American exceptionalism, resonated loudly enough with the people and politicians to make it the primary approach to sex education policy from the mid-1990s into the mid-2000s.[5]

President Obama's administration swung the pendulum back again by dropping all funds for abstinence-only programs from its 2010 federal budget and overturning the "global gag rule" that banned the distribution of federal funds to foreign nongovernmental family planning organizations that offer information other than about abstinence. Such cyclical policy shifts characterize backlash politics, which reach beyond conservative forces focused on protecting certain moral traditions and lock national debates into a gendered moral logic framed by virtue and vice. Relating the contemporary debate over sex education to the early republican debate over women's education illustrates how the dualistic logic of virtue and vice perpetuates backlashes in a democratic politics held hostage by the ideals of purity, chastity, and modesty. The early republican debate indicates how women's moral guardianship translates into their double burden of moral responsibility for public and private life. As made evident in the contemporary debates over sex education, women's political identity as moral guardians becomes an essential feature of backlash politics, which blames an entire society's decay on the sexual behavior of individual women.

Understanding how virtue and vice function in a political community helps us track how it distributes moral responsibility between men and women and map out the topography of the moral terrain that defines women's citizenship as suspect. Responsibility is defined here as the moral decision making that involves interrogating the standing assumptions that determine how, when, why, and to whom personal, social, economic, and political resources are distributed to meet the needs, wants, and desires of the self and others in community.[6] The unequal distribution of moral responsibility between men and women allows men to exercise what Joan Tronto calls privileged irresponsibility, or the power to "ignore certain forms of hardships that they do not have to face."[7] Instead of responsibilities, male citizens assume obligations, the more rigid requirements and specifications, most explicitly laid out in contracts, arising from the formal rules and promises characteristic of political and economic life. Obligation aligns with the male public sphere and responsibility with the female private sphere. Female finite moral virtues acquire a civic dimension during the republican era that transforms women's moral responsibility into an obligation to uphold, through their infinite moral virtue, the common good. This circumstance sets American women up for failure, given their lack of formal political power to carry out this obligation, which makes them scapegoats for democracy. The female double burden of responsibility and male privileged irresponsibility, then, act as two gendered moral dynamics that construct women as moral guardians but suspect citizens and targets vulnerable to backlash politics.

Backlash politics draws attention to this political status premised on a set of gendered moral assumptions that generate mistrust in women's legitimacy as members of the political community. Virtue and vice represent and categorize a range of standing assumptions that perpetuate the stereotypes, biases, and prejudices that people, knowingly or not, use to assess each other's moral worth. Political communities rely on these codified standing assumptions to determine membership. The distribution of responsibility within a community puts the political dynamics of moral categories into motion. Margaret Urban Walker identifies assignment, negotiation, and deflection as three ways that communities distribute responsibility.[8] Assignment charts the distribution of moral responsibility among different categories of people according to standing assumptions about identity that define social roles. Negotiation refers to the process by which people, individually and collectively, interrogate through deliberation with the self and others the standing assumptions behind the choices involved in determining the distribution of moral responsibilities. Deflection illustrates how the emphasis of one category over another creates a default for moral assumptions that justifies excluding categories of information and groups of people. These three processes are used here to track how male and female virtue and vice determine the distribution of responsibility that charts the standing assumptions deployed in backlash politics.

Trust, a fundamental political act in democracy that binds each person through a promise to consent to the social contract, involves an assessment of moral character based on either accepting or interrogating the standing assumptions categorized as virtue and vice. Backlash discourse deflects attention from interrogation toward unreflective acceptance of moral assumptions that maintain women's political status quo as virtuous moral guardians of the common good. Any real or perceived challenge to these assumptions represents a breach of political trust. Women's struggles for gender equality and sexual liberation equate, then, with the traitorous act of rejecting their allegiance to the nation. Backlash politics effectively awakens suspicions deeply embedded within the American political script. Such backlashes operate on sets of moral assumptions designed to ensure stability by resisting the changes associated with women's economic, social, and political advancement.

The suspicion that jeopardizes women's legitimacy as full citizens holds broader implications for American democracy. Backlashes capitalize on a paradox of American citizenship that entrusts women with the nation's common good while mistrusting their ability to make decisions about their bodies and intimate relationships and entrusts men to protect women, while denying men the moral capacity to ensure the nation's future. Mistrust in men's and women's moral capacity to fulfill their responsibilities to democracy results in a privileging of irresponsibility that characterizes American citizenship. Citizens turn away from interrogating standing moral assumptions that perpetuate bias and prejudice, seeking neither structural solutions to national problems nor active political engagement. Privileging irresponsibility as a trait of membership in a democratic community indicates that American citizenship may be suspect.

Debating Women's Education and Moral Guardianship in the Republican Era

A national debate over women's education emerged at the turn of the nineteenth century in response to the idea of motherhood as politically important to the American republic. Since wives and mothers can maintain the common good by conveying moral virtues to their husbands and children, republican motherhood grants American women citizenship based on their moral superiority in the private sphere and exclusion from public life's corruption and vice. The Family Man characterized republican manhood. American men sustained political power through patriarchal control over women in the private sphere, a strategy used to tame disorderly men by motivating them to marry and start families. Male civic virtue depended on managing female moral vices such as deceit and corruption. Politicians hoped that men, focused on ruling their families, would then leave governing to them.[9] Direct political engagement loses its moral value as male civic virtue derives from ruling over a man's wife and female civic virtue emanates from a woman's political exclusion. A serious challenge to democratic citizenship arose during the republican era. Proposals to advance women's education threatened to dislodge a gendered moral logic strategically deployed to deflect people's attention away from exercising power in the political arena.

Opponents to reforming women's education, echoing Puritan ministers and magistrates, engage in a version of backlash politics that frames such social change as a threat to God's natural patriarchal order. The infinite female moral virtues of piety, wisdom, and meekness anchor this discourse in a Christian belief system. Piety combines with wisdom in assertions that women's education should cultivate only the reason necessary to strengthen their devotion to God and enhance their social appeal. Reverend John Bennett advises, in his widely read *Letters to a Young Lady*, that a young American woman's "proper pursuit of knowledge . . . will aid and inflame your *piety*, and render you much more valuable and interesting to all your acquaintance. When the *foundation* is laid in virtue, the *superstructure* may have every graceful embellishment."[10] Republican women's acquisition of the ornaments or virtues adorning the daughters of Zion takes a more secular turn by extending faith in God to reason and valuing intellect along with physical beauty. Reverend James Fordyce, a minister in England whose *Sermons to Young Women* became quite popular there and in America, fears women's education will embolden them with the reason to abandon the infinite female virtue of meekness, which enables women to obey God's command to serve as helpmeets and challenge His natural patriarchal order.

Meekness also acts as the cornerstone for constructing the finite virtues that form the female character of moral guardianship. Finite female virtues, Reverend Fordyce outlines, include "decency of character, dignity of conduct, the honours due to temperance, integrity, benevolence, magnanimity, and other qualities of that order are ideas as solid as they are refined, and which ought certainly to be cherished by all who are capable of comprehending their moment."[11] These virtues reflect the high normative value placed on women's generous, forgiving nature in response to insult or injury, and their ability to temper their passions. Republican women become guardians over their moral character by controlling self-expression and emotions for the benefit of others, personal traits conducive to social harmony and stability.

In return for their meekness, women receive the reward of male guardianship. "Nothing can be more certain than that your sex is, on every account, entitled to the shelter of ours," Reverend Fordyce explains. "Your softness, weakness, timidity, and tender reliance on man; your helpless condition in yourselves, and his superior strength for labour, ability for defense, and fortitude in trial; your tacit acknowledgement of these, and frequent application for his aid in so many winning ways, concur to form a plea, which nothing can disallow or withstand but brutality."[12] Submission to male protection fulfills God's law, affording women "the guardianship of Omnipotence, as that which must give efficacy to all the rest; but which can only be obtained by something more and better than them all, I mean, True Religion."[13] Basic reading and writing, opponents argued, sufficed to cultivate the reason necessary for the female virtues of meekness and submission. Education beyond these fundamentals threatens to provide women with knowledge that could encourage them to challenge their submission to God and man. Women's dependence on the protection of men and God limits their moral guardianship to keeping a vigilant watch over their own virtue.

Reformers such as Benjamin Rush and Judith Sargent Murray replace piety with wisdom as the primary infinite female virtue to advocate for a broader course of study and access to education for women while retaining the role of male guardianship. Rush maintains an explicit tie between virtue and America's biblical tradition. "The only foundation for a useful education in a republic is to be laid in RELIGION," Rush proclaims. "Without this there can be no virtue, and without virtue there can be no liberty, and liberty is the object and life of all republican governments."[14] Religion, then, provides the moral grounds for virtue and freedom.

Murray, perhaps the most radical of the reformers, takes a more secular approach but ultimately upholds male guardianship and the patriarchal order. Advancing a position echoed by Mary Wollstonecraft, Murray contends that equal education will reveal women's capacity for memory, judgment, reason, and imagination as equals to men. Yet Murray, in line with her opponents, sustains men's natural superiority over women. "O ye arbiters of our fate! Murray decries. "We confess that the superiority is indubitably yours; you are by nature formed for our protectors; we pretend not to vie with you in bodily strength; upon this point we will never contend for victory." Unlike Reverend Fordyce, Murray then introduces some equality into the relationship between men and women. "Shield us then, we beseech you, from external evils and in return *we* will transact *your* domestick [*sic*] affairs."[15] Equal education grants women access to reason and the infinite virtue of wisdom, which enables them to assume a "separate but equal" role in the private sphere. Submission to male guardianship transforms into an exchange relationship that presumes a greater level of sexual equality that challenges patriarchy without completely abandoning it.

Meekness essentially disappears from the reformers' discourse since education would develop women's reason, enabling them to exercise the independence needed for women to meet the republic's changing political demands as its moral guardians. Focus on the finite realm of family, education, and the republic shifts reformers' attention away from the infinite spiritual realm of religion. Murray builds her arguments using historical, instead of biblical, female figures. According to Murray, Jane of Flanders and Queen Margaret of Anjou, who lost their lives fighting and leading military battles to defend their countries, should serve as models of virtue for American women. Drawing on such figures, Murray attributes male civic virtues of courage, bravery, and fortitude to women, bolstering her claim that, although they may never actually engage in military feats, women's minds and wills equal men's in strength, which positions them to contribute to political life.

By exhibiting a great love of country, American women also acquire the civic virtue of patriotism crucial to binding a republic together. Wives and mothers who watch their husbands and sons head to battle and endure their deaths with fortitude, for Murray, exhibit a level of patriotism unrivaled even by soldiers and their commanders much less the average male citizen. Mothers sacrificing their sons for the greater good exceed the commitment to the nation made by military and political leaders. As Murray explains, "Nor is the patriotism of the chief arrayed for the battle; nor his, who devotes himself with all a statesman's integrity to the public weal, condemned to an ordeal more severe."[16] Such comparisons construct women as participating in guardianship of the nation. Patriotism grants American women political legitimacy by linking the courage, fortitude, and bravery exercised by wives and mothers in private life to this civic virtue that extends from the finite realm of the family to an infinite capacity to sacrifice for the nation's common good as its moral guardians.

This national debate captures how spiritual devotion to God begins to merge with a love of country that assigns women a sacred political status as moral guardians. Protecting the common good requires an infinite capacity to understand how individual moral actions intertwine to bind a nation's moral fabric together. Murray captures the expansive nature of women's morality:

> The pleasures of women must arise from their virtues, these great expressions of nature—these heart-rending emotions, which fill us at once with wonder, compassion and terror, always have belonged, and always will belong, to women. They possess, in those moments, an inexpressible something, which carries them beyond themselves; and they seem to discover to us new souls, above the standard of humanity.[17]

Virtues grounded in reason combine with women's natural capacity for the emotions necessary to reproducing and nurturing human life to give women a unique ability to transcend the self and material reality. Murray values women's devalued emotions in order to grant them moral superiority. Access to this infinite plane of existence assigns women's emotions a sacred role in upholding a nation's commitment to the common good that transcends the people's everyday experiences. Women's moral guardianship evolves in this republican context by directly linking finite female virtues such as fortitude and courage with a God-given natural emotional capacity that empowers them to see the infinite, abstract common good and to protect it.

The profane operates in tandem with the sacred as these debates over women's education turn to the matter of Eve, who causes humanity's downfall by eating from the Tree of Knowledge of good and evil, an act that burdens all women with original sin and an infinite capacity for vice. Reverend Fordyce opposes expanding women's education beyond basic skills by interpreting Eve's fall as resulting from an inability to temper her passions and exercise the self-denial and restraint that should define a woman's moral character. Eve lost the battle between "the finest sentiments and the grossest passions [that] have been observed to meet in the same mind," Fordyce explains. "Our First Mother was betrayed by the pride of knowing."[18] Uncontrolled desire for knowledge, then, causes Eve's and ultimately humanity's downfall. Women's pursuit of wisdom, categorized as an infinite moral virtue, transforms into an act of pride, one of the Seven Deadly Sins. Eve's fall serves as a cautionary tale that American women's access to an education beyond developing the reason necessary to temper their passions and strengthen their piety will lead to the nation's moral decay.

Benjamin Rush, alternatively, frames expanding women's education as essential to cleansing away Eve's original sin in order to protect America from the deteriorating effects of male vice and European influence. A course of study for American women must move from Europe's focus on female manners to classical texts about mathematics, geography, history, astronomy, and natural philosophy. Such an education, Rush argues, will prepare American women to "be the stewards and guardians of their husbands' property" in their absence, help protect the family from vacillating economic cycles, and teach their sons how to be citizens.[19] Educating women to meet the pragmatic needs of the private sphere as men increasingly left it for the public arena of economic life allowed women to assume greater responsibility for morality. "It will be in your power, LADIES, to correct the mistakes and practices of our sex by demonstrating that the female temper can only be governed by reason and that the cultivation of reason in women is alike friendly to the order of nature and to the private as well as public happiness," Rush declares.[20] Female reason grants women a more expansive or infinite capacity for virtue that extends well beyond controlling one's own actions to correcting the mistakes of others. Republican men, then, acquire the privilege to exercise moral irresponsibility.

Advancing a position premised on relative equality between men and women, Murray rejects such a redistribution of moral responsibility by accounting for Adam's role in the biblical story of human origins. Adam succumbs to the commonplace carnal desire for a woman, whereas Lucifer must use all his sinful powers to tempt Eve to eat from the Tree of Knowledge. This interpretation identifies men's moral weakness and spotlights women's strength of character in order to counterbalance the heavy weight of sin attributed to female morality. "His soul is formed in no sort superior, but every way equal to the mind of her, who is the emblem of weakness, and whom he hails the gentle companion of his better days," Murray asserts.[21] Men and women, according to this interpretation of Adam and Eve, assume equal moral responsibility for the Fall, which makes women's pursuit of knowledge no greater a threat to the nation or humanity than men's.

Rush asserts a more moderate position in which women's infinite moral virtue further extends their double burden of moral responsibility for the nation's "public happiness" or common good to all humanity. Allowing the daughters of Eve the education to cultivate virtue enables American women to restore the United States to its exceptional status as the Garden of Eden in the New World. "At least one spot of the earth," Rush states, "may be reserved as a monument of the effects of good education, in order to show in some degree what our species was before the fall and what it shall be after its restoration."[22] This biblical dimension references the continued weight of the profane embedded in American women's political identity as moral guardians but suspect citizens, assigned a double burden of responsibility for original sin and cleansing it away through an infinite moral virtue capable of protecting the republic and humanity from moral downfall.

Suspicion remains a central factor in building women's relationship to political life during the republican era despite the emphasis placed on their moral guardianship over the common good. Reformers and their opponents in the debates on women's education agree that female vice entails an infinite dimension capable of bringing down the whole nation. The era's growing social problems of women's poverty and prostitution, unlike men's finite vices of gambling, drinking, and sexual promiscuity, signified a moral abomination with infinite political implications. Identifying female vice as the indicator of America's demise, Benjamin Rush predicts that, "we shall probably too soon follow the footsteps of the nations of Europe in manners and vices. The first marks we shall perceive of our declension will appear among our women. Their idleness, ignorance, and profligacy will be the harbingers of our ruin."[23] Women's education, though differing in form and content, both sides of this debate contend, will rein in female moral vice by cultivating their reason. This, Reverend Fordyce argues in a puritanical fashion, will enlist American women on the side of virtue and against sin and vice. Rush advances this position on the grounds that female reason will make them easier to control. "If men believe that ignorance is favorable to the government of the female sex," he explains, "they are certainly deceived, for a weak and ignorant woman will always be governed with the greatest difficulty."[24] Men, regardless of their privileged irresponsibility, retain the power to govern women, indicating a higher degree of mistrust in female virtue despite women's infinite capacity as the nation's moral guardians.

The gendered logic of the virtue-vice dualism operating in these debates over women's education illustrates how suspicion lingers just beneath the dominant discourse of republicanism. As women acquire infinite civic virtue that allows them to protect the republic's common good, this concept's dualistic logic translates infinite moral into civic vice by holding American women accountable for any sign of national decay. Infinite civic vice acts as a default category for any behavior, real or perceived, that, breaking with the standards of excellence necessary to maintain public-spiritedness, may contribute to the nation's moral and political decline. Attributing infinite civic vice to women locks suspicion of their political legitimacy into place.

Focus on men's and women's morality in these debates deflects attention away from the broader shifts occurring in the political structures of the republic. Women's moral and civic virtue derives from their role in private life as republican wives and mothers while men access moral and civic virtue as husbands who govern their wives. Maintaining the natural patriarchal order over the family, as opposed to direct political engagement, represents the average man's primary source of political power. Although men and women gain enough reason to cultivate virtue, their political power remains confined to moral capacities exercised in the private sphere of the family, leaving governance outside the average, non-property-owning person's grasp. Suspicion of men's privileged irresponsibility and women's ability to fulfill the double burden of moral responsibility cements societal doubt into the moral foundation of American citizenship. This unequal distribution of responsibility, however, keeps the spotlight on women as the source of national decay, and as backlash politics focus on female moral misbehavior, it effectively deflects attention away from broader political concerns.

Debating Contemporary Sex Education:
Resurrecting the Daughters of Eve and Zion

Late twentieth- and early twenty-first-century debates over abstinence-only-until-marriage and comprehensive sex education operate according to the virtue-vice dualism's gendered moral logic, which channels the legacy of the Puritans and republicans into contemporary American discourse, in which women remain moral guardians but suspect citizens. Abstinence-only advocates advance a "back to virtue" backlash politics to save America from its moral decline caused by the Sexual Revolution from the late 1960s into 1980s when second wave feminists won reproductive rights for women and sex education became part of the public school curriculum. Abstinence, as President George W. Bush declared in his 2004 State of the Union Address, represents the new "revolution of conscience, in which a rising generation is finding that a life of personal responsibility is a life of fulfillment."[25] Abstinence-only curricula encapsulates returning to a moral tradition grounded in Christian beliefs and reviving an exceptional political heritage built on stable heterosexual families. Comprehensive sex education curricula, in contrast, include a range of sexual identities, behaviors, and choices to shift moral decision making away from a particular tradition and toward the young person who lives in relationships with others. Both curricula provide sites for tracking the two other ways that communities distribute responsibility—assignment and negotiation—in order to identify how backlash discourses redeploy standing assumptions about women and men through the virtue-vice dualism.

Purity, the infinite moral virtue central to Puritan discourse, establishes abstinence-only curricula on America's biblical tradition as a means to secure young people's commitments to abstain from any sexual activity until heterosexual marriage. The *Heritage Keepers* manual describes a couple's wedding day as a celebration of a young woman's sexual purity symbolized by her white dress and veil. Purity balls, a staple of abstinence-only programs, serve as rituals in which young women publicly commit to remain virgins until marriage. Fathers often take their daughters to these balls, usually held in churches, and pledge "to choose before God to cover my daughter as her authority and protection in the area of purity."[26] Standing before a large cross, each daughter then kneels beneath two crossed swords and accepts a purity ring from her father, who will take the ring back and give it to her husband on their wedding day. Manhood ceremonies, though much less popular than purity balls, provide young men a rite of passage. Their fathers give them a purity ring to represent their commitment to protect women and honor God and a sword that enlists them in the battle for God on earth. Linking manhood with male guardianship over women maintains a patriarchal order established by the Puritans and continued during the republican era. A young woman's sexual purity remains the finite marker of her infinite moral virtue and marriage to God before man, which, in keeping with backlash discourses, means to connect current generations to moral traditions deeply embedded in the American political script.

These commitment ceremonies entail a religious component that also echoes Puritan moral discourse by intertwining the infinite moral virtue of piety with purity. True Love Waits, a leading campaign in the abstinence movement, developed commitment cards that read, "Believing that true love waits, I make a commitment to God, myself, my family, my friends, my future mate, and my future children to a lifetime of purity including sexual abstinence from this day until the day I enter a biblical marriage relationship."[27] Over two million young people from the United States and abroad have, according to True Love Waits, made this pledge at thousands of events and online, allowing them to swear before God that they will abstain from sex until marriage. Young people who voluntarily or involuntarily engaged in sexual activity can also commit to secondary virginity, which abstinence-only curricula defines as a physical, mental, and emotional recommitment to saving sex for marriage. This pledge cleanses away their past sexual activity and enables them emotionally and spiritually to reclaim their virginity. Abstinence-only programs reconfigure the physical act of sexual intercourse as a religious matter that retains a sacred link between people and God. Piety and purity function as infinite moral virtues in this backlash discourse that effectively taps into America's biblical tradition to recast Puritan beliefs in the twenty-first century.

Assigning young men and women different finite moral virtues based on the responsibilities attributed to their respective sex roles function to preserve their sexual purity in abstinence-only curricula. Young women in a *Heritage Keepers* lesson plan, for example, receive a "Be a Man!"

handout that lists the four traits of a "real man" as strong, respectful, courageous, and protective. These traditional finite male virtues teach young women to accept standing assumptions about men's natural role as women's guardians whose independence and power derive from men's greater physical strength.[28] The "Be a Real Woman!" handout given to young men addresses positive self-esteem and body image by describing "a real woman" as knowing who and what she wants to become. Part of this confidence in her self-identity, however, requires that "a real woman" sends a clear message about herself through her speech, dress, and actions that, the handout explains, rightly or wrongly, leads people to assume who she is on the basis of how she looks.[29] This lesson redeploys a moral legacy rooted in Puritanism by perpetuating the assumption that modest appearance and behavior indicate a woman's moral virtue of chastity.

These male and female finite virtues serve to justify the unequal distribution of moral responsibility assigned to traditional sex roles. "A Real Woman," the *Heritage Keepers* handout further explains, must also "remember that most guys are more visually stimulated than girls, and they might mistake your fashion statement for a sexual statement." It then warns, "Make sure your sexual messages match your sexual values."[30] Any reference to guys controlling their sexual behavior remains absent from the "Be a Man" handout. These young men and women learn from this lesson to accept the sexual double standard that assigns women the moral responsibility for their sexual behavior while men, despite their male guardianship, exercise privileged irresponsibility for controlling their sexual desire. Women, abstinence-only curricula teach, should act based on the standing moral assumptions that perpetuate sexual objectification by casting male strength in terms of controlling women's sexuality. Modesty and chastity act as protective measures that women must take to preserve their sexual purity, the marker of female virtue, until heterosexual marriage.

Heterosexuality functions as the standing assumption about sexuality in these programs premised on the biblical moral tradition. Zero percent of authentic abstinence-only curricula include the subject of homosexuality.[31] Homosexuality is a sin according to the biblical interpretations informing these programs, which makes gay and lesbian sexual identities the wrong moral choice for young people, who will suffer punitive consequences such as HIV/AIDS and STDs.[32] This moral logic frames homosexuality as an irresponsible decision, aligning it with infinite vice and sin. Heterosexuality, as a result, retains its place as the assumed normative standard of virtue.

Distributing moral responsibility according to the traditional sexual division of labor in abstinence-only curricula perpetuates the standing assumptions supporting the sex roles necessary for heterosexual marriage and families. Sixth graders, a *Why kNOw?* lesson instructs, learn about these sex roles by first writing down on token chips the household responsibilities of their mothers and fathers, such as cleaning, cooking meals, employment outside the home, and bill paying. Then they place each token in one of two jars marked "Mother" and "Father."[33] If confusion arises, the manual directs, teachers should explain the "right" jar into which students should drop the token in order to educate them that men and women possess unique and different abilities. The lesson ends with the teacher removing one jar to show that only two heterosexual parents can meet the responsibilities of a family. The *Heritage Keepers* "Be a Man!" handout discussed earlier focuses on the traits of the male breadwinner and, in keeping with this model, omits any reference to male responsibility for care of the family. The "Be a Real Woman!" handout, alternatively, spotlights women's caregiving role by identifying "caring" as definitive of female moral character.[34] The heterosexual division of labor in these curricula sustains the unequal distribution of responsibility for care in families, which remains assigned to women. Men are freed to maintain their privileged irresponsibility as care receivers who decide if, when, how, and for whom they will care.

Abstinence-only curricula effectively redeploy the storyline evident in the Puritan and republican contexts by constructing twenty-first-century American women as moral guardians assigned the burden of taking care of themselves, their husbands, and their families *and* responsibility for their own sexual behavior and that of men. Men retain the privilege to exercise irresponsibility for their sexual behavior and the care of others. Despite this unequal distribution of responsibility, these curricula fail to identify that other men pose the danger from which they are entrusted to protect women. A *Heritage Keepers* lesson about weddings, for instance, teaches the young man that the woman whom he will marry "loves you and trusts you with all that she is and all that she has." The young woman, the lesson then explains, must be "ready to trust him with all that you have and all that you are, and, because you have waited, you have it all to give."[35] Trust, then, flows only from the woman to the man, which establishes this marital bond on patriarchal assumptions that wives enter this unequal relationship in return for their husbands' protection. Transferring trust to men, even though they retain the privilege to act irresponsibly, conveys the underlying suspicion of women who, although assigned the double burden of moral responsibility, require protection first by their fathers and then their husbands.

Comprehensive curricula challenge this unequal distribution of moral responsibility. "In a sexual relationship," the SIECUS *Guidelines* state, "both partners, regardless of gender, have equal rights and responsibilities."[36] Men lose their privilege to exercise irresponsibility. Young people actively participate in challenging the gendered assumptions behind traditional sex roles. Students in an Advocates for Youth lesson, for example, work in same-gender groups to list the most damaging gender stereotypes associated with "male" and "female." Groups then discuss the advantages and disadvantages of membership in the opposite gender. The class ends with all the students discussing exceptions to gendered traits such as male strength and female caring assigned by society to men and women.[37] Disrupting traditional sex roles corresponds with showing how the sexual division of labor no longer reflects contemporary workforce realities. The facilitator in one Planned Parenthood lesson invites men and women who perform jobs considered nontraditional for their sex such as male nurses and female construction workers to the class to demonstrate that most women work in the paid labor force and that men do perform "unconventional" labor.[38] Such experiences engage young people in critically assessing the assumptions behind gender stereotypes and how they limit full human expression and opportunities.

Heterosexuality also no longer remains a standing moral assumption. Comprehensive programs integrate the full spectrum of orientations, from heterosexual, gay, and lesbian to transsexual, bisexual, and questioning throughout their curricula. Sexuality, as the SIECUS *Guidelines* explain, constitutes a part of human development, not a choice, which distances this approach from the religious moralism advanced in abstinence-only curricula.[39] Students in a Planned Parenthood lesson, for example, identify and critically examine stereotypes and myths about gays and lesbians, such as their appearance, sexual promiscuity, and AIDS as a "gay" disease.[40] Such activities allow young people to encounter how moral assumptions function to categorize those who diverge from society's normative standards of virtue as vice-ridden and sinful. Interrogating sexuality, sex roles, and the sexual division of labor enables comprehensive programs to reframe certain societal structures premised on heterosexual two-parent marriage and redistribute moral responsibility for sexual behavior from women to men to achieve greater gender equality.

Comprehensive sex education, despite its critical stance toward gender and sexuality stereotypes, fails to interrogate directly the female moral virtues of purity, chastity, and modesty, which remain standing assumptions that drive how the political culture engages with young women's and men's sexuality. Together, these three virtues justify male privileged irresponsibility for their sexual behavior, which leaves women carrying the double burden of moral responsibility and perpetuates moral assumptions supporting gender inequality. Purity, chastity, and modesty represent three defining virtues for women deeply embedded in the American political script's gendered moral tradition. The dualistic moral logic operates politically in this context to locate those who directly challenge the female virtues upholding sexual purity as promoting the vices of female impurity, immodesty, and promiscuity. Advocates for comprehensive sex education, by avoiding female virtue, sidestep a moral landmine that all opponents to backlashes in the United States encounter. American society assigns vice to those who interrogate standing moral assumptions about virtue, which undermines the legitimacy of their position with the broader public and can effectively cast them as causing the nation's moral fabric to decay.

Attention to moral decision making in abstinence-only and comprehensive programs illustrates the second way that communities distribute responsibility: through negotiation, a process that entails navigating the range of choices involved in determining the best course of action. Suspicion about young people's ability to negotiate decision making about their sexual lives characterizes abstinence-only programs. A zero-tolerance approach toward any information in the curricula about reducing risks of sexual activity through contraception or other means aims to avoid sending young people a mixed message that real alternatives to abstinence exist. To communicate this "risk elimination" message, Focus on the Family's *No Apologies* manual associates teen sexual activity with the other high-risk behaviors of drugs, alcohol, violence, and smoking.[41] Such character-based curricula also equate any form of sexual activity among young people with sin, evil, and vice that will bring them shame, guilt, and harm. Abstinence until marriage, accordingly, represents the only choice for young people as the path to virtue. The True Love Waits Bible-based curriculum draws explicitly on apocalyptic religious language to categorize premarital sex as evil. "Satan's plan is for you to be sexually disoriented and confused," a church sermon on teen chastity included in their manual declares. "God's plan is to reveal His true nature through your commitment to purity."[42] Such language, echoing that of Puritans and republican opponents to women's education, raises teen sex to the level of a struggle between God and Satan, good and evil. The wrong decision can condemn the young person for eternity. Portraying teens confused about sexuality as morally wrong and evil intentionally uses fear and shame to instill a commitment to abstinence.[43] Negotiating moral decisions narrows the choice either to abstain from sex or endure steep moral, social, and even religious consequences.

Obedience to authority and tradition as the way for young people to engage in moral decision making eliminates negotiating choice and exercising freedom and self-determination from abstinence-only curricula. A *Why kNOw?* "What Is Freedom?" lesson sums up this approach in the formula "F = D + R," in which "F" stands for freedom, "D" for discipline, and "R" for rules. "True freedom," students learn, results from "disciplining oneself to follow the rules to achieve self-mastery or dominance in a given situation."[44] The rules emanate from certain traditions in which abstinence represents a moral standard that young people must obey if they hope to achieve virtue. The *Heritage Keepers* manual invokes America's Judeo-Christian tradition. The *Why kNOw?* curriculum turns to a patriarchal tradition of marriage. The True Love Waits program imposes the will of God. As authority figures, parents, certain educators, and religious leaders convey to young people these traditions and the consequences imposed for deviating from the moral dictate of abstinence. "Responsibility is built upon obeying consistently," a Teen-Aid lesson teaches, since it "brings order to situations and prevents health and relationship problems."[45] Such obedience to authority eliminates negotiating a moral decision-making process in which assuming responsibility for one's actions amounts to accepting the right choice of abstinence as determined by tradition. Shutting down negotiation in this way also prevents young people from critically engaging the standing assumptions behind the traditions determining their decisions. Standards of behavior, as a result, appear as natural or God-given and beyond question. Suspicion of young people's ability to negotiate moral decision making extends to authority figures such as parents, who should only convey rules established by traditions instead of teaching their children how to navigate the complexities of assuming responsibility for their choices.

Comprehensive curricula take a value-neutral, instead of a character-based, approach. Developing trust in themselves and their ability to assess situations and make choices using a deliberative process anchors this approach, which focuses on teaching young people how to negotiate moral decision making. Suspicion then shifts from people's ability to make moral choices to the standing assumptions behind tradition and authority, which become sites of interrogation as young people learn, instead of obediently accepting rules dictated by tradition, to reach normative judgments by negotiating many factors. Considering social contexts and the people in them becomes essential to "making responsible decisions about sexuality because those decisions affect individuals and the people around them," the SIECUS *Guidelines* state.[46] A Planned Parenthood lesson on healthy sexuality enacts this guideline by asking young people to assess different scenarios such as a young man rejecting responsibility for his girlfriend's pregnancy and a young woman deciding to ask her health teacher about protection for oral sex with her girlfriend.[47] Such curriculum educates young people about accounting for the complex moral terrain of social contexts that they must negotiate to determine if and to what degree they will assume responsibility in response to a given situation. This value-neutral approach to moral character reflects a level of trust in, rather than a suspicion of, young people's capacity to exercise the freedom necessary for self-determination marked by moral decision making.

The moral logic framing comprehensive and abstinence-only curricula deflects attention away from how the virtue-vice dualism shapes the negotiation and assignment of responsibility. Debates over social policies such as sex education, as a result, lock into an oppositional dynamic determined by underlying standing assumptions that remain unquestioned. Abstinence-only programs stake a claim to a moral tradition deeply aligned with the Puritan and republican legacies. American women, these curricula teach, must recommit to assuming the double burden assigned to them as moral guardians aligned with the moral and civic finite female virtues of chastity and modesty, which grant women the infinite virtue of purity that enables them to preserve the nation's common good. These daughters of Zion retain their original moral position as the daughters of Eve, however, and those who question this moral tradition are aligned with the vice, sin, and evil of which society already suspects them. This moral dynamic drives backlash discourse and frames opponents as suspicious by locating them on the side of vice for critically engaging standing moral assumptions in the American political script, a position that can be seen as traitorous.

Comprehensive programs still teach abstinence as the best choice for young people despite the fact that most American teens have sex before their high school graduation.[48] Standing assumptions that derive from the female finite and infinite virtues of purity, chastity, and modesty maintain a high barrier that prevents groups from advocating for a healthy active sexuality for all people, including those under the age of eighteen. Public dialogue about desire, passion, and playfulness as part of a complex, healthy sexual life remains aligned with the vice of sexual promiscuity, locating it outside the moral bounds of political deliberation. The gendered virtue-vice dualism continues to stymie such public engagement with social policies in which the female virtues of purity, chastity, and modesty set the terms for debate. Sex and sexuality trigger assumptions of vice-ridden behavior that shut down consideration of both as essential elements that form relationships necessary to community. This moral dynamic framing debates between backlash forces and their opponents indicates a broader societal suspicion about whether the American people can engage in a public dialogue about healthy sex and sexuality that moves beyond the confines of purity and chastity for women and a "boys will be boys" attitude toward men.

Scapegoats for Democracy: Trust, Blame, and Irresponsibility in American Citizenship

Debates about education in the early republican and contemporary contexts reveal the dualistic logic of virtue and vice operating behind standing moral assumptions, which continue to perpetuate backlash politics by deflecting attention toward morality and away from political engagement and structural solutions to social problems. The republican era debates over women's education illustrate how women's double burden of responsibility grants men privileged irresponsibility. This dynamic generates societal doubt about the capacity of average men or women to participate fully in public life. Women's construction as virtuous moral guardians indicates a deeper suspicion of granting the people full citizenship. Focusing national attention on male and female moral and civic virtue and vice in cycles of backlash politics deflects attention away from this societal distrust that ultimately devalues active political engagement as essential to democratic citizenship.

Societal suspicion also shapes contemporary debates over sex education in which standing assumptions about sex and sexuality as vice-ridden shut down public dialogue about their importance to a healthy life and community. Structural solutions to addressing social problems related to young people's sexual behavior remain excluded from a public debate defined by individuals assuming moral responsibility independent of context. Broader social, political, and economic factors that influence young people's decision making about their sexual behavior fall outside the scope of consideration. Most European nations, in contrast, locate their comprehensive sex education programs within a set of government policies designed to transition young people into the job market and higher education, provide easy access to medical services, and guarantee universal health insurance—three factors that contribute to their lower teen pregnancy and STD rates.[49] Addressing structural factors and personal decision making in this comprehensive approach also affects abortion rates, which remain much lower than those in the United States.[50] In stark contrast, legislation on sex education policy in the United States fails to account for such structural factors and focuses instead on personal responsibility. The Responsible Education for Life Act, which died in committee, limited its proposal to adding contraception to the information about abstinence provided in family life education. The Patient Protection and Affordable Care Act, passed in 2010, allows the states to choose between the Title V Abstinence-Only-Until-Marriage Program and the Personal Responsibility Education Program, the first-ever dedicated funding stream for comprehensive sexuality education.[51] This comprehensive program, as its name suggests, emphasizes individual decision making based on information about abstinence and contraception. Structural factors remain unaddressed. This commitment to personal responsibility as the answer to social problems deflects attention away from political solutions based on a set of moral assumptions framed by virtue and vice.

These debates, spanning two centuries, reflect a deeper challenge to democratic citizenship. Women's political identity still conforms to their construction as moral guardians who must acquire female moral virtue to achieve any political standing. Any departure from this path, such as education or sexual liberation, triggers a backlash that equates these advances in women's freedom and equality with an entire society's decay. The infinite female virtues of piety and purity intertwine to sustain the moral conditions necessary for this societal suspicion, yet this normative standard for judging women requires a level of perfection that transcends human ability and experience. This paradoxical moral status perpetuates societal mistrust of women's capacity to maintain their tenuous grasp on citizenship as members whose loyalty to the political community remains in question. Male vices, alternatively, are not seen as dangers to the nation or humanity, allowing males the privilege of irresponsibility as citizens. American society, then, trusts those deemed irresponsible and denies that trust to those held morally responsible for its future.

The gendered dynamics of the virtue-vice dualism operating in the American political script enable backlash politics to trigger this societal mistrust in such a way that people turn to established moral tradition as the way forward. Politics is an arena abandoned to moral assumptions instead of one that engages democratic citizens in deliberative dialogue and recognizes the government as a necessary component in addressing the structural aspect of social problems. Standing moral assumptions deeply embedded in the American political script cast political engagement and political solutions as suspect. Societal distrust extends from women, the scapegoats and moral guardians of democracy, to the people and government policies necessary for democracy to function. American citizenship characterized by privileging irresponsibility frames all the people as suspect.

4 | Suspect Citizenship

From Lowell Mill Girls to Lesbian Feminists and Sadomasochism

Battles over sex roles, sexual practices, and sexuality become "wars" at turning points in U.S. political history when women, knowingly or not, stand in opposition to moral guardianship. The Lowell mill girls—the first nearly all-female labor force in the United States between 1826 and 1850—challenged mid-nineteenth-century conceptions of True Womanhood merely by stepping onto the factory floors of textile mills in Lowell, Massachusetts. A belief system dominant in the northern states during this period, True Womanhood based its moral standards on white upper- and middle-class wives and mothers serving as pillars of moral stability and domestic tranquility amid cycles of political, social, and economic change. The Lowell mill girls' failure to fit into this traditional sex role led to their appearance in the national debate at the time over "the labor problem." Reformers such as Orestes Brownson and Catharine Beecher opposed defenders of corporate policies such as Dr. Elisha Bartlett regarding whether female workers strengthened or damaged U.S. industry and society.

Another, often overlooked, debate simultaneously raged among the Lowell mill girls and broke them into two camps.[1] The loyalists supported the corporation's policies and conveyed how female laborers upheld the values of True Womanhood in the *Lowell Offering*, a monthly literary magazine that published editorials, poems, short stories, and essays by female textile workers. The *Offering* was financially backed by the Boston Associates, who owned the Lowell textile mills. The rebels argued for the right of women to decent wages and working conditions in their pro-labor newspaper, *Voice of Industry*, and eventually formed their own union, the Lowell Female Labor Reform Association (LFLRA). Doing so required the rebels to abandon the protections of female virtue, which, according to this dualism's logic, aligned them with vice.

Fast-forward to the sex wars that raged from the late 1970s into the early 1990s. Second wave feminists abandoned many remaining tenets of "True" or Traditional Womanhood by asserting women's right to sexual and reproductive freedom, which dramatically broke with conventional sex roles and politicized sexuality. Homosexuality and sadomasochism (S/M), usually relegated to the backwaters of national political debate as vices, moved into the mainstream of second wave feminism. This move triggered a backlash outside and inside the movement. The "lesbian issue," National Organization of Women (NOW) president Betty Friedan proclaimed, represented a "lavender herring" for the women's movement, and lesbians a "lavender menace." The gay-straight split within the movement emerged as a result.

Homosexuality and S/M collapsed into one category of vice, lumped together as extreme forms of sexual deviance, in mainstream national discourse during this time. S/M refers to a set of practices ranging from spanking and bondage to 24/7 slavery. It involves participants whose sexualities extend across the spectrum and communities that engage in specific and differing sexual and emotional practices.[2] Five key components differentiate S/M from other sexual practices: an explicit power relationship between a dominant and submissive pair, role-playing, consent, shared understanding between parties about the activities in a scene, and a sexual context.[3] S/M became a means for framing the gay and lesbian movement as a heightened threat to the moral fabric of American society because it was believed that the gay community advanced such deviant sexual practices, which would become rampant in America and cause many people to die, a depiction conveyed nationally by the CBS documentary *Gay Power, Gay Politics*. Vice squads in major cities such as San Francisco and New York City frequently targeted leather bars, where S/M practitioners in the gay community gathered, and arrested them for lewd and indecent behavior. The Alcoholic Beverage Commission (ABC) also threatened to revoke the licenses of every leather bar in San Francisco. The *Diagnostic and Statistical Manual of Mental Disorders* (*DSM*) in the 1970s listed homosexuality and S/M as mental disorders. Although the American Psychiatric Association removed homosexuality from the *DSM* in 1986, "sexual sadism" and "sexual masochism," referencing S/M, remain. Defining S/M practitioners and supporters as deviant, perverse, and mentally disabled aligns them explicitly with vice in political and social discourse.

Lesbian S/M practitioners, amid these violent external attacks on their communities, became more visible and vocal, which escalated a backlash response from radical and lesbian feminists. Attacks launched by Women against Violence in Pornography and Media (WAVPM) targeted the S/M content in pornography. To defend the lesbian S/M community from this frontal assault by anti-S/M radical and lesbian feminists, a group called Samois began organizing in 1978. It held informational presentations at local women's bookstores in San Francisco and at lesbian bars and public events such as the first Women's Leather Dance, Ms. Leather Contest, and Lesbian Pride Leather Dance.[4] LSM in New York City, Leather and Lace in Los Angeles, and Urania in Boston also organized to give voice to the pro-S/M position. *Coming to Power: Writings and Graphics on Lesbian S/M*, published by Samois in 1981, frames this sexual practice among lesbians as one of many ways women might explore desire in a conception of sex and sexuality liberated from patriarchy. Radical and lesbian feminists responded in *Against Sadomasochism: A Radical Feminist Analysis*, asserting that S/M reenacts patriarchal power dynamics of domination and subordination that undermine lesbian struggles for equality and freedom. Anti-S/M lesbian feminists, ironically, redeploy moral guardianship to frame their opposition to S/M as a sexual practice inconsistent with lesbianism and feminism.

This chapter brings these two seemingly disparate debates between the Lowell mill girls and lesbian feminists together into the same analytic space to understand how the moral logic of the virtue-vice dualism generates backlash politics within marginalized communities. Breaking with the dominant standards of female virtue, whether by working in a factory or loving other women, aligned the women involved in these internal debates with vice.[5] Anti-S/M lesbian feminists and loyalist Lowell mill girls, respectively, frame pro-S/M lesbian feminists and rebellious Lowell mill girls as vice-ridden despite their shared marginalization in American society. Thus, already vulnerable women transform into suspect citizens accused of betraying their own female communities. These internal debates redeploy the dualistic moral logic of virtue and vice used by the dominant political culture to oppress these communities of women. This dynamic indicates the deeply embedded nature of backlash politics that even operates within marginalized political groups.

Charged with vice by their opposition, the pro-labor Lowell mill girls and pro-S/M lesbian feminists occupy a libratory space that allows them to escape the dominant moral paradigm where they question the virtue-vice moral framework, consider other ethical possibilities, and effectively organize political action against the status quo. The rebellious Lowell mill girls adapt the rights-based discourse of Jacksonian democracy to address their specific issues as working women and advance quite revolutionary claims about women's rights well before the 1848 Seneca Falls *Declaration of Sentiments and Resolutions*. Pro-S/M lesbian feminists turn critical attention to fantasies as an essential component in S/M role-playing that provides a point of departure for examining moral imagination in a democratic feminist ethics. The position of both groups on the political and social margins of society enables these suspect citizens to act as "innovating ideologists" with a particular capacity "to see," or to have vision beyond an immediate reality in order to imagine the horizon of possible futures and ways to attain them.[6]

Lowell Mill Girl Debates: The Trap of True Womanhood

Young women throughout New England left family farms to work in the textile mills that began popping up along the coast between 1810 and 1860. The mill towns' remote locations and the fact that many men were migrating West made it difficult to recruit workers. The Boston Associates solved this labor shortage problem by taking the relatively unusual approach of recruiting young women—a cheap labor pool—from nearby farms to join the paid labor force in its Lowell, Massachusetts, textile mills. Breaking with the separate spheres ideology put the Boston Associates in the position of ensuring its female workers' moral virtue in order to satisfy the demands of True Womanhood that dominated the political culture. Idyllic portrayals of virtuous women working in factories came into conflict with the increased participation of mill girls in the labor movement, propelled by an economic depression that hit the textile industry in 1837. Women joined men in protesting poor working conditions and fighting for a ten-hour workday in the Ten Hour Movement. Loyalists and rebels initially responded to this contentious political context by appropriating the dominant discourse of True Womanhood to stake their separate claims to moral guardianship over the Lowell mill girls.

Loyalists did so by focusing on the mill girls' moral and intellectual cultivation. The lead proponent of the loyalist's position, Harriet Farley, describes the *Offering*'s mission in the following terms: "Factory girls have their faults, as well as their virtues. The latter we shall point out to the community, the former to themselves. We should like to influence them as moral and rational beings—to point out their duties to themselves and to each other."[7] Promoting the factory girls' virtues to the public and pointing out their faults or vices to the mill girls would enable loyalists to rectify the girls' moral shortcomings and elevate the female laboring class. A focus on moral instead of material issues, then, would most effectively advance the Lowell mill girls' cause. The *Offering*'s contributors, Farley declares, "have shown that their first and absorbing thought was not for an advance of wages or a reduction of labor hours. They have striven for improvement of head and heart before that of situation. They have attended more to self-reformation, than to the reformation of society."[8] Instead of concerning themselves with material matters beyond their control, mill girls should reform their moral character. Loyalists equate the rebels, because of their struggle for higher wages and a ten-hour workday, with vice, portraying them as greedy women pursuing individual self-interest. "Selfishness we have often thought to be a vice increased, if not engendered, by factory life," Farley declares, "where all are so isolated, so self-dependent, and so liable to be jostled by the bold and overbearing from their proper places, the degrading motto, 'Take care of Number One.'"[9] Standing firmly on the side of female moral virtue allows loyalists to act as moral guardians capable of molding the mill girls into True Women by directing their attention inward toward personal moral development.

Corporate wrongdoing, much less structural economic problems, disappear from the loyalists' moral calculus that holds each mill girl morally responsible for her job dissatisfaction. Loyalists never attribute the vices of wealth, greed, or selfishness to the Boston Associates, who profit financially at the expense of workers. Poor working conditions, they imply, actually derive from the mill girls' lack of virtue. Failure to care for themselves properly by seeing a doctor and purchasing the clothing necessary to endure factory conditions cause the mill girls' bad health. This moral equation factors out poor ventilation, dangerous working conditions, long hours, or wages so low that seeing a doctor or buying clothes was unaffordable. "Throughout the wide world there is wrong, injustice and oppression," Farley explains, "and we have no hope but it will remain so, until sin and selfishness have ceased."[10] Mill girls must cultivate their moral virtue and assume personal responsibility for their working conditions instead of fighting collectively for political change since their vice of selfishness, not corporate policies or economic pressures, creates the evils of factory life.

Female virtue served as a prerequisite for employment in the Lowell textile mills, and female vice a just cause for termination. The Boston Associates designed a system supported by the loyalists to guard the morality of the young, unmarried women whom it recruited. Regulation papers codified the rules of moral conduct for the mill girls, stipulating a 10 P.M. curfew, denial of visitors at "unreasonable" hours, regular church attendance, and complete abstinence from alcohol on all company property. Male overseers enforced this code inside the mills by firing and even blacklisting female workers who committed moral infractions. The Boston Associates held the landladies who ran their boardinghouses responsible for reporting any problems with the mill girls' moral conduct to the overseers. Boardinghouse keepers, overseers, and other corporate agents exercised so much power over the mill girls that many commonly referred to them as the "moral police." Loyalists advocated for such corporate paternalism and extended it to the mill girls by advising them to exercise "despotic" oversight over one another to protect themselves from vice and to keep each other on virtue's narrow path.[11] Aligning with the overseers, landladies, and corporation secured for loyalists the protections of virtue granted True Women at the cost of sacrificing their own basic freedoms as mill girls. Such moral policing illustrates how society distributes power based on an assessment of women's moral character as virtuous.

Rebels similarly adapted the moral guardianship discourse of True Womanhood but with the very different aim of advancing the fight for more freedom and equality for the Lowell mill girls. They frame their fight for a ten-hour workday in terms of granting the mill girls more freedom by giving them more time off to cultivate their morality and intellect by attending Lowell's abundant lectures, music recitals, and religious services and using its many libraries. Such activities would allow these young women to develop the faculties necessary to become mothers capable of passing virtue on to future generations. The Boston Associates' opposition to a ten-hour workday, according to this argument, prevents the mill girls from becoming educated moral mothers. "They tell us that our 'free institutions' are based upon the *virtue* and *intelligence* of the American people, and the influence of the mother, to form and mould the man," Sarah Bagley, a leader of the rebels, explains, "and in the next breath, that the way to make the mothers of the next generations virtuous, is to enclose them within the brick walls of a cotton mill from twelve and a half to thirteen and a half hours a day."[12] Women taking such political stands against an employer broke dramatically with assumptions of a True Woman's passivity. This dominant ideology, however, prevented rebels from challenging the confinement maintained by the moral police because it limited them to claiming virtue for Lowell's mill girls as future mothers. Abandoning moral guardianship discourse to advance their argument for a shorter workday would have intensified the rebels' association with vice and rendered them mute in the public debate.

Focusing on female moral virtue deflects attention away from broader structural change. Loyalists' sole concern with the mill girls' individual moral character, rebels contend, leads them to ignore broader material issues, such as shorter workdays, increased wages, and better ventilation systems in the factories, necessary to improve female virtue. On these grounds, rebels reject loyalist claims to moral guardianship over the Lowell mill girls. Bagley charges that, "as a guardian and friend of the moral and intellectual prosperity of factory operatives, the *Offering* should have taken high and independent grounds, recollecting that tedious, protracted labor, in a confined and impure atmosphere, was not calculated to fill its bright pages with free, healthy, and virtuous senti-ments."[13] Identifying such material conditions as essential to intellectual and moral well-being makes rebels the mill girls' true moral guardians. "With us and us alone," Bagley states, "rests the great responsibility of *the standard of female virtue in Lowell*."[14] Virtue, then, belongs to the rebels who fight against, instead of passively accept, human oppression. "Every *Female* who realizes the great necessity of a *Reform* and improve-ment in the condition of the worthy, toiling classes, and who would wish to place woman in the elevated station . . . is most *cordially* in-vited to attend and give her influence on the side of *virtue* and *suffering humanity*," proclaims Huldah J. Stone, secretary for the Female Labor Reform Association.[15] Stone calls women to use their "elevated station" and virtue to help humanity's virtuous laboring class. Aligning female reformers with virtue assigns vice to loyalists and the Boston Associ-ates, who oppose changes designed to improve working conditions. This inversion of who belongs to which moral category fails to challenge the structural framework and logic of moral guardianship. This strategy, in the long run, undermines the rebels' position by maintaining the in-equality and constraints of the virtue-vice dualism.

Loyalists redeploy the hierarchical logic of virtue and vice to argue for raising the mill girls, seen as social pariahs, up to the moral stan-dards of True Womanhood by cultivating their virtue and intellect. "We wished to show the world, that labor which has been thought most de-grading, was not inconsistent with mental and moral cultivation," Har-riet Farley explains. "We would have taught a lesson to those in the Old World, who say that democratic institutions level downward, but *never* upward."[16] Framing their position in the egalitarian terms of leveling "upward" perpetuates inequality by maintaining the True Woman as virtuous and the mill girl as vice-ridden. "We would not pull down the superior to the position of the more humble, but would raise the humble to the elevation of the superior," Farley maintains.[17] Morally and in-tellectually inferior mill girls, then, must work to achieve the level of wealthy, well-educated women who embody the standards of female vir-tue in the era's dominant ideology of True Womanhood.

Working within this moral framework, rebels approach "leveling upward" by resorting to the same strategy of inverting who belongs to each category. They reject the wealthy class as a standard for virtue and expose the irony of loyalists, who celebrate the leisure class and degrade the mill girls. "The elevation and promotion of the real producers of our country to that station and standing in society which they were by a beneficent God designed to occupy!" Stone exclaims. "Too long have the virtuous poor been looked down upon as a lower race of beings, while vice and crime of the darkest hue, rolled in luxury and splendor through our streets."[18] Moral standards, rebels contend, should realign to grant virtue to workers, who produce the nation's goods and services, and vice to the wealthy, who live off of the backs of "the virtuous poor." Bagley reframes Farley's position on leveling upward by proposing that "we would not seek to bring them [the wealthy] down (God knows that all such are already low enough in the scale of moral excellence) but we would seek to elevate, to ennoble, to raise higher the standard of moral excellence and human attainments."[19] Inverting the moral valuing of workers and the wealthy to achieve class equality, however, leaves the logic of the virtue-vice dualism justifying inequality in place.

The dualistic logic of virtue and vice undermines the rebels' struggle to advance mill girls' freedom and equality. When pushing for material change, morality diverts rebels away from economic proposals and concerns. When calling for equality, rebels invert the virtuous rich and vice-ridden poor without challenging the premise of this moral hierarchy. When arguing for freedom, they limit their fight to reducing the workday by two hours and leaving the moral police unchallenged. Rebels, recognizing the limits of moral guardianship for advancing their cause, turn away from its virtue-based discourse and toward the rights-based discourse increasingly used by workers in Jacksonian America. Bagley conveys this discursive shift when explaining that the *Voice of Industry*'s "Female Department" "will also defend women's rights, and while it contends for physical improvement, it will not forget that she is a social, moral, and religious being."[20] Rights for women move into the foreground as rebels shift the ideology of True Womanhood to the background.

The Rebels: Weakening the Bonds of Virtue

This shift reflects how rebels became what James Farr calls "innovating ideologists," who respond to the "extended implications or unintended consequences of two or more beliefs" by attempting to resolve their apparent contradictions.[21] Given the ideological context of True Womanhood, rebels and loyalists act innovatively by arguing that women who worked in factories could achieve the virtue reserved for wealthy women. Loyalists broke with the separate spheres ideology premised on the idea that women's virtue derived from their roles as wives and mothers, not as paid laborers. Yet rebels went further by attempting to resolve the apparent contradiction between their democratic commitment to human equality and freedom and the inequality and constraint characteristic of the True Womanhood ideology. Focusing on the mill girls' moral character failed to address the structural and material issues related to their struggle for decent working conditions, hours, and wages. Such changes, the rebels came to realize, require collective pressure on the corporation to improve workers' lives. As a result, rebels abandon the virtue-based discourse and adapt the democratic rights-based discourse gaining traction among workers during the Jacksonian period to meet the particular demands of female laborers organizing for social change on the grounds of natural rights, freedom, equality, and justice for women.

Rebels tailor the Declaration of Independence to advance labor reform for female workers. Echoing Wollstonecraft's arguments, rebels reframe reason and equal rights as allowing women to attain "true" moral virtue. Moving away from female moral virtue enables the rebels to claim that women, and mill girls specifically, possess the reason necessary to know their natural rights, the cornerstone of a rights-based discourse. Invoking the Declaration, Stone states, "All men are created free and equal; not free to starve, or work for a mere pittance, but free to work reasonable hours and receive a reward proportionate with the real production of the labor performed."[22] Corporations such as the Boston Associates, by failing to pay the mill girls decent wages and give them reasonable hours, deny them the inalienable rights granted to all humans equally by the Declaration. Women as humans should enjoy the protections granted to them by natural right and law. Factory owners deny workers their natural right to life, liberty, and the pursuit of happiness, rebels argue, by paying poverty wages and leaving them to work in life-threatening conditions. Such practices justify the mill girls' right to rebel against the Boston Associates by organizing to oppose injustices that jeopardize their self-preservation.

Claiming women's "indefeasible and inalienable rights" led rebels to break through the barriers of the separate spheres ideology that upheld women's inequality to men in the private sphere. The financial and social independence experienced by mill girls, who earned their own wage and lived away from their families, located them in male public life and led some to question women's inequality in private life. Rebels began extending their rights-based position to the institution of marriage. They argued that women should have input equal to men in all domestic decisions, freedom in friendship and affection, free intercourse, and unrestrained expression of language and address.[23] Claiming independence for women pushes this argument even further away from a virtue-based discourse. "Woman has lost her individuality, in the marriage relation," explains one *Voice* contributor.[24] Natural rights, this rebel continues, ensure women the freedom to pursue their individual destiny, which requires equality in marriage. "No relation is true that *makes* one soul subservient to another, none is true which does not rather tend to the elevation and equalization of both parties. The same lie which reveals itself in slavery, is at the bottom of our marriage institution."[25] Framing women as inferior to men, similar to slaves to their masters, makes marriage contrary to natural rights as an unequal, constrained, and oppressive institution. Such conditions, whether in marriage or the factory, degrade women and undermine their capacity for virtue. Attributing inalienable rights to women locates them within a broader struggle for equality, freedom, and justice under the rubric of human rights for all people.

Rebels embody the independence, freedom, and equality for which they argue by engaging in direct political action and adopting an aggressive discourse with a revolutionary overtone that transforms moral guardianship. Rebels formed their own union, participated alongside men in the broader Ten Hour Movement, testified before the Massachusetts state legislature, spoke at political rallies, and published the *Voice*. One rebel captures their sense of empowerment: "'What can the operatives do to change the conditions of industry and reduce the hours of daily labour?' We answer, 'what cannot the operatives do?' Our oppressors well know our strength. Ask the capitalist, if you please, what the operatives have done for him. Then we will ask what cannot we do for ourselves."[26] This claim to strength and independence emboldens rebel calls to action that invoke the American Revolution, proclaiming that "the blood of the revolution has not yet been washed from the hearts of our fathers and brothers."[27] Drawing on this cultural memory expresses the rebels' shared commitment to fight for equality, freedom, and independence, and their readiness for battle against the Boston Associates. "Operatives! Let us not be discouraged!" one rebel exclaims. "Our cause is a righteous one, and we have every reason to believe it must triumph. . . . No never shall we hold ourselves exempt from responsibility, never shall we cease our efforts in the warfare against evil."[28] A rights-based discourse locates rebels as part of the nation's democratic project. That position aligned them with protecting the common good against the evil of corporate injustice and reconfigured the double burden of moral responsibility attributed to American women based on their infinite capacity for female virtue.

Fighting for equality, independence, and rights enlisted rebels in a war for workers' rights that paralleled the American Revolution's struggle for the democratic goals in the Declaration of Independence. Rebels, in doing so, transformed moral guardianship from its passive construction of women as True Women who accept the status quo to revolutionaries who stand against the injustices that jeopardize self-preservation. "No, never while we have hearts to feel and tongues to speak will we silently and passively witness so much that is opposed to justice and benevolence," one rebel declares, "never, with the awful facts of female degradation, under our present system of industry, staring us in the face."[29] Rebels assume moral guardianship, yet now they do so using a rights-based position that grants them the reason to identify their natural rights as the basis for their female virtue. Although the double burden of moral responsibility remains in place, rebels make a claim to protect the nation's democratic future by taking direct political action against the corporate injustices that threaten it.

This aggressive political position located the rebels outside the dominant moral framework as women in the paid labor force collectively organizing to advance national reform for workers' rights. Exiled even by loyalist Lowell mill girls, whom the broader society also aligned with vice, pushed the rebels so far to the political margins that alternatives to a masculine rights-based discourse and feminine virtue-based discourse became visible. This position outside the dominant moral framework's boundaries allowed rebels to assume an epistemological position from which they could identify the ideological limitations of True Womanhood for women's struggles for equality and freedom. From this vantage point, rebels began to imagine a revolutionary rights-based discourse adapted to advance women's freedom, equality, and inclusion, which, while retaining some latent elements of female virtue, empowered these suspect citizens to transform moral guardianship.

Lesbian Feminist S/M Debates: The Moral Bondage of Moral Guardianship

Similar to the Lowell mill girls, lesbians represent a category of women marginalized by both the broader society and other women for breaking with its normative heterosexual standards. These standards align lesbians with female vice as sexual deviants who intimately love other women. Struggles for sexual freedom throughout the 1960s and 1970s opened a space where lesbians who actively participated in second wave feminism believed that they could come out publicly, at the very least, within the movement. They collectively organized in the face of resistance most clearly captured by Betty Friedan's infamous proclamation that lesbians represented a "lavender menace" for the feminist movement. The Radicalesbians formed in response. Lesbian feminists who practiced S/M thought that their commitments to sexual freedom and exploring pleasure, desire, and intimate human relationships corresponded with those of other lesbian feminists. They were wrong. Despite their shared marginalization within the women's movement and American society as sexual deviants, the most vice-ridden label for women, many lesbian feminists strongly opposed those supporting or practicing S/M. A backlash against them resulted that, oddly enough, redeployed the moral logic of virtue and vice and resurrected True Womanhood.

This internal debate emanated from lesbian feminist opposition to S/M on the grounds that all power represents the patriarchal exercise of control defined by male domination and female submission. Women's liberation, then, requires eradicating all forms of power, including S/M practices among consenting lesbians. Feminist transformation of society, Karen Rian argues, demands "not the expression—or even equalization—of power, but rather the *elimination* of power dynamics in sexual, and other relationships."[30] This position distances anti-S/M lesbian feminists from the role of power in human relationships by narrowly defining it as an evil that must be eliminated because of its masculine construction. The dualistic logic of virtue and vice frames this discourse in a way that closes off the space for considering other perspectives on power by categorizing it as an evil or vice. Anti-S/M lesbian feminists, then, stand on the side of virtue, which enables them to transcend the corrupt world of power and act as moral guardians protecting their superior moral beliefs. S/M lesbians, instead of deflecting attention away from the power dynamics involved in sex and sexuality, argue for examining them from a woman's perspective before reaching conclusions based on assumptions of masculinity. "The challenge of talking personally and explicitly about all the ways we are sexual, and about how our sexuality differs, is not so much destructive as it is corrective, and necessary," Katherine Davis states. "The logical place to begin is to talk about our sexuality *as it is*."[31] Attending to existing material contexts, as was the case for the rebellious mill girls, identifies women, even woman-identified women, with male power and corruption, a realm that True Women deem beneath them.

Anti-S/M lesbian feminists assume a position as moral guardians over lesbians to exercise political power in a way reminiscent of the loyalists. Moral policing in this context took the form of censorship. Some feminist bookstores banned Samois's *What Color Is Your Handkerchief* and *Coming to Power*. Many feminist and lesbian newspapers published devastating reviews of both books, refused to print supportive commentary, and rejected paid advertisements for the publications. These lesbian feminists defended such censorship by framing S/M books and pamphlets as forms of hate speech. "We do not print speeches and papers by Nazis. We do not print essays advocating a return to slavery, or essays justifying white or male supremacy," Sarah Hoagland explains. On these grounds, she then claims the right to exclude those with opposing beliefs. "The simple fact that we have set up Lesbian-feminist newspapers, journals, magazines, research newsletters, presses, publishing houses and bookstores in and of itself is a declaration that there are limits, that we have a set of values, and that we want to explore ideas within these values."[32] Lesbians who practice S/M threaten the moral fabric of the lesbian community just as homosexuality contradicts

America's traditional values. Anti-S/M lesbian feminists assume the protective posture of moral guardians to defend the clear boundary around their virtuous moral high ground and to police those who might breach its walls. "It is just not true that all areas of eroticism should be explored by Lesbian-feminists or anyone else," Hoagland states.[33] Erecting such a clear barrier against the free exploration of sex and sexuality shuts down the critical analysis necessary to interrogate moral assumptions used to categorize groups as unworthy of understanding and inferior.

S/M lesbian feminists, similar to the rebellious Lowell mill girls, are aligned with vice, the default moral category into which all those who do not subscribe to the dominant group's values fall. Without clear definition, vice retains an infinite capacity for categorizing anyone who deviates from a given political community's normative standards of virtue as deviant, less than "normal," and, thereby, less than fully human. "Our sexual system contains a vast vague pool of nameless horror," Gayle Rubin explains. "This reservoir of terror has several effects on our ability to deal with sex politically. It makes the whole subject touchy and volatile. It makes sex-baiting painfully easy."[34] Comparing S/M lesbians with Nazis and white supremacists submerges them in the "vast vague pool of nameless horror" identifiable as infinite vice that categorizes S/M lesbians, along with other sexual deviants such as pedophiles, boy lovers, and even rapists, as less than human and, as such, less deserving of full rights and freedoms. The expansiveness of infinite vice creates an ambiguity that prevents differentiating among those located in this moral category. Anti-S/M lesbian feminists draw on this moral logic, which propels the very backlash politics used against all lesbians to dehumanize them, in order to equate S/M lesbians with those who represent the extremes of the human capacity for evil.

S/M lesbians destabilized the sexed and gendered moral framework of virtue and vice by demystifying the "nameless horror" attributed to sexual practices categorized as perverse and dangerous. Gayle Rubin interrogates the moral assumptions behind society's differentiation of good from bad sex. Based on the premise of Western cultures that all "sex is inherently sinful," Rubin argues, a moral hierarchy evolves that elevates superior forms of sex, defined as heterosexual, married, monogamous sex for procreative purposes above all other practices including homosexual, unmarried, promiscuous, non-procreative, commercial, and S/M sex.[35] Western societies attribute complexity and moral nuance to "good" sex. "Bad" sex, alternatively, lumps together all other practices as simply off limits, which makes them morally homogeneous as vices beyond the need for critical analysis. S/M "is dark and polarized, extreme and ritualized, and above all, it celebrates difference and power," Rubin states. "If S/M is understood as the dark opposite of happy and healthy lesbianism, accepting that happy and healthy lesbians also do S/M would threaten the logic of the belief system out of which this opposition was generated."[36] This belief system requires a lack of knowledge about the category of vice that must appear nameless and without clear definition in order to operate as a default category for those who deviate from a political community's normative standards. Naming, contextualizing, and analyzing the material reality of deviant sexual practices grants them a level of complexity. Such nuance disrupts the moral assumptions that deflect attention away from the importance of even understanding what constitutes "bad" sex. The infinite nature of vice as a default moral category, then, acquires the finite definition necessary to deconstruct such sexual practices as understandable, nuanced, and complex and humanize those who engage in them.

Anti-S/M lesbian feminists reject the position that the material reality of sexual practices should be examined and assume moral guardianship over the purity of lesbian love, which they frame as a female virtue that S/M lesbians threaten to taint. Hoagland's *Lesbian Ethics* challenges the traditional feminine finite virtues of altruism, self-sacrifice, and vulnerability as moral bonds that secure women's dependence on men and prevent them from valuing one another. These feminine virtues deny women direct access to power, which makes them deceitful and manipulative, since, to survive, they must resort to channeling power through others, particularly their husbands and children. "When lesbians use the virtues among each other," Hoagland explains, "we wind up using our survival skills against each other; thus our survival skills go awry. I want to suggest that the feminine virtues are a means of exercising control in relationships—whether as lovers, friends, or collective members—and that as a result they function to interrupt rather than promote lesbian connection."[37] Hoagland advances a structural critique of feminine virtues as directing women's emotional and physical resources away from other women, which "actually interrupt[s] attempts among lesbians to connect and interact ethically by promoting control and distance and by erecting barriers."[38] To overcome these limitations, Hoagland argues for a lesbian ethics that replaces "mothering" with "amazoning," a concept of motherhood as creation that encompasses a range of choices, instead of barriers and sacrifices. Female virtue, despite Hoagland's structural critique of feminine virtues, remains the moral foundation of "amazoning" and her lesbian ethics.

Anti-S/M lesbian feminists such as Hoagland redeploy female virtues to define the parameters of lesbian community in a way that excludes those practicing S/M, who come to represent what Rubin calls "the leather menace." S/M lesbians reenact domination and subordination in their sexual practices, which classifies them as masculine for engaging in such exercises of power. Categorizing them in this way locates S/M lesbians outside the protections granted "real" or True Women within the lesbian community. Hoagland denies S/M lesbians the opportunity to engage in deliberations about sex, sexuality, and power on the basis of their deviance from assumptions about the normative standards governing lesbian love, the same moral strategy used to deny lesbians membership in the broader society. "The exclusion of women from the conceptual community simultaneously excludes them from the political community," Hoagland recognizes. "So the manipulation here is designed not just to dodge particular applications of moral principles but they narrow the moral community itself, and is therefore particularly insidious."[39] However, she excludes S/M lesbians from the lesbian community on the basis of predetermined moral beliefs from which those who practice S/M are denied a voice in shaping. Anti-S/M lesbians rely on the moral logic of virtue and vice, despite their awareness of how the broader society uses it to oppress them, to categorize S/M lesbians as vice-ridden deviants from "true" lesbian love achieved by "real" women. This position brings the full weight of female virtue grounded in assumptions of sexual purity to bear on their opposition.

Being pushed to the margins of the broader society and the lesbian community allows pro-S/M lesbians to see how anti-S/M lesbian feminists assume the virtuous position of True or Traditional Womanhood, an icon of oppression in early second wave feminism. The moralistic dynamics of the S/M debates trap lesbians in the virtue-vice framework that deflects attention away from women achieving liberation from patriarchy. "The re-emphasis on feminine values, especially sexual chastity, had led to a shift in the mode of argument for feminist goals," Rubin explains. "Instead of arguing for justice or social equality, much feminist polemic now claims a female moral superiority."[40] Sexual chastity, a female finite virtue, assumes a place in the anti-S/M lesbian discourse that defines the normative standards for their community's acceptable sexual practices as absent of exercising power. "Man the Id and Woman the Chaste are Victorian ideas, not feminist ones," Rubin proclaims, associating anti-S/M lesbian feminists with the oppressive moral ideology of True Womanhood.[41] The underlying moral logic of virtue and vice continues to operate in Rubin's argument, which, while aiming to move beyond its confines, claims moral superiority over anti-S/M lesbians by framing their position in terms of Victorian chastity. Within the women's liberation movement, such associations align anti-S/M lesbians with vice. This moral dynamic in the lesbian S/M debates illustrates the deeply embedded nature of the virtue-vice dualism and its power to perpetuate backlash discourse even among those who explicitly try to challenge it.

Locating this debate within the broader context of moral guardianship reveals how the double burden of moral responsibility assigned to women functions in such internal debates to frame one group as knowing the interests of the other group better than they do themselves. Anti-S/M lesbian feminists adopt this position when they deny that lesbians can consent to S/M, a cornerstone of this sexual practice. S/M, by definition, Bat-Ami Bar On explains, contradicts women's sexual freedom, since "there is no true liberation where there is abuse, humiliation and exploitation, not even when they occur in a context that is voluntary, chosen and of mutual interest."[42] Predicating S/M on an exercise of force that prevents self-determination and choice denies the possibility that S/M, as its lesbian practitioners assert, involves pleasure, desire, and romantic intimacy. S/M lesbians, it is further claimed, suffer from false consciousness, or a false belief that they could consent to participating in a sexual scene where the parties determine how they will exercise their sexual power given the broader patriarchal society, which actually denies such consent for women. "Professing to embrace 'consensual choice,' and abstracting themselves from the real, shared world, sm lesbians leave behind the possibility for concrete personal and political choice," Judith Butler explains. "Instead we get a playing-out of sexual fantasies as if the historical and political world did not exist."[43] Consent to rules within a role-playing context creates a fantasy world separated from reality that negates real agreement between the parties. This position presumes that S/M lesbians cannot differentiate fantasy from reality, know their motivations and intentions, and exercise the power to consent to a set of sexual practices. Denying S/M lesbians the capacity to reason and knowingly consent dehumanizes these women and portrays them as unable to determine a rational plan of life, which invokes conventional backlash arguments designed to exclude women from the public sphere. Anti-S/M lesbian feminists, alternatively, suggest that they possess the capacity to escape false consciousness and see the oppressive reality of S/M from which they must protect the "true" lesbian community's common good.

Abandoning such claims to moral guardianship, which can justify imposing one's belief system on others, S/M lesbians embrace their categorization by society and other lesbians as sexually deviant and perverse, the very embodiment of female vice. "Sexual diversity exists," Rubin explains, "not everyone likes to do the same things, and people who have different sexual preferences are not sick, stupid, warped, brainwashed, under duress, dupes of patriarchy, products of bourgeois decadence, or refugees from bad child-rearing practices. The habit of explaining away sexual variation by putting it down needs to be broken."[44] Despite their moral marginalization, members of S/M lesbian communities consent to the rules, norms, and behaviors defining their sexual practices. "We believe that S/M must be consensual, mutual, and safe," the Samois statement of purpose proclaims. "S/M can exist as part of a healthy and positive lifestyle."[45] Before a lesbian S/M scene begins, the parties discuss their sexual likes and dislikes and establish safe words to ensure that the scene stops or changes to suit the needs of the sadist and masochist. Granting each party power in determining the boundaries for engagement equalizes their relationship. Clear communication further establishes the trust necessary to engage in sexual practices such as bondage, corporeal punishment, and erotic torture that hold the potential for danger. Sharing techniques and information about health issues and safe practices through workshops and publications such as *What Color Is Your Handkerchief* and *Coming to Power* served as a main purpose for organizing S/M communities such as Samois. S/M lesbians reject the premise that those labeled as deviants from a dominant community's normative standards lack the capacity to make voluntary agreements that enable them to achieve a good life. Essentially, S/M lesbians assert their humanity in the face of dehumanizing forces from inside and outside the lesbian community. Claiming their deviance from female virtue and moral guardianship made S/M lesbians into suspect citizens who then asserted their ability to reason and consent as human beings and formed political communities, posing a direct threat to the established moral logic dictating American women's lives.

Fantasy and Imagination in Lesbian S/M and Contemporary Feminist Ethics

Fantasy in the lesbian S/M debates intersects with consent, power, and freedom in ways that contextualize the role of imagination in the process of moral decision making, which advances contemporary feminist ethics' understanding of the politics of normative judgments. Role-playing in scenes constructed by those involved frames S/M practices in terms of fantasies. Developing characters, storylines, settings, and entire narratives that extend beyond the boundaries of a given material reality evolve from the imagination of S/M practitioners, who translate their fantasies into actions. Fantasy and role-playing in lesbian S/M give shape and form to the amorphous arena of vice, where the imagination encounters taboos, deviance, perversity, and unacceptable behaviors. Instead of avoiding this abyss of the unknown, S/M lesbians engage the moral space they occupy and, by describing and explaining it, give meaning and structure to sexual practices usually left to an uninformed imagination, which generates fear.

Opponents of S/M generally dismiss fantasy as an escape from the difficult material reality against which feminists must struggle to effect political change. Robin Morgan's "Politics of Sado-Masochistic Fantasies" breaks with that position to argue against S/M lesbians' view of power as an inherent part of human relationships. Morgan writes a parable designed to help readers understand the fantasies evolving from strong sexual desires despite the dangers that such fantasies pose for women. The parable begins with an imaginary where a man and a woman meet and engage sexually. The woman wants the man to know and understand her. The man impersonates this ability, and the woman slowly accepts this impersonation. Eventually, the woman realizes her degradation in accepting this form of love in sex and sees that her only exercise of power can be in demanding the man's degradation. The woman assumes the position of a sadist to oppress the man as the masochist. The woman's exercise of patriarchal power over the man serves as the only form of sexual engagement available within the confines of patriarchy, and it negates the woman's ability to find the love and joy that she wants. Fantasies, then, remain confined to material reality, which limits women to understanding sexual pleasure in masculine terms of domination as a sadist. This implies that S/M among lesbian partners simply reenacts the very masculine power dynamics used to perpetuate women's oppression.

This parable ends with a utopian vision for this woman and man: *"the possibility of their naked minds and bodies engaging one another—a joyous competition which must include any assumption of defeat as (1) temporary and (2) utterly lacking in humiliation; of any triumph as, obversely, impermanent and meaningless. The taking and giving of turns."*[46] Such fluid power dynamics establish equality between woman and man by eradicating dominance and submission and ensuring freedom. Ending patriarchy represents the only means to these utopian ends. "In patriarchy men have power. In patriarchy women are powerless," Morgan explains. "It is from this viewpoint, this *fact*, that we can start to imagine how we got here, to understand why, and thereafter to invent the way out for all of us."[47] The material and structural reality that defines patriarchy acts as the point of departure for imagining an alternative political community premised on gender equality. S/M fantasies pose serious dangers for women by embedding masculine power so deeply into their imaginary that it shapes their desires and hopes. Advancing this position prevents Morgan from recognizing this parable's heterosexism, which retains the gendered dynamics of conventional sexuality instead of disrupting them by examining lesbian sexual relationships. Imagination remains tethered to the existing moral and political framework of heterosexuality under patriarchy, which limits the freedom to envision an alternative future premised on reconceptualizing power in ways other than those operating within a male-dominated context.

S/M lesbian fantasies in *Coming to Power*, alternatively, start with fantasy as the premise for satisfying sexual desire in which power plays an inherent part. These fantasies about sexual practices break dramatically with romantic visions of heterosexual sex. Consent intersects with fantasy as S/M lesbians exercise reason when they voluntarily agree to create and enact scenes designed by the participants to derive sexual pleasure from practices labeled deviant. "Fantasy is, by definition, consensual," Katharine Davis explains. "If you don't like what you're fantasizing, you have total power to change the scene."[48] S/M fantasies apply imagination to role-playing scenes that simulate realities associated with pain, harm, and danger—the sources of participants' sexual pleasures. Transforming sexual fantasy into a material context created by those participating in the scene empowers these women to take control over their sexual desires instead of repressing them. "It is giving, trusting, opening my mind and my body to possibilities, to fantasies I never dreamed possible," Barbara Rose explains. "I can be her slave, her servant, her teacher, her mother—I can be anything, anyone. I am my own lover. She is part of me, and I am part of her."[49] Fantasies offer a space of shared freedom for both partners who engage in a form of sexual intimacy that reaches into each other's dreams, hopes, and imagination. Such conceptualizations deepen a feminist understanding of how sexual intimacy shapes the relational self and the ways in which relationships often blur our vision of the boundary between self and other.

The line between pain and pleasure also blurs within S/M lesbian fantasies, which explore the place where these experiences meet. "I'm learning more and more about gentleness within the structure of roughness," Crystal Bailey states. "I like learning how far I can push someone before their body resists. It's so important to find out where someone feels safe, then I can ask them to step away from it until they get scared; we pull back again where it's safe and then I push them to step out a bit further."[50] Explaining the S/M lesbian experience directly engages the moral abyss of sexual practices that strategically employ pain to generate pleasure, a space usually marked as off limits and dangerous. Safety, however, characterizes these practices among lesbian partners, who establish clear boundaries that grant them the freedom to move outside conventional moral constraints on sex and sexuality. Framing S/M practices in terms of safety, consent, and empowerment deconstructs the simplistic dismissal of its practitioners as deviant, vice-ridden threats to feminism, lesbianism, and society.

Lesbian S/M fantasy simulates experiences through role-playing that, when applied to forming normative judgments, provide insight into structuring this process from a feminist perspective. Patrick Hopkins compares simulations in S/M to riding a roller coaster. "The simulation itself is the goal, not a lesser copy of the goal," he explains. "The SM practitioner may find actual violence and humiliation repugnant and horrible, but finds the simulation of that event thrilling and exciting— not as a stand-in but as a goal in itself."[51] Simulations enable people to experience emotions and sensations outside the bounds of an everyday lived reality such as the thrill generated by a roller coaster ride. Moral decision making entails imagining the consequences of particular choices and how they will affect others individually and collectively as well as how they align with our vision of the world. The moment people decide if, for whom, to what degree, how, and why they will assume moral responsibility they are fantasizing the possible outcomes that simulate the experiences resulting from the decisions made. Role-playing simulates these moments in the moral imaginary, allowing people to grasp the role of others and contexts in their decision making, deepening the relational dimension of feminist ethics.

Fantasy can further inform this process as freeing people to imagine courses of action outside the boundaries determined by a dualistic moral framework limited to virtue and vice. S/M lesbian fantasy disrupts this boundary and offers a way to simulate experiences relegated to the moral hinterlands of vice by securing the safety to do so through negotiation of rules by participants. This deliberative strategy prevents developing a scene based on predetermined rules and moral assumptions. The conventional framework of the virtue-vice dualism fades and traditional normative judgments nearly disappear as the moral decision-making process actively engages the imagination through deliberation and negotiation with the self and others.

S/M lesbian fantasy offers insight into how the imaginary can play a more effective role in moral decision making in a way that reconceptualizes this process as escaping the set of moral assumptions upholding the dualistic framework of virtue and vice. "Judging without the mediation of a concept is a quotidian skill we would do well to learn and practice,"

Linda Zerilli states, arguing that feminists must go outside given conceptual constructs to achieve freedom in making normative judgments.[52] How feminists actually do this, she acknowledges, is a very difficult and perhaps utopian task. Lesbian S/M fantasy provides some clues. These women claim the power to explore their sexual desire freely with other women, and without the moral limits of chastity, modesty, and purity. Moral guardianship is shattered, and the last vestiges of protection afforded by female virtue are removed. Fantasy through simulation untethers normative judgment from a reality grounded in a set of moral assumptions and traditions that ossify morality into locating people and decisions into clear categories of virtue and vice. An alternative moral decision-making process emerges that begins with consent and rules for engagement based on the negotiation and deliberation of participants who share their desires and fears to determine certain boundaries that secure the safety necessary to explore fantasy. Imagination acts as the foundation for this deliberative process designed to empower its participants, who constantly negotiate the context instead of relying on preexisting moral limitations that prevent envisioning a range of possibilities.

The role of S/M fantasies in the lesbian feminist debates illustrates how the virtue-vice dualism determines the level of disruption caused by freedom, since this moral framework can be used to either harness or liberate the imagination. Fantasy, broadly speaking, exists in one's imagination outside of societal constraints, which constitutes an exercise of freedom that, Zerilli explains, "disturbs the use of politics as a means to an end; it is always 'out of order.'"[53] Fantasy, then, causes a breach in reality that opens up the possibility for creation understood as the power of beginning, which generates the political act of constructing meaning through conceptual and discursive shifts in language. Utopian thinking employs fantasy and imagination as theoretical tools for envisioning alternative political communities and ideologies outside existing governing or rule-making structures. "Fancy neither proves nor disproves; it seeks, instead, to illuminate, to help us become wiser about political things," Sheldon Wolin explains. "Imagination is the theorist's means for understanding a world he can never 'know' in an intimate way."[54] Fantasy and imagination function politically to grant the freedom to see beyond the constraints of individual, contextual, and structural internal and external boundaries.

Suspect Citizens as Innovative Ideologists

Changing political, social, and economic structures, whether in the nineteenth or twentieth century, put the Lowell mill girls and lesbian feminists in a similar context where the discourse available to them no longer fit their circumstances. In different ways and to different degrees, these women attempt to relate their experiences, either by adaptation or abandonment, to the dominant belief system of moral guardianship. The loyalists tried to alter the ideology of True Womanhood by integrating female laborers into a belief system premised on women's role as virtuous wives and mothers that confined them to the private sphere. Anti-S/M lesbian feminists opposed True Womanhood, broke with its heterosexist assumptions, and rejected patriarchy to fight for a world without power where gender equality and freedom would reign. These ideological innovations encounter the limitations of the virtue-vice dualism that results in excluding members of their marginalized communities by claiming moral superiority over them. Loyalists and anti-S/M lesbian feminists, respectively, redeploy the moral logic of backlash politics used against them by the dominant society to expel the rebels and S/M lesbians from their communities.

Dynamics within the American political script facilitate such internal backlashes. A critical distance emerges between the dominant ideology of moral guardianship and women such as the loyalists, who work outside the home, and anti-S/M lesbian feminists, who love other women and reject patriarchy. Suspicion about their commitment to the broader political community results. As their proximity to female virtue as heterosexual wives and mothers decreases, societal doubt about women's ability to uphold their political obligation for maintaining the nation's common good through moral responsibility increases. Trust in women diminishes, which jeopardizes their legitimate membership in the political community as the nation's gendered moral groundwork shifts to transform moral guardians into suspect citizens. Moral ambiguity derives from these political moments as the categories of female virtue and vice become less defined. Some women, such as the loyalists and anti-S/M lesbian feminists, resort to the readily available discourse of moral guardianship, which enables them to reclaim enough political trust to maintain a tenuous hold on citizenship by distancing themselves from those who break even more dramatically with the standards of female virtue.

Exclusion from their own female communities as vice-ridden located the rebels and pro-S/M lesbian feminists so far beyond the boundaries of legitimate citizenship that the dominant moral framework came clearly into view as one antithetical to freedom, equality, and inclusion. The rebels abandoned moral guardianship for a liberal rights-based discourse and innovatively applied it to female laborers and other women, claiming political legitimacy not as wives and mothers but as human beings who exercise reason. Heterosexuality and feminine submissiveness prevent pro-S/M lesbian feminists from even making a claim to moral guardianship. Freed from its moral bondage, pro-S/M lesbians occupy a particularly vulnerable political space stripped of moral legitimacy for engaging in vice-ridden sexual practices that break with the sexual and social contract. This dangerous location, nonetheless, provides a vantage point uniquely suited for identifying how moral dynamics justify oppression and inequality. "The sexual outlaws—boy-lovers, sadomasochists, prostitutes, and transpeople, among others—have an especially rich knowledge of the prevailing system of sexual hierarchy and of how sexual controls are exercised," Rubin explains.[55] Outlaws banished to the moral borderlands, pro-S/M lesbians are liberated from thinking in terms limited to the dualistic logic of virtue and vice. Embracing their deviant status opens up possibilities for imagining a world inclusive of diversity that extends to sexuality and sexual practices. Pro-S/M lesbians, to an even greater degree than the rebellious Lowell mill girls, lacked an alternative discourse to help them resolve the contradiction between their belief systems and existing political context. Freedom from existing conceptual restraints enabled them to become innovating ideologists by claiming vice and suspicion as legitimate standpoints from which to envision moral and political alternatives.

Suspicion can generate the innovation necessary to challenge the moral and political status quo. Such innovation, ironically, is critical to the ingenuity and flexibility required of democratic citizens. Located outside the protection of moral guardianship, women such as the Lowell mill girls and lesbians disturb and disrupt the nation's equilibrium, which wedges open a space for exercising the freedom necessary for imagining alternative political futures. These suspect citizens threaten the nation's exceptional future as its moral guardians, which mobilizes backlashes inside and outside these communities. Exercising fantasy and imagination, these suspect citizens provide a set of practices essential to developing the vision to see past the existing moral paradigms that propel backlashes and move toward alternative processes of moral decision making on the basis of negotiation and deliberation. Imagination and fantasy, in a political script characterized by suspicion of change, may hold the potential to advance a moral revolution by promoting, within collectively determined boundaries, the disruption, disorder, and disturbance necessary for citizenship in democracy.

5 | "Ozzie and Harriet" Morality

Resetting Liberal Democracy's Moral Compass

D isorder and chaos were spiraling Jacksonian America into a whirl-wind of change when Alexis de Tocqueville and Gustave de Beau-mont stepped onto U.S. shores in 1831. Universal white manhood suffrage, immigration, urbanization, and early industrialization were driving economic and political transitions that also transformed the family from a social institution shaped by European aristocracy into one fitting American democracy. Equality, Tocqueville observed, essentially dismantled the hierarchical aristocratic family to the degree that "in America the family, if one takes the word in its Roman and aristocratic sense, no longer exists."[1] Tocqueville links the family to broader political change as he declares that "democracy which destroys or obscures almost all social conventions and . . . makes it harder for men to es-tablish new ones, leads to a complete disappearance of almost all the feelings originating in such conventions."[2] The egalitarian family evokes deep concerns for Tocqueville, since, freed from this mooring of social convention, democracy could drift toward an abyss of disorder. Alter-natively, Tocqueville saw separate spheres for public man and private woman as the force necessary to meet this threat by effectively preserv-ing the natural equality and economic efficiency necessary for social or-der and prosperity. "The Americans," Tocqueville claims, "do not think that man and woman have the duty or right to do the same things, but they show an equal regard for the part played by both and think of them as beings of equal worth, though their fates are different."[3]

This separate spheres approach informs contemporary backlash politics. Communitarians, in particular, often redeploy Tocqueville's view of the American family in their efforts to reset America's moral compass back to the 1950s and what I call "Ozzie and Harriet" morality. The popular 1950s *Ozzie and Harriet* television show illustrates the separate spheres occupied by Ozzie Nelson and his wife, Harriet. Wearing a lovely dress, heels, and pearls, Harriet prepares breakfast before sending her husband off to work and her two sons, Ricky and David, off to school. These two clean-cut young men encounter various teenage problems and ultimately require their father's guidance, which centers on a conventional moral code and resolves Ricky's and David's dilemmas. Harriet, meanwhile, appears from time to time, cooking meals, cleaning the house, and occasionally getting into a marital situation with Ozzie that resolves happily by the show's end. The Nelson family symbolizes the traditional heterosexual white two-parent middle-class family to which Americans should return, communitarians say, in order to reverse the nation's moral decay as indicated by increased rates of divorce, single motherhood, teen pregnancy, and school violence. The 1950s, for leading communitarian Amitai Etzioni, represents "the model of the orderly society we lost, one in which virtues were well in place" and when Americans adhered to strong beliefs such as anticommunism, Christianity, family unity, sexual codes, and respect for authority.[4] "Ozzie and Harriet" morality here captures how the virtue-vice dualism channels Tocqueville's separate spheres ideology into contemporary debates over the family that frame American women's mass exodus from the kitchen to the workplace as the indicator of the nation's moral demise.

For communitarians, the Sexual Revolution of the 1960s catalyzed America's decline as excessive freedom, individualism, and a general disregard for moral tradition caused massive social upheaval and generated an identity-based politics that fragmented the common good. These societal changes destroyed the separate spheres ideology in which "the roles of men and women were relatively clearly delineated" and enforced by a society that "chastised" those who challenged these norms, stigmatizing unmarried women as spinsters and married women without children.[5]

Second wave feminism's attack on Traditional Womanhood as a relic of a repressive Victorian moral code enforcing female purity, chastity, and modesty "led quite a few Americans to a state of normless anarchy," which caused rates of divorce, single motherhood, and date rape on college campuses to increase dramatically.[6] "Traditional virtues," as a result, "lost much of their power, and no strong new shared values arose."[7] American women's return to Harriet Nelson's role in private life, the argument goes, will revive the female finite virtues nearly destroyed by the women's liberation movement. Resetting the moral compass to align with the separate spheres ideology described by Tocqueville as central to American democracy's success will enable American women to resume moral guardianship for the family and the common good.

Agreeing with the communitarians, Alasdair MacIntyre proclaims, "Morality today is in a state of grave disorder," when comparing contemporary liberal democracy with the Dark Ages before the Roman Empire fell.[8] According to MacIntyre, reordering democratic life requires a "thicker" conception of morality than that offered by John Rawls's "thin" moral premise in Kantian ethics, which advances justice as the first virtue. MacIntyre, alternatively, presents a multiple virtues position grounded in an Aristotelian view of a *telos*, or concept of human nature as having an end without which it cannot be determined, understood, or defined. America's moral decay, then, results from moral relativism replacing a *telos* that grants an understanding of the "good life" or *eudaimonia* achieved in the *polis* where the internal goods of practices, not external goods or rewards, motivate man's virtue or moral excellence. Contemporary liberalism locates political and moral life in a natural rights framework that reduces the "good life" to the individual pursuit of self-interest without interference from other people, communities, or traditions. Morality anchored in a *telos*, for MacIntyre, will provide the American people with virtue, a standard for making clear moral judgments and resolving political conflicts within a shared understanding of the "good life," which will generate multiple virtues to guide daily life as a community.

To mend liberal democracy's moral fabric, worn thin by the identity-based politics generated in the 1960s, these political theorists agree, requires reviving a moral tradition anchored in multiple virtues that orients the people toward a common good. The traditions on which

Alasdair MacIntyre, Amitai Etzioni, and William Galston draw function according to hierarchies that exclude most people and all women from political life and the creation of tradition. Gender neutrality veils a range of assumptions regarding women's unequal power, constraint, and exclusion. This chapter turns from the broad idea of tradition to the particulars of male and female virtue and vice in this multiple virtues position. A set of moral assumptions antithetical to women's full citizenship undermines these thinkers' claim to reenergizing civic engagement in liberal democracy by actually deflecting attention away from the people's active participation in it.

Positioning this multiple virtues argument in relationship to Tocqueville's depiction of male and female virtue and vice in *Democracy in America* creates an analytic space for considering how these moral assumptions shift attention away from democratic life. "Habitual inattention," Tocqueville states, "must be reckoned the great vice of the democratic spirit."[9] The gendered moral logic of the virtue-vice dualism functions to perpetuate a vision of democratic life predicated on a suspicion of active and sustained engagement in it. The "Ozzie and Harriet" morality advanced in contemporary backlash politics holds broader implications for American liberal democracy by turning attention toward the family and civil society and away from public life to resolve structural political problems. Habitual *attention* to politics, then, becomes devalued and a marker of suspect citizens.

The Separate Spheres Paradox: Alexis de Tocqueville's *Democracy in America*

Democratic despotism deeply concerned Tocqueville as he observed Americans' habitual inattention to politics. The scant amount of time spent on political issues made them susceptible to their passions and prompted hasty opinions. Habitual inattention perpetuates an insidious form of oppression in which the state softens and bends the wills of its citizens until "each nation is no more than a flock of timid and hardworking animals with the government as its shepherd."[10] As Americans, focused on individualistic concerns, conform to popular opinion when bothering with politics, the increase in the equality of conditions will, Tocqueville fears, result in a proportional loss of freedom. The tyranny of the majority, which leads to democratic despotism, results when the force of equality overtakes freedom to raise conformity to the level of omnipotent power. The people then abandon reason for passion, majority for minority voices, and formal laws for mores. This "majority is invested with both physical and moral authority," Tocqueville explains, "which acts as much upon the will as upon behavior and at the same moment prevents both the act and desire to do it."[11] This form of tyranny, differing from that of traditional tyrants who rely on explicit physical force to control their people, results from an insidious power to control inner thought and external action. The people's habitual inattention to political life ultimately leads to liberal democracy's decay.

Analyzing male and female virtue and vice in Tocqueville's *Democracy in America* reveals a paradox in the separate spheres position with important implications for women and democratic citizenship. Tocqueville fosters the very habitual inattention to politics that he fears will destroy democracy by defining what men and women do and why they do it in terms that devalue direct political engagement. This paradox emanates from the moral logic deeply embedded in the American political script, captured in Tocqueville's work, that shows how American women remain locked into *either* accepting their role as moral guardians of virtue *or* being held morally responsible for America's decline into vice and eventual acquiescence to democratic despotism. This dualism creates the tenuous moral context for women's suspect citizenship. The separate spheres paradox illustrates how women's political identity as moral guardians but suspect citizens confines the American people to a thin conception of citizenship antithetical to democracy's demands.

The virtue of courage characterizes Tocqueville's American men and women, who all struggle daily with the volatile changes accompanying nation building, whether pioneering the West or industrializing the East. Attributing this traditionally masculine virtue to women indicates the permeability of the sexual division of labor that facilitates transforming republican into democratic virtue in the American context. Tocqueville particularly admires the pioneer man and his wife for exhibiting courage when exchanging the luxury and safety of civilization for the deprivation and danger of the wilderness. Their motivations for doing so, however, differ. An unwavering commitment to her family motivates the pioneer woman. The pioneer man endures "for a time the life of a savage in order to conquer and civilize the backwoods" to pursue his fortune in the West. Economic gain, not political ambition or patriotism, drive this pioneer and his Eastern counterpart alike.[12] Whether pioneers, businessmen, or wage laborers, Tocqueville's American men possess the courage to face dangers inherent to a lifelong pursuit of wealth in a cyclical market economy.

This economic imperative also influences female courage marked by the capacity for endurance. Indicating this gendered dynamic, Tocqueville explains that "in no country of the world are private fortunes more unstable than in the United States. It is not exceptional for one man in his lifetime to work up through every stage from poverty to opulence and then come down again. American women face such upheavals with quiet, indomitable energy. Their desires seem to contract with their fortune as easily as they expand."[13] This depiction illustrates Tocqueville's admiration for female courage as an unwavering ability to stand up to adversity, enabling the American woman to endure the upheavals caused by the American man's ongoing pursuit of wealth.

American women's responsibility for the family provides them with a source of steadfast strength unavailable to men, who are carried on the tides of the market. Marriage, of course, establishes the family. This act, for Tocqueville's American woman, demands perhaps her greatest courage, since "it is the very enjoyment of freedom that has given her the courage to sacrifice it without struggle or complaint when the time has come for that."[14] Young American girls, unlike American men, sacrifice their freedoms when entering marriage. As wives, American women withstand whatever trials result from their husbands' adventures, even the poverty faced by pioneer women. Tocqueville describes how the pioneer woman's "want, suffering, and loneliness have affected her constitution but not bowed her courage."[15] Such moral fortitude in the face of physical deprivation captures the spirit of courage in Tocqueville's account of American women whose quiet strength of will sustains their families as a pillar of order amid chaos. Tocqueville identifies American men and women as possessing the courage needed to confront the challenges of building a nation. Male courage, however, derives from actively participating in the market that generates the very instability against which female courage acts as a countervailing force. Neither form of courage requires aggressive bravery in politics or on the battlefield, since virtue arises either from the market or from the family, not from politics.

Differences in Tocqueville's account of male and female chastity exemplify the double burden of moral responsibility placed on American women, whose virtue, rather than their husbands', preserves marriage as the cornerstone of the family and the common good. Male chastity tempers the American man's mercurial spirit, regulating his habits enough to preserve domestic harmony since family disputes draw man's attention away from accumulating wealth. Public opinion cajoles American men into acting chastely. "To win the esteem of their fellows," Tocqueville states, Americans "are bound to conform to regular habits. In that sense one can say that it is a point of honor to be chaste."[16] Male chastity does not extend to sexual constraint. American men who visit prostitutes, according to Tocqueville, only engage in a minor vice that does not amount to a general failure of moral character or a threat to the common good.

Woman's chastity requires her sexual constraint, which, coupled with the finite female virtue of fidelity, bases her morality on sexual purity before marriage and the unfailing commitment to her spouse afterward. American women's association with religion, in contrast to the external honor motivating male chastity, gives them the internal strength of will to adhere to the female virtues of chastity and fidelity. The broader community, Tocqueville observes, places such importance on women's morality that American legislators legally protect female virtue by making rape, a crime judged by public opinion more severely than all others, punishable by death.[17] Women's chastity requires legal protection, then, since it preserves the family and the common good. This sexual double standard indicates how Tocqueville's Americans view women with suspicion by associating their failure to uphold the dictates of virtue with endangering democracy.

The disproportionate weight placed on male and female chastity reflects the burden of moral responsibility assigned to American women, which Tocqueville conveys in his account of the pioneer husband and wife. Upon meeting the pioneer husband, Tocqueville expresses near astonishment at the cold, methodical hospitality with which he is received. Yet he appreciates this pioneer who belongs "to that restless, calculating, and adventurous race of men who do with the utmost coolness things which can only be accounted for by the ardor of passion."[18] Rationality regulates his temperament enough to channel the pioneer's energy into the difficult labors of frontier life, which demand passion to be disciplined by chastity.

This same trait evokes a romantic sense of loss when Tocqueville describes the pioneer woman. Before moving West, she received an American girl's typical education that made "her morals . . . pure rather than her mind chaste," which, he laments, tends "to make women chaste and cold rather than tender and loving companions of men."[19] In an isolated log house where an entire family shares one room, Tocqueville still fails to see any intimacy between the pioneer husband and wife, whom he never describes in direct relationship to one another. Their chaste disposition, though rendering private life less charming, represents "a secondary evil, which should be faced for the sake of the greater good."[20] American women, unlike men, give up their passions to satisfy the demands of the greater good, which establishes a double standard extending to men's sexual desire that frees them from the double burden of moral responsibility for the broader community.

Hard work, the central finite male virtue, entails a level of pragmatism that transforms republican virtue into democratic honor and results in a comparatively thin male moral code. Tocqueville observes that "in a democratic society . . . where fortunes are small and insecure, everybody works and work opens all doors. That circumstance has made the point of honor do an about turn and set it facing against idleness."[21] Americans honor men who, in the absence of inherited wealth, work incessantly to achieve fragile fortunes. Tocqueville reserves some respect for the Protestant work ethic driving America's economic growth. Americans, however, decouple the work ethic from its religious origins to devote themselves to pragmatism and materialism, the key beliefs in the American man's "new religion." Financial gain, instead of receiving glory for serving God or the greater good, earns men honor, which Tocqueville defines as "nothing but this particular rule based on a particular state of society, by means of which a people distributes praise or blame."[22] Honor, then, "is only effective in full view of the public, differing from sheer virtue, which feeds upon itself, contented with its own witness."[23] Public opinion replaces internal religious or moral conviction as the factor determining the American male's honor, which exposes his personal character to the forces of conformity that promote the tyranny of the majority.

Men's participation in political and civic associations, as a result, becomes vital to protecting against these dangers to democracy by preserving the individual's everyday liberties that limit pressures to conform to public opinion. Civil associations, for Tocqueville, bind the nation together by joining men collectively for intellectual and moral reasons that allow their feelings and ideas to expand to encompass others. This sense of morality and community counters the individualism and materialism that cause many ills in the democratic body politic. Political associations derive from man's self-interest, which, on occasion, drives him to band together with others to secure government assistance. American men's relationship with the state remains conflicted. "The inhabitant of the United States," Tocqueville explains, "learns from birth that he must rely on himself to combat the ills and trials of life; he is restless and defiant in his outlook toward the authority of society and appeals to its power only when he cannot do without it."[24] Political engagement represents a last resort for American men, who define themselves in terms of self-reliance and independence from governing authority.

Politics serves an instrumental means to American men's economic ends. "The passions that stir the Americans most deeply are commercial and not political ones," Tocqueville observes. "One must go to America to understand the power of material prosperity over political behavior, and even over opinions."[25] Politics transforms into a business that fulfills the pragmatic purpose of maintaining the order necessary for economic prosperity. Men's moral worth in this context depends on their financial success rather than contributing to the nation's common good. The male finite virtues of courage, chastity, and hard work reflect how American men achieve moral status by turning their attention toward economic matters and away from political or civic concerns. Habitual inattention, the vice that Tocqueville saw as most destructive to democracy, results from a view of political engagement as an instrumental obligation necessary to achieve individual material goals.

Framing political participation as an obligation deserving habitual inattention grants American men the power to exercise privileged irresponsibility toward politics. Tocqueville's American men possess the capacity to temper individualism enough to act with an awareness of the broader community, which can motivate them to join civic and political associations. "The doctrine of self-interest properly understood," Tocqueville explains, "does not inspire great sacrifices, but every day it prompts some small ones." This capacity lacks a vision of the common good and "by itself it cannot make a man virtuous, but its discipline shapes a lot of orderly, temperate, moderate, careful, and self-controlled citizens. If it does not lead the will directly to virtue, it establishes habits which unconsciously turn it that way."[26] "Self-interest properly understood" entails a rational calculus in which American men assess when, how, and to what degree small everyday sacrifices may benefit the community and, as a result, their self-interest. American men can then exercise privileged irresponsibility toward matters disconnected from their immediate self-interest such as the nation's common good.

Representative democracy structurally contributes to a citizenry's ability to exercise such a privilege and neglect the daily business of politics since responsibility for this work falls to elected officials. American men, given their instrumental view, conflate politics with business, which leads to bribery of politicians and a view of government as corrupt and vice-ridden.[27] Politicians deserve no honor because of their lack of virtue and dedication to a sphere narrowed to serving economic interests. Political participation for its own sake loses moral value, which enables American men to justify exercising the privilege of irresponsibility in determining when politics deserves their attention. Such habitual inattention perpetuates sporadic participation and ill-informed opinions and conflates economic with political issues. Devaluing political activity for its own sake jeopardizes the people's participation in their government, which places democratic citizenship under suspicion.

American men's privilege to exercise irresponsibility for the common good derives from American women's self-sacrifice, the infinite moral virtue that allows them to assume responsibility as the nation's moral guardians. The pioneer wife, for Tocqueville, embodies this unlimited capacity for self-sacrifice. Abandoning her youth, lifestyle, and personal interests for a pioneer's hard life requires absolute devotion to her marital duties. The pioneer wife literally transfers her physical strength to her children to the extent that "one might think that the life she has given them exhausted her own, and yet she does not regret what they have cost her."[28] Never communicating regret or suffering, this woman possesses a peaceful angelic quality. "Her whole physiognomy bore marks of religious resignation," Tocqueville describes, "a deep peace free from passions, and some sort of natural, quiet determination which would face all the ills of life without fear and without defiance."[29] This "deep peace" acts as the pioneer woman's moral backbone that enables her to confront life's challenges with the active, though quiet, determination necessary to meet the ever-changing circumstances of frontier life.

A close affiliation with religion grants American women an infinite capacity for self-sacrifice, which leads Tocqueville to attribute great political importance to them as the guardians of the nation's common good. Men's focus on material, economic matters rendered religion "powerless to restrain them in the midst of innumerable temptations which fortune offers."[30] The church, increasingly separated from the state in American democracy, moves into the female private sphere where religion "reigns supreme in the souls of women." The American wife conveys religious morality to her family and her husband, who "derives from his home that love of order which he carries into affairs of state."[31] Women secure the moral order by exercising the restraint necessary to counterbalance the instability and freedom of liberal democratic life.

Female virtue acquires an infinite civic dimension through American women's responsibility for mores (*moeurs*). For Tocqueville, this term references "the habits of the heart, but also to the different notions possessed by men, the various opinions current among them, and the sum of ideas that shape mental habits . . . the whole moral and intellectual state of a people."[32] This expansive dimension represents the common good that extends well beyond a nation's formal laws and constitutions and the material reality of each individual's life to join them together in a belief system that forms the democratic spirit. American women, charged with shaping the mores necessary to maintain public order and the common good, assume the double burden of moral responsibility for female private and male public life. Infinite moral and civic virtue add a heavy spiritual weight to the burden that transforms this responsibility into a sacred political obligation, which women, denied full citizenship, remain unable to fulfill, framing them as suspect citizens.

This sacred obligation for democracy's future encompasses American women's responsibility for protecting against finite male vice, which facilitates the democratic despotism against which female virtue must protect. The chaos, ambition, and greed characteristic of democratic public life, while providing fertile ground for American men to pursue economic gain, creates a thin obligation to politics and the opportunity for democratic despotism. New male immigrants to the United States embody the dangers posed by unmarried men who, without wives to bind them to the common good, cause extreme political disorder, such as the riots, largely arising from racial and ethnic tensions, that broke out in Philadelphia and New York City throughout the 1830s. For Tocqueville, these events epitomize vice.[33] Restraining the male vice that threatens such political disorder becomes the responsibility of American women. Their infinite moral and civic virtue empowers them to assume moral responsibility for themselves, their families, and men, which transforms into a political obligation for protecting against the democratic despotism that results from unfettered male vice. American women attain this ability as young girls schooled in the ways of democracy. "The vices and dangers of society are soon plain to her," Tocqueville explains, "and seeing them clearly, she judges them without illusion and faces them without fear, for she is full of confidence in her own powers, and it seems that this feeling is shared by all around her."[34] Firsthand knowledge of public vice enables American women to identify it and protect the family and democracy from its insidious capacity to corrode the common good.

Marriage, as the cornerstone of political stability, demands extensive protections from vice and corruption. "All those vices which tend to impair the purity of morals and the stability of marriage," Tocqueville observes, "are treated in America with a severity unknown in the rest of the world."[35] Anchoring democratic order, marriage erects a barrier against the vice of instability, one solely defended, not by the male citizen's honor, but by the female moral guardian's finite virtues of chastity, fidelity, courage, and infinite moral capacity for self-sacrifice. Alternatively, promiscuity, infidelity, cowardice, and selfishness represent possible female vices, although Tocqueville never specifies them. This omission indicates the political significance of the infinite moral and civic weight placed on female virtue that women exercise through marriage and the family to protect democracy.

Tocqueville's American men and women operate according to the gendered logic of virtue and vice, exposing the separate spheres paradox:

the sexual division of moral labor necessary to protect against democratic despotism results in the very habitual inattention to politics that causes it. Industry demands the attention of male citizens, who earn the finite virtue of honor for economic achievement. Women focus on the family as the source and site of their virtue, where they preserve infinite and finite moral and civic virtue for the entire nation. This sexual division of moral labor between the economy and the family creates the context in which the people's inattention to politics becomes habitual. Only great political matters capture their attention. Everyday freedoms, as a result, gradually disappear without the people noticing, which leads to democratic despotism. Direct attention to politics falls to elected politicians, who occupy a morally devalued public space. The civic obligation to protect the common good belongs, not to politicians or male citizens, but to female moral guardians, whose political identity depends on their exclusion from the corrupt sphere of public life. Citizen participation in formal politics, devoid of female virtue or male honor, becomes, at best, amoral and, at worst, vice-ridden.

This combination elevates direct political *inactivity* to a standard of moral excellence in American democracy. Tocqueville's support for the separate spheres ultimately perpetuates, instead of prevents, the conditions of democratic despotism. A morally impoverished sense of citizen engagement as only an obligatory and instrumental means to economic and social ends, as opposed to an end in itself, promotes habitual inattention to politics, which diminishes the importance of direct, consistent activism to democratic citizenship.

A "Curl Back" to Virtue: Neutralizing Gender in Contemporary Morality

Contemporary thinkers Alasdair MacIntyre, Amitai Etzioni, and William Galston share Tocqueville's concern that decaying morality leads to disorder and decline in democracy. These scholars, from differing perspectives, hope to "curl back" to 1950s America before rampant individualism and unrestrained freedom advanced by the women's and civil rights movements of the 1960s and 1970s, they argue, effectively replaced moral tradition with relativism. Without a moral compass, identity-based politics results in an unchecked pluralism that fragments the political community. A "curl back" did begin in the 1990s to regenerate moral virtues that would turn the nation to "face in the other direction" and "to push the pendulum back to stave off anarchy and to restore social order."[36] Feminists often refer to this swing as a backlash that entails returning to a separate spheres ideology captured here by the 1950s *Ozzie and Harriet* television show. The "back to virtue" position taken by MacIntyre, Etzioni, and Galston frames a return to a virtue-based tradition as essential to unifying a disorderly nation on the verge of moral anarchy. Virtue represents the link necessary to reconnect individuals to a sense of self and the people to a community, where a shared tradition binds them together in the common good. This quest for unity to save liberal democracy from excessive difference leads these three thinkers to neutralize the gendered power dynamics inherent to a virtue-based moral tradition by deflecting attention away from power. Contrary to their interest in reinvigorating civic engagement, these scholars, like Tocqueville, advance a position that promotes the vice of habitual inattention to politics, a sphere designed for navigating the conflicts inherent to human life.

In *After Virtue*, MacIntyre diagnoses contemporary liberalism as suffering from a thin conception of the moral subject defined by a level of self-interest that negates a true idea of the "good life." Aristotelian virtue tradition serves as MacIntyre's cure for this social malady. Aristotle clearly differentiates between men's and women's capacity for virtue. While both remain capable of moral goodness, he states, "the fact still remains that temperance—and similarly courage, and justice—are not, as Socrates held, the same as in a woman as they are in a man. One kind of courage is concerned with ruling, the other with serving; and the same is true of other forms of goodness."[37] Temperance defines female virtue, enabling women to control their desires enough to function in service to men. Their reason allows men to attain the justice and wisdom that grants them access to the *polis* where they govern. Women remain in the *oikos* where they fulfill the community's demand for productive and reproductive labor. This functionalist position assigns men and women different tasks in these separate spheres on the basis of their differing moral capacities. The moral order that results secures social stability. MacIntyre omits this dimension of Aristotle's ethical tradition to adopt a position that appears gender neutral in order to avoid introducing difference into his teleological argument for virtue, which would undermine his view that this moral path can unify Americans.

Difference in a political world shaped by identities based on race, class, gender, ethnicity, sexuality, age, ableism, and religion, for MacIntyre, generates a moral relativism causing contemporary liberalism's decline. He traces this problem to the Enlightenment's construction of the autonomous self as denying the individual access to a moral identity predetermined by a theistic and teleological world order. Disconnected from tradition and a *telos* by reason and self-determination makes modern man a creature of social context defined by personal preferences and self-interest. Without a *telos*, an individual's identity "can then be anything, can assume any role or take any point of view, because it *is* in and for itself nothing."[38] This "democratized self" possesses no essential identity or defined nature and, therefore, no means to create meaningful standards of moral judgment for the individual much less the community.[39] Moral character in modern liberalism amounts to living within the rules of a law-abiding society, which ensures the security necessary for individuals to pursue their self-interest and external goods. Man's "good life" no longer equates with that of the *polis*, and citizens lose any meaningful link to the political community. For MacIntyre, the *telos* unifies the individual's moral self and, as a result, the fragmented moral and political order.

Virtue focuses MacIntyre's vision of political life as emanating from moral subjects unified in a shared moral tradition that provides the teleological means for repairing liberalism's shattered self. Power disappears from this vision as people return to virtue to resolve the dilemmas of diversity generated by moral relativism. A shared virtue tradition brings people together around a common understanding of "the good life" and displaces differences, conflicts, and disorder. To overcome the association of tradition with the static status quo of the past, MacIntyre argues for "a living tradition" that "is an historically extended, socially embodied argument, and an argument precisely in part about the goods which constitute that tradition."[40] Changing contexts and historical circumstances may require people to make moral judgments by negotiating between already existing cultural and religious traditions and a foundational Aristotelian virtue tradition. Narrowing negotiation in this way negates how these traditions grant virtue to the dominant governing class, which acquires moral authority over the subordinate, less virtuous, and often vice-ridden class that serves it. Virtue deflects attention away from the politics operating in these moral traditions that justify inequality between categories of people on the basis of predetermined conceptions passed from one generation to the next through the virtue-vice dualism.

This focus on virtue results in a gender neutrality that overlooks the inherent role of vice. Women's exclusion from public life on the basis of their moral inferiority disappears as a factor denying them a voice in shaping these moral traditions. Yet the moral traditions now upheld as virtue traditions continue to justify gender inequality. MacIntyre does claim that women should acquire full citizenship; however, the virtue tradition on which his argument rests imports women's inequality, constraint, and exclusion into the political community's idea of the "good life." The question then remains: *For whom* would this be the good life? Failure to account for how virtue justifies dividing people into dominant and subordinate categories redeploys a tradition actually premised on difference and inequality instead of unity, the goal of MacIntyre's project. The dualistic logic of this moral tradition equates difference in moral identity or political belief with vice as suspicious and potentially traitorous behavior that threatens the community's order and unity. Virtue functions to exercise political power to construct a political community's "good life" based on unity rather than difference and a predetermined tradition predicated on a level of homogeneity and conformity antithetical to democracy.

Deflecting attention away from the power dynamics inherent to a virtue tradition creates what I call the problem of insularity, which characterizes political communities built on the moral scaffolding of the virtue-vice dualism. MacIntyre's framing of practice illustrates the problem of insularity. Practice, within ethical contexts, generally refers to the actions and relationships of those within a specific community that provide the basis on which the community builds its normative standards. MacIntyre defines practice as

> any coherent and complex form of socially established cooperative human activity through which goods internal to that form of activity are realized in the course of trying to achieve those

standards of excellence which are appropriate to, and partially definitive of, that form of activity, with the result that human powers to achieve excellence, and human conceptions of the ends and goods involved, are systematically extended.[41]

Practices, according to MacIntyre, pertain to the internal goods derived from engaging in a practice already established by those participating in it. Practitioners set the terms for the practice, excluding all outsiders from participating in any negotiations and effectively insulating the practice from external forces. Individuals achieve a higher standard of excellence when an activity belongs to a practice or predetermined tradition that over time establishes, often through trial and error, the best means for achieving set goals. Bricklaying, for MacIntyre, is not a practice, but architecture is because designing and building large structures belongs to a tradition with standards of excellence. This virtue tradition prevents MacIntyre's conception of practice from being applied to bricklayers, who, in reality, like architects, belong to a tradition that informs their practices, which provide the skilled labor necessary to erect the large structures designed by architects. Under a veil of neutrality created by presumed standards of excellence, virtue imports a range of moral assumptions that perpetuate inequalities premised on valuing one dominant group, such as architects, over another, such as bricklayers.

The problem of insularity refers to the way in which virtue erects a protective wall around categories of people whose moral excellence emanates from such a well-established tradition that it appears to be natural rather than deriving from exercises of power to maintain dominant and subordinate classes in society. Locating virtue tradition in practice would suggest MacIntyre's orientation toward accounting for such power dynamics. MacIntyre specifically aims to overcome the limits of Rawls's Kantian ethics, which suffers, in his estimation, from a universalism and transcendence that provide a thin view of the moral subject. By grounding virtue tradition in human actions that occur in material contexts, MacIntyre advances a more fully contextualized moral subject embedded in a complex, changing social and material reality.[42]

Virtue, however, insulates these moral subjects within specific sets of practices that, for the most part, fail to meet the standards of excellence assigned to practices such as architecture. Their voices as members of a community affected by the structures designed by architects remain silenced, since, as outsiders to the practice, they lack legitimacy. Even practitioners must accept the authority of the preexisting tradition as the standard of excellence against which they judge each other, insulating them from active engagement in determining their practices. Those who explore new practices, such as alternative bricklaying methods or architectural designs, challenge this tradition, which readily locates them on the side of vice, a fact that perpetuates "bad" or outmoded practices. Virtue tradition also makes it difficult for new groups such as women to engage in, much less participate in, developing those practices closed off to them by tradition. Failure to account for such political dynamics develops a thinner understanding of the moral subject and the way that virtue tradition upholds divisions in society predicated on inequality between categories of people. These divisions appear as "givens" or natural because of their longevity and insulation from interrogation.

Focusing on liberal pluralism rather than moral relativism, Amitai Etzioni and William Galston turn to Alexis de Tocqueville to advance a functionalist argument for virtue similar to MacIntyre's that also omits gendered power dynamics. Etzioni outlines a "sociology of virtue" based on the primary virtues of autonomy and order that allow the individual to live in active tension with the community. This active tension would create social stability without government intervention. Moral tradition integrates with modern concepts of freedom to achieve a "virtuous equilibrium" that supports Etzioni's new golden rule: "respect and uphold society's moral order as you would have society respect and uphold your autonomy."[43] Informed by Tocqueville, this idea that morality anchors American democracy against the chaos of democratic freedoms also grounds William Galston's argument for liberalism as inherently possessing the virtues necessary for democracy to function successfully.[44] Galston codifies these virtues into five categories—general, general political, liberal, political, and liberal economy—to clarify that courage, loyalty, independence, tolerance, patience, hard work, and self-restraint, among others, constitute the moral backbone of contemporary liberal democracy. Despite their reliance on Tocqueville's political thinking about virtue's essential part in sustaining American democracy, neither

Galston nor Etzioni address the separate spheres ideology characterizing Tocqueville's view that American men and women possess different
virtues. Avoiding the sexual division of labor that secures women's role
in the private sphere by placing the heavy weight of moral responsibility
on female virtue attempts to neutralize gender difference by deflecting
attention away from the power dynamics operating within this moral
tradition.

This gender-neutral position omits female moral virtue from a liberal tradition that, as Tocqueville argues, requires women's morality
to act as a counterbalance to democratic freedom. On these grounds,
Tocqueville goes so far as to attribute great political significance to
American women. Etzioni and Galston remove women and female virtue
from this equation. Etzioni advances order as a primary virtue needed
in American democracy. Galston frames self-restraint as the liberal virtue necessary for citizens to limit their individual freedoms voluntarily
in order to accommodate others' needs based on a community's shared
moral understanding. Such temperance, for Galston, requires the liberal individual to exercise self-control in conjunction with the virtue of
self-transcendence, which frames personal restraint in terms of meeting
the demands of the common good.[45] The female virtue of self-sacrifice
disaggregates into the two liberal virtues of self-restraint and transcendence that extend from finite individual action to the infinite realm of
reaching beyond the self for the community's greater moral and political good. Neutralizing gender in this way could be read as redistrib-
uting the double burden of moral responsibility traditionally assigned
to women through the female virtue of self-sacrifice to all American
citizens, who would collectively become democracy's moral guardians.

Removing the gender attributed to these virtues by Tocqueville,
however, belies the fact that Etzioni and Galston share his view of
the traditional American family as necessary to anchoring democracy
against its inherent chaos. This position assumes that women's primary
responsibility remains to their husbands and children in the private
sphere, where they carry the weight of protecting the entire nation from
moral decay. Second wave feminism, for Etzioni and Galston, brought
America to the precipice of social anarchy because this movement
pushed women to abandon the family for jobs in the public sphere, leaving the "seedbeds of virtue" untended. As democracy's foundation, the

heterosexual two-parent family establishes the mores and social institutions necessary to protect the people from intrusive government intervention and extensive centralization. Resurrecting the "Ozzie and
Harriet" family will rebuild this crumbling foundation. Children,
importantly, will again acquire from their parents the civic character
necessary to assume their responsibilities as future citizens. The moral
weight placed on the family by Tocqueville for upholding the nation's
common good remains, since, Galston explains, "it follows that if families become less capable of performing that role, the well-being of the
entire community is jeopardized."[46] Meeting the demands of this double
burden requires protecting the traditional family from the deteriorating
forces of high divorce rates, single motherhood, illegitimate births, and
gay and lesbian marriage and adoption.[47] Galston and Etzioni oppose
nontraditional family structures and efforts that strengthen day care
programs while they support imposing stricter divorce laws that entail
"braking mechanisms" and cooling-off periods. Gendered power dynamics operate beneath the veil of moral neutrality to return American
women to their place beside Harriet Nelson in the kitchen.

American women's supposed mass exodus from the private sphere as
a result of second wave feminism assigns them the responsibility for the
traditional family's decline, which leaves liberal pluralism unchecked by
strong moral virtues that bind people to a common good. Blame for
the nation's decay falls to women for abandoning their virtuous role as
moral guardians in private life. Galston and Etzioni fail to account for
the double shift of labor that American women perform inside and outside the home as mothers and workers, the lack of men's contribution to
reproductive labor in the home, or the structural shifts in society that
require two parents to work outside the home just to support their families. Privileging male irresponsibility features in such arguments that
frame women as solely responsible for morality through their role in the
family. Any deviation from that virtuous path makes American women
vulnerable targets in backlash politics that blames them for the nation's
decline and denies them a part in positively contributing to solutions in
ways other than returning to the family. Focusing on virtue attends to
a person's moral character while shifting attention away from structural
economic changes, women's gains in equal education and employment,
and increased female political representation. Habitual inattention to

politics results from such "back to virtue" arguments that, in this case, reframe virtue in gender-neutral terms despite the fact that their operation aims to resurrect the separate spheres ideology and return women to the private sphere. Backlash politics, in this way, appears to support democratic values of difference, diversity, and tolerance while actually redeploying the virtue-vice dualism to frame women as suspect citizens for abandoning their post as the nation's moral guardians.

Reading MacIntyre, Etzioni, and Galston against the traditions on which they rely to unify Americans against the forces of liberal pluralism and moral relativism illustrates how their multiple virtues position redeploys a separate spheres ideology consistent with backlash or "curl back" politics. Virtue functions to lower a veil of gender neutrality since, as a standard of excellence emanating from tradition, this concept appears devoid of the power dynamics characteristic of politics as an arena for negotiating difference. A gendered perspective, however, reveals how virtue redeploys traditional moral beliefs deeply embedded in Western political thought into the American political script, where these beliefs continue to justify women's exclusion from public life in order to maintain social order. Reliance on virtue tradition without critically engaging its gender dynamics perpetuates the problem of insularity that protects such moral traditions from interrogation given their apparent "goodness" or excellence. Feminist theorists and others who interrogate these traditions may be regarded with suspicion for questioning them, particularly as a group excluded from predetermined practices. Assuming virtue's gender neutrality as a means of promoting unity through a shared understanding of a common good as opposed to valuing difference insulates the political community and its moral subjects from the realities of power exercised through a morality premised on inequality.

Habitual Inattention to Democracy: The Power of Vice

The "back to virtue" politics advanced by Etzioni, Galston, and MacIntyre hopes to prevent American democracy's moral decline that fragments the political community. Their attention focuses on recommitting the people to a virtue tradition that promotes unity instead of difference, agreement instead of discord. The moral subject displaces the citizen as a matter of interest in reviving democracy. Returning to a predetermined tradition replaces political negotiation and deliberation with acceptance. Politics as a means for determining the distribution of resources by exercising power in various ways ranging from negotiation and deliberation to force disappears from this "back to virtue" position.

Such habitual inattention to politics, Tocqueville warns, represents the greatest vice in a democracy. Americans are "often carried away, far beyond the bounds of common sense, by some sudden passion or hasty opinion. . . . Unable to be expert at all, a man easily becomes satisfied with half-baked notions."[48] The people, overwhelmed by an extensive amount of information about the issues and little time to digest it, tend simply to adopt the majority's opinion, thereby creating conditions conducive to the tyranny of the majority, which dictates public opinion and silences minority voices. To protect democracy from such forces of despotism, Tocqueville advises Americans to attend to political matters ranging from voting for representatives to the "petty affairs" of everyday life.[49] Constant attention to the everyday life related to family and civil society can prevent democracy from slipping into despotism by establishing the private sphere as a zone of personal freedoms protected from government intervention.

Preserving the common good through moral unity does not lead MacIntyre, Etzioni, or Galston to address how politics actually operates in everyday life, which involves accounting for differences among the people. Gender neutrality indicates this inattention to power dynamics and ultimately the omission of vice that connotes moral disorder and frames women as suspect citizens instead of moral guardians. Vice, a default category for all behaviors outside the standards of excellence, equates with moral difference and divergence from a political community unified around a shared moral understanding of the common good. Vice puts the complicated, messy aspects of everyday ethical life into stark relief as a critical part of a political community in which the people negotiate conflicts related to differing identities, beliefs, material needs, wants, and interests. Habitual inattention to politics characterizes the multiple virtues position that avoids the realities of vice to advance an "Ozzie and Harriet" morality, which promotes consensus as the optimal political outcome without accounting for dissent and disagreements as necessary to liberal democracy. Similar to *Ozzie and Harriet*, moral dilemmas and minor conflicts end with a positive resolution emanating from shared moral beliefs predicated on a separate spheres ideology.

Attending only to virtue perpetuates an unrealistic, incomplete picture of the moral subject and the moral ambiguities inherent to the diversity and pluralism prized in democratic societies. This complex political terrain requires enough moral ambiguity for the people to meet the hard demands of liberal democracy. "Liberalism imposes extraordinary ethical difficulties on us," Judith Shklar asserts, "to live with the contradictions, unresolvable conflicts, and balancing between public and private imperatives which are neither opposed to nor at one with each other."[50] Ordinary vices contribute to a democratic ethics capable of negotiating these complexities. Snobbery arises from justifying the inclusion of some and exclusion of others that creates inequality—the price, according to Shklar, that a liberal society pays for diversity and difference. Hypocrisy naturally occurs in representative democracy, which creates a gap between politicians and their ability to represent constituent interests and results in a healthy skepticism by the people toward their government. Such ordinary vices play a necessary civic role in liberal democracy by accounting for the complex realities of political life that empowers citizens with an ethics capable of helping them to navigate it. *Civic* vices make citizens attentive to the behaviors that can damage and destroy the common good. Thus vice prevents the habitual inattention to the realities of everyday political life that Tocqueville worried would erode democracy's freedom. Vices often trigger public attention that engages deliberation about perceived wrongdoing and its relationship to the political community.

Analyzing the gendered dynamics of virtue and vice in the multiple virtues position illustrates how a façade of neutrality erected by moral assumptions of excellence passed from one era to the next makes a separate spheres ideology difficult to discern. Gender neutrality also characterizes Shklar's work on ordinary vices, which indicates how virtue and vice appear as "givens" insulated from differences among people and changing contexts by traditional moral beliefs. This insularity poses a problem by deflecting attention away from a set of gendered power dynamics operating through the virtue-vice dualism that directly affect American women's full citizenship. Despite the focus of "back to virtue" advocates on women's role as moral guardians of the nation's common good, vice remains the defining feature of their relationship to politics since even their finite vices hold an infinite capacity to threaten the nation's future. Female moral vice, as a result, entails this civic dimension that ties a woman's individual behavior to a nation's success or failure. Indeed, women's engagement in public and political life equates with civic vice, since it involves abandoning their post as moral guardians, which causes disorder and disruption.

Backlash politics capitalizes on this gendered moral dynamic, which enables its proponents to frame a woman's increased access to education, jobs, and political office as destroying American democracy. Such societal doubt about women's loyalty to the nation emanates from a virtue tradition built on a separate spheres ideology that narrows women's value to political life in terms of moral guardianship and places all other avenues to full citizenship under suspicion. Backlashes channel a broader and deeper societal suspicion of politics as a morally valued, much less virtuous part of American democracy. Valuing such skepticism of politics perpetuates the very habitual inattention to public life that, Tocqueville warns, must be protected to preserve everyday freedoms. Vice in this moral calculus equates with political power to signal moral corruption, which devalues the engagement critical to sustaining liberal democracy.

6 | The Legacy of Virtue and Vice

Mary Wollstonecraft and Contemporary
Feminist Care Ethics

C hanges in the family, whether in the eighteenth or twenty-first
century, generate highly charged debates over women's role as
moral guardians assigned to protect the nation's future, and they
arouse societal suspicions about women's citizenship that fuel backlash
politics. Mary Wollstonecraft, in *A Vindication of the Rights of Woman*,
challenged the eighteenth-century European ideal of the sentimental family as depicted in Jean-Jacques Rousseau's *Emile*, in which romantic love between husband and wife in the domestic realm prevails
against public life's harsh realities. This sentimental view of the family
maintained women's place in private life even as the philosophy of the
Enlightenment granted reason to all human beings—which logically
should include women. Female reason, however, threatened to justify
women's entrance into public life and to introduce emotions, sexuality,
and irrationality into this supposedly asexual sphere characterized by
male rationality. Instead of confining women to the sentimental family,
Wollstonecraft argues that women should receive an education equal to
men, which would enable women to cultivate their reason and achieve
"true" moral and civic virtue. Women would then abandon vice-ridden
behavior such as gossip, sexual flirtation, and reading romance novels
for their virtuous duties as wives and mothers. Equal education would,

Wollstonecraft contends, cultivate women's private or "natural" virtue that emanates from their biological ability to give birth in such a way as to benefit the public spirit. Such "natural" female virtues fall under the broader concept of care, a pivotal dimension of contemporary feminist ethics and political theory. Feminist care ethics, in this sense, carries Wollstonecraft's work forward by reframing care as representing women's ethical standpoint in private life and as possessing the potential to transform how democratic citizens envision political life.

The sentimental family's ideological remnants continue into the twenty-first century despite dramatic shifts in how male public and female private life are configured. Sixty-seven percent of women with children under the age of eighteen in the United States work in the paid labor force outside the home, and since 1990, 70 percent of children live in a family in which every parent works.[1] A crisis in care results as American women who pull a double shift between work and home still cannot meet all the demands on their time. Their accelerated entrance into the paid workforce makes publicly visible all the unpaid care work still done by women in the private sphere, such as cooking, cleaning, raising children, and assisting elderly parents. "For four decades, American women have entered the paid workforce," Ruth Rosen explains, "on men's terms not their own—yet we have done precious little as a society to restructure the workplace or family life."[2] Feminist theorists and philosophers respond to this care crisis by challenging the position of "back to virtue" thinkers, who deploy female moral virtue to assert that a woman's primary responsibility, regardless of whether she works outside the home, is to uphold her civic obligation to care for her family.

Feminist care ethics emanates from Carol Gilligan's *In a Different Voice: Psychological Theory and Women's Development*, which demarcates the separate moral sphere of men's ethic of rights associated with public life from women's ethic of responsibility related to care and compassion in the private sphere. Men, accordingly, rely on reason and objectivity in an individualistic rights-based approach that reflects their experience in liberal democratic and capitalist public life. Women, in contrast, employ a responsibility-based approach related to their role as caregivers in private life, which requires attention to relationships, emotions, and contexts in reaching normative judgments. Early work on care ethics identified the mother-child relationship as the paradigm for caring practices. Revisioning care from a feminist perspective led to developing an alternative to the dominant liberal ethical framework premised on justice, individualism, universal principles, and rationality. This trajectory moves outside the mother-child paradigm to define care more broadly as a practice inherent to meeting basic human needs. Joan Tronto and Berenice Fisher redraft care as "a *species activity that includes everything that we do to maintain, continue, and repair our 'world' so that we can live in it as well as possible.*"[3] Care becomes a political concept by locating its practices as integral to the complex web of interdependent relationships between caregivers and receivers that allow a political community to function. "Public care" evolved from this perspective to emphasize how these practices apply explicitly to social policies, various political institutions, and democratic processes. Contemporary feminist care theorists generally agree that care, though still grounded in the context of human relationships, encompasses a set of practices extending from private to public life.

No similar consensus emerges around the question of whether care should be defined as a virtue. This situation creates a "slippage problem" with regard to the various alternative terms used in care ethics. Some accept care as a virtue, while others raise concerns about such a framing of care. Selma Sevenhuijsen attempts to salvage virtue from its patriarchal tradition as a tool, when carefully employed, for establishing the standards by which the entire community can judge good care from bad. Sevenhuijsen indicates some reservations about this approach, however, by interchanging "virtue" with "value," "disposition," and "emotion."[4] Virginia Held identifies virtue as a patriarchal concept and turns to "value" to capture how care emanates from relationships as opposed to individuals. Yet Held still insists that although "caring is no doubt a virtue, the ethics of care is not simply a kind of virtue ethics."[5] Tronto avoids virtue. She explains that "those who have written eloquently about care as a virtue, whether a social virtue as in [Charlotte Perkins] Gilman or a private virtue as in [Nel] Noddings, have been unable to show a convincing way of turning these virtues into a realistic approach to the kinds of problems that caring will confront in the real world."[6] Alternatively, Tronto identifies the "ethical elements" of attentiveness, responsibility, competence, and responsiveness as the normative dimensions of care in order to operationalize these "ethical elements" as practices.[7] Slippages between virtue and terms such as "value," "disposition," "emotion," and "ethical elements" in feminist care ethics indicate the challenges posed by the virtue-vice dualism to moving outside this dominant ethical framework.

This chapter places Mary Wollstonecraft in dialogue with feminist care ethics in order to address the question of whether care *should* be defined as a virtue.[8] Wollstonecraft, though never explicitly identifying care as a virtue, focuses on the public and private virtues attributed to women's role as wives and mothers, who, by fulfilling their caring duties, secure social order. Reading contemporary feminist care ethics against Wollstonecraft's work on female virtue exposes how the legacy of virtue and vice prevents theorizing a feminist ethics consistent with the democratic values of equality, freedom, and inclusion by creating three intractable problems: moral perfectionism, parochialism, and inequality. *Moral perfectionism* references the penultimate expression of virtue as an ethical view of the moral subject transcending the physical world. Exercising reason and drawing on moral tradition enables the individual to escape everyday life's material constraints and achieve virtuous ideals such as justice. *Parochialism* conveys the narrow applicability of an ethical perspective grounded in virtue and vice that sets boundaries within and around this dualism to establish a moral framework premised on exclusion. *Inequality* derives from the dualistic nature of virtue and vice, which perpetuates a moral logic that locates people based on their normative value in hierarchical relationships of domination and subordination that determine how a political community distributes power and resources.

Structuring this analysis around these issues illustrates two central ways in which the legacy of virtue and vice undermines the purpose of feminist ethics. First, Wollstonecraft's work advances moral perfectionism as the goal for men and women that can be achieved by adhering to the virtuous standard of excellence. This position, inherent to a virtue-based ethics, contradicts the grounding of feminist ethics in the contextual realities of everyday life. Second, Wollstonecraft's attention to sex and sexuality, particularly given her Victorian moral context, starkly contrasts with the marginality of both issues in feminist care ethics, which focuses on relationships, emotions, contexts, and basic human needs. The tendency of feminist care ethics to marginalize sex and sexuality as important elements of care in human relationships indicates how the virtue-vice dualism's moral logic deflects attention away from two central aspects of human life generally aligned with female vice. This dualistic logic imports certain moral assumptions from one historical context to the next through the concepts of virtue and vice, which, as this analysis of feminist care ethics reveals, seriously inhibits freedom, equality, and inclusion. Care, this chapter ultimately argues, should not be framed as a virtue.

Sex, Sexuality, and Suspicion in Mary Wollstonecraft's Political Thought

Mary Wollstonecraft, similar to other women who question the reigning moral paradigm, represents how society identifies women as moral guardians but suspect citizens. Wollstonecraft broke with traditional Victorian womanhood when she crossed the high barriers between the male public and female private spheres by engaging in paid labor throughout her life to support herself and her family. Her writing further pushed through this boundary when, as a woman making claims to gender equality, Wollstonecraft challenged leading male thinkers of her day such as Edmund Burke in her *A Vindication of the Rights of Man* and Jean-Jacques Rousseau in *A Vindication of the Rights of Woman*. The latter catapulted Wollstonecraft to the forefront of the European Enlightenment. After her death during childbirth in 1797, Wollstonecraft's intimate private life became public when her husband, William Godwin, published *Memoirs of the Author of "A Vindication of the Rights of Woman"* in 1798. This memoir, though meant to pay tribute to her memory, conveys information about her romantic life that included premarital sexual relations with Godwin. The public scandal generated by the *Memoirs* "plunged Wollstonecraft and her proto-feminist philosophy into disrepute."[9] Wollstonecraft's life and legacy depict the ease with which society moves women, particularly when they claim a voice within the public arena and argue for equality and freedom, across the moral boundary between virtue and vice.

Suspicion characterizes Wollstonecraft's work in terms of the serious doubts that she raises about Victorian morality, which, she argues, actually promotes manners instead of "true" virtue. Female modesty in the Victorian era determined a woman's reputation for virtue, which she exhibited by wearing the appropriate dress, keeping the appropriate company, and obeying a range of social norms that dictated appropriate behavior. "It has long since occurred to me," Wollstonecraft states, "that advice respecting behaviour, and all the various modes of preserving a good reputation, which have been so strenuously inculcated on the female world, were specious poisons, that incrusting morality eat away the substance."[10] The façade of polite Victorian society hid a range of inappropriate activities in which women engaged, such as incessantly reading romantic novels, gossiping, and participating in lewd behavior with other women. Cultivating a reputation for good manners combined with unequal education prevented women from pursuing real virtue and morality. This chasm between women's manners and morals results in societal doubt about women's ability to fulfill their civic obligations as moral guardians of the family, which justifies their ongoing confinement in private life.

Sentimentalism anchors Wollstonecraft's criticism of Victorian morality and foreshadows the problem of parochialism identified in feminist care ethics as narrowly confining caring practices to family relationships. Women's social, economic, and political dependence on men focuses their energy on achieving happiness through romantic love, which leads "them shamefully to neglect the duties of life, and frequently in the midst of these sublime refinements they plump into actual vice."[11] Self-preservation drives women to compete against each other to get and keep a husband by capturing his sexual interest. Society mistakes women adorning their bodies with clothing that subtly accentuates their physical beauty as female modesty. This finite female virtue narrows a woman's emotional range to romantically pleasing men with her physical appearance. For Wollstonecraft, this behavior results in, at worst, vice and, at best, a vacuous moral sense limited to manners. Denying women access to equal education and public life creates this parochial moral viewpoint that inhibits the "true" virtue necessary for protecting the common good from moral decay. "Females . . . denied all political privileges," Wollstonecraft states, "have their attention naturally drawn from the interest of the whole community to that of the minute parts." Rectifying this problem requires nothing less than a "REVOLUTION in female manners," which would transform them into true virtues by cultivating women's reason.[12] Husbands and wives could ground their relationships on mutual respect and friendship instead of fleeting passions and physical attraction. Sentimentalism weakens Victorian society's moral foundation by building the family institution on the shaky grounds of a marital relationship defined by manners instead of male and female virtue.

Overcoming the parochialism of the sentimental family required that women receive an education equal to that of men, the basis for Wollstonecraft's "revolution," which dramatically shifts the gendered distribution of moral responsibility. Education alongside men grants women the opportunity to acquire the knowledge necessary for developing their reason and, most importantly, their virtue. Women's ignorance maintains their childlike behaviors in pursuit of fulfilling base desires, which, for Wollstonecraft, perpetuates their inferiority to men. Such hierarchy between men and women denies the Enlightenment's promise of equality. "To render the social compact truly equitable, and in order to spread those enlightening principles, which alone can meliorate the fate of man," Wollstonecraft explains, "women must be allowed to found their virtue on knowledge, which is scarcely possible unless they be educated by the same pursuits as men."[13] Knowledge leads to the understanding and rationality necessary for women to escape the narrow confines of physical and emotional dependence on men, freeing them to become better wives and mothers capable of fulfilling their domestic duties. Equal education would provide women with the means to overcome societal doubt regarding their ability to reason sufficiently to carry out moral guardianship's civic obligations and social responsibilities and to build the trust necessary for women to be recognized as full citizens contributing to the common good.

Inequality between the sexes breeds the vice and corruption that eats away at the community's moral substance. Men and women must cultivate "true" virtue in order to transform Victorian manners into morality. "The two sexes mutually corrupt and improve each other," Wollstonecraft asserts. "This, I believe to be an indisputable truth, extending to every virtue. Chastity, modesty, public spirit, and all the noble train of virtues, on which social virtue and happiness are built should be understood and cultivated by all mankind, or they will be cultivated to little effect."[14] Men lose their privileged irresponsibility by assuming an equal responsibility for morality, which shifts the double burden assigned to women as moral guardians. Men should become better husbands and fathers as their moral scope expands to include the private virtues associated with the domestic duties of care. Alternatively, as women, develop their reason, they should come to understand that their private virtues contribute to the broader public spirit. Wollstonecraft dismantles male moral privilege by equalizing the gendered distribution of moral responsibility between men and women who, though still in separate spheres, develop their reason through education to cultivate the "true" virtue necessary for preserving the common good.

Chastity and modesty, finite moral virtues traditionally attributed to women, further equalize the sexual division of moral labor as Wollstonecraft revisions these virtues and assigns them to men. Victorian society lays the responsibility for female chastity and modesty on the weaker sex. These virtues become manners when women fain bashfulness and coquetry while men present themselves as gallant and chivalrous. Reputation and the appearance of virtue publicly erect a façade hiding the vice and immorality that infects the entire society. "It is vain," Wollstonecraft asserts, "to expect much public or private virtue, till both men and women grow more modest."[15] Chastity conventionally reflects a woman's sexual purity, which she protects until marriage when she engages in sexual intercourse with her husband for the sole purpose of procreation. Wollstonecraft redrafts chastity to reference a purity of mind that women will acquire by gaining access to an education equal to men and by cultivating their reason. "In defining modesty, it appears to me equally proper to discriminate that purity of mind, which is the effect of chastity, from a simplicity of character that leads us to form a just opinion of ourselves."[16] Modesty transforms, for women and men, into a "soberness of mind" premised on the purity of reason that leads them to a self-denial based on a rational decision-making process guided by "true" virtue.[17] Self-governance becomes viable for men freed from their sexual desires, and for women granted the reason to make rational, virtuous decisions. These virtues, traditionally framed in terms of sexual behavior, become asexual reflections of reason exercised by men and women.

Resolving inequality and overcoming the parochialism of the sentimental family enables Wollstonecraft's men and women to achieve the "true" virtue indicative of moral perfectionism. Reason uncovers the true moral principles that men hide "to justify prejudices" by burying virtue beneath the manners that confine women to domestic life.[18] Freed from human opinion and exercises of power, reason and knowledge clear the way to virtue in its purist form. "The perfection of our nature and capability of happiness," Wollstonecraft asserts, "must be estimated by the degree of reason, virtue, and knowledge, that distinguish the individual, and direct the laws which bind society."[19] Virtue's expansive capacity to encompass the infinite enables individuals to understand themselves as part of a broader society, which captures the transcendent quality of moral perfectionism. Further underscoring transcendence, Wollstonecraft grounds her moral viewpoint in religion by identifying "true" virtue as emanating from "the perfection of God."[20] God, not people, serves as the final judge in determining virtuous behavior, which makes Him the ultimate source of the moral self. Instead of living according to manners determined and measured by society, moral perfectionism, for Wollstonecraft, allows men and women to develop "true" virtue by using the human reason granted to them by God to understand and live by moral principles.

Moral perfectionism usually deflects attention away from vice. Wollstonecraft, however, addresses the relationship of female vice to women's sex and sexuality, breaking dramatically with Victorian society's repressive attitudes toward the subject. "I here throw down my gauntlet, and deny the existence of sexual virtues, not excepting modesty," Wollstonecraft declares.[21] Determining female, as well as male, morality on whether finite behaviors and appearances signal sexual desire immerses virtue in the realm of material reality and human relationships clouded by opinions, assumptions, and prejudices that hide the truth. Men and women should employ their reason to engage in self-denial to control their sexual appetites, which only should lead to procreation as a necessary feature of the political community. Sexuality, for Wollstonecraft, should be limited to heterosexuality as indicated by her reference to indecent practices at boarding schools where girls sleep and wash together, leading women to adopt vice-ridden, immodest habits.[22] Wollstonecraft—surprisingly, given her historical context—engages directly with sex and sexuality as central to transforming male and female manners into true virtue that would allow men and women to better fulfill their respective duties in private life and in the political community.

Moral Perfectionism in Feminist Care Ethics: The Problems of Infinite Virtue, Patriarchal Moral Standards, and Omitting Vice

In stark contrast to Wollstonecraft, sex, sexuality, and vice disappear from feminist care ethics despite its careful attention to basic human needs and practices in human relationships. Such omissions indicate how assumptions of moral perfectionism pull care ethics away from its foundation in the relationships, practices, and emotions of people's everyday experience. Attention to these material aspects of life drives feminist care ethics, in contrast to liberalism's narrow focus on reason and independence, to develop the fullest possible understanding of the moral subject. Without a clear alternative, virtue acts as the controlling concept in feminist care ethics as an assumed ideal ethical standard against which the community measures citizens to determine their moral worth. As such, the infinite dimension inherent to virtue demands that people transcend the finite, material trappings of everyday life in pursuit of moral perfection. The moral logic of the virtue-vice dualism imports infinite virtue and moral perfectionism into feminist care ethics, which maintains ideals as essential to judging the moral subject, sustains certain patriarchal moral standards, and omits vice as part of understanding human life's complexities.

Nel Noddings's *Caring: A Feminine Approach to Ethics and Moral Education* illustrates how building care ethics on the mother caring for her child as the female moral subject's ethical ideal results in moral perfectionism. The dyadic relationship between the mother, understood as the "one-caring," and the child, identified as the "one cared-for," orients Noddings's feminine ethics toward the material practices of mothering. Caring requires the engagement of two people and thus establishes relationships as essential to an ethics envisioned from a feminine perspective. "Taking *relation* as ontologically basic," Noddings asserts, "simply means that we recognize human encounter and affective response as a basic fact of human existence."[23] This position directly challenges the

"Father's" language of liberalism, which represents the dominant masculine ethics premised on individualism, reason, and universalism. The "Mother's" language, alternatively, conveys a feminine ethics emanating from women's experiences as mothers in the private sphere based on relationships, emotions, and particular practices. Active virtue anchors this feminine ethics and incorporates the sentiments of natural caring into an ethical framework that does "not let 'virtue' dissipate into 'the virtues' described in abstract categories," which would undermine Noddings's feminine alternative to liberalism's masculine ethics.[24]

A tension exists in Noddings's ethics between establishing caring as a virtue—a moral standard of excellence against which practices can be measured—and preventing it from becoming one abstract virtue among many others. This tension reflects the dynamic internal to virtue between the finite and infinite. Since Noddings works within the virtue-vice framework defined by the masculine moral paradigm that she critiques, the female practices of caring associated with motherhood must be elevated from their devalued location in the private sphere to the level of an ethical ideal aligned with the infinite. "For many women," Noddings emphasizes, "motherhood is the single greatest source of strength for the maintenance of the ethical ideal."[25] Joy represents an "exalted" emotion that sustains the person who performs the difficult labor of caring.[26] Referring to joy in this way signals the infinite and spiritual element of virtue that emotionally rewards people for "good" behavior by allowing them to escape finite reality. Noddings enlivens the tension between the infinite and finite by rooting her ethics in the tangible relationships of caring. Mothering, however, remains the ethical ideal of feminine caring against which society measures women. Framing care as a virtue imports preexisting standards of moral excellence into this feminine ethic, located squarely within a moral logic that places greater value on the infinite and perfectionism than on finite human practices. Virtue prevents Noddings from establishing an ethics on relational, rather than universal, grounds.

Defining mothering as a virtue carries a patriarchal moral tradition into Noddings's feminine ethics, which, as a result, retains strong ties to moral guardianship and its corresponding separate spheres ideology. Mothering belongs to a constellation of female moral virtues such as purity, piety, chastity, and modesty. Historically, these virtues require women to remain in the private sphere, protected from public life's vice and corruption. The mother-child relationship as the paradigm of care in Noddings's feminine ethics maintains the separate spheres of male public and female private life while elevating care to the level of moral value granted to justice. Equating female care as a virtue to male justice redeploys a separate but equal status into contemporary ethics that morally justifies segregating men and women and retains women's moral guardianship, a construction premised on their exclusion from direct access to political life.

Justice, as Noddings's work suggests, serves as the preexisting standard of virtue against which feminist concepts such as care are measured in a liberal democracy, which speaks to the continued dominance of a virtue-based moral framework. Feminist political theorists who debate the relationship between justice and care focus on the question: How does care, freed from the conceptual confines of the private sphere, relate to justice, understood as the primary virtue of liberalism? Susan Moller Okin, following John Rawls, defends justice as the primary virtue from which care naturally flows in systems premised on fairness and equality.[27] Joan Tronto responded to Okin by arguing that care and justice represent compatible standards for liberal democracy. The distributive function of justice prioritizes which human needs caring practices meet on the basis of fairness and equality instead of parochial interests.[28] The debate then moved toward a dialectic view of care and justice in order to integrate meeting human needs more seamlessly with distribution of resources.[29] Integration, however, commodifies care as a resource, which diminishes its relational value in order to fit care into a distributive mold and, Julie Anne White argues, weakens the impartial nature of justice that can counteract the paternal impulse of care.[30] Bringing this debate full circle, Virginia Held inverts Okin's original claim that justice supersedes care. She contends that care trumps justice as the basic moral value, since the people and political community depend on care needs to be met for their survival.[31]

The cyclical nature of the justice-care debate operates according to the moral logic of dualisms, in which two oppositional categories limit theoretical moves to upholding, inverting, or equalizing their hierarchical relationship. As the primary virtue of liberalism, justice carries more weight than care in a moral tradition designed to attribute lesser value to women's practices. Revisioning care within this dominant dualistic framework requires feminist political theorists to follow predetermined rules that maintain hierarchical moral categories, which contradict these theorists' commitments to equality, freedom, and inclusion. Dualisms erect an insurmountable barrier to achieving equality between justice and care and limit these concepts to narrow confines. Virtue and vice function in the moral background to perpetuate inequality, constraint, and exclusion, placing these concepts in direct opposition to the goals of liberal democracy and feminism.

Virtue as the standard of moral excellence focuses attention on moral perfection, which leads feminist care ethics, in its quest to achieve a moral status equivalent to justice, to omit serious consideration of vice. Noddings, while recognizing that vice, harm, and feminine evil exist, sidelines their importance to her ethical project, which focuses on care as a feminine virtue essential to human flourishing.[32] Harm and "bad" caring practices enter into feminist care ethics in terms of the moral decision-making process needed to judge "good" from "bad" care.[33] Omitting vice advances the goal of morally valuing care, long associated with the devalued labor of women in private life. Yet a feminist care ethics grounded in actual human relationships, everyday practices, and social contexts needs to include negative emotions, corruption, violence, oppression, and abuse as part of human experience and governance. An idealistic view of care emerges without a clear account of vice. The moral perfectionism inherent to virtue deflects attention away from a range of moral assumptions categorized as vice, which prevents feminist care ethics from developing the fullest understanding of the moral subject and how to navigate the "good" and "bad" moral terrains that make up the reality of human life.

Parochialism: Practice and the Limits of Finite Virtues

Practice in care ethics shifts attention from infinite virtue and moral perfectionism to finite virtues and parochialism. Virtue and care ethics similarly focus on practice as essential to basing moral standards on visible actions judged in a societal context. Grounding care in concrete practices narrows its applicability to those whom we physically encounter, potentially limiting care to private relations. This creates the problem of parochialism in care ethics. Care on a national, much less global, scale becomes difficult, if not impossible, since it occurs only through concrete engagement with immediate others. Virtue links finite individual behavior to an infinite collective moral consciousness, which makes this concept seem capable of resolving the problem of parochialism by binding citizens to a system of moral beliefs reflecting political and cultural contexts. While capable of expanding the ethical scope of care beyond concrete others, virtue narrowly defines moral and political identities, and the process of moral judgment necessary to political decision making.

Sara Ruddick's *Maternal Thinking: Towards a Politics of Peace* develops a feminist ethics based on the finite virtues of motherhood that narrowly defines women's political identity as moral guardians and generates a parochialism that undercuts Ruddick's goal to advance global peace politics. Emphasizing the practices in maternal relations focuses on the finite reality of caregivers who strive to manage conflicts and tensions without letting them degenerate into negligence or harm to care receivers. Moral standards emerge from those who participate in these caring practices as "mothers develop *conceptions* of abilities and virtues according to which they measure themselves and interpret their actions."[34] Practitioners developing virtues based on actual caring grounds virtues in a finite context that escapes the moral perfectionism arising from infinite virtue and retains the conceptual capacity of virtue to extend from individuals to the broader community. The internal dualistic logic of virtue and vice identified as the infinite and finite, however, locks Ruddick's maternal thinking into a parochial moral legacy that confines women to moral guardianship.

Women as mothers serve as "custodians of the promise of birth," signaling their role as moral guardians, which Ruddick develops further by building maternal thinking on four female virtues central to the moral legacy of virtue.[35] Humility, a finite female virtue, pertains to a mother accepting her lack of control over an uncontrollable world, a moral perspective that resonates with the Puritan view of humility as a woman's complete submission to the Lord, who controlled her destiny.[36] Cheerfulness allows mothers to persevere against difficult circumstances. This virtue reflects that of the happiness attributed to Puritan women who joyfully submitted to God and their husbands.[37] Attentive love reframes the ideal of a mother's love in finite terms as being active and careful to prevent women from sacrificing the self to their husbands and children.[38] Recasting the female infinite virtue of self-sacrifice as attentive love captures the affection and friendship that Wollstonecraft identifies as an alternative to Victorian sentimentalism in the family, linking this finite female virtue to Traditional Womanhood. Proper trust, the fourth finite virtue, requires that a mother, instead of expecting blind obedience to parental authority, accept her child's indignation at betrayals of trust.[39] Such trust falls outside the pantheon of female virtues that determine the political identity of women as moral guardians. The societal trust placed in women as mothers charged with protecting the nation's common good from their location in the family, however, creates the conditions necessary for distrust or suspicion of their ability to fulfill this obligation. The finite female virtues of humility, cheerfulness, attentive love, and proper trust belong to the legacy of virtue and vice that embeds maternal thinking within the moral guardianship tradition.

This tradition locks in a parochialism based on granting women moral virtue and some political recognition for their confinement to private life and prevents Ruddick from successfully transferring these finite female virtues of maternal thinking to global peace politics. Humility, for instance, may cause people to relinquish control instead of performing the hard work in the political arena necessary to organize and advance a broader movement for peace. Cheerfulness negates the value of anger and discontent in motivating people to take political action. Attentive love works against activists immersing themselves completely in movement building, which often demands a high level of dedication in moments of intense political change. Proper trust disregards the healthy distrust and skepticism of citizens who actively question and scrutinize their government's policies to produce the information and analysis needed to persuade people to support a peace movement. Framing these traits as female virtues narrows the scope of maternal thinking by locking it into a moral guardianship tradition and dualistic moral logic that deflects attention away from an array of dynamics required to overcome the mother-child relationship's parochialism and meet the broader moral demands of global peace movements.

Moving away from the mother-child paradigm expands the scope of care ethics but can still limit it to the moral framework of the virtue-vice dualism that sustains a parochial viewpoint. Julie Anne White decouples social roles such as wife and mother from "character traits," a phrase that she uses in place of virtue, in order to liberate care from a moral tradition antithetical to accounting for the dynamics of fluid social roles. Framing care as a private virtue essential to the mother-child relationship, White argues, sets up a paternalistic model of authority that transfers into how the state engages with those receiving social welfare.[40] Alternatively, White recasts care receivers, usually identified as needy dependents in the social welfare context, as copartners with caregivers in an interdependent process that grants all participants an equal voice in determining how best to meet their needs. Such a democratic politics of public care demands recognizing the interdependence of relationships and replacing the solidity of character traits with the fluidity of social roles.[41] Separating social roles from character traits, however, leaves the moral framework of the virtue-vice dualism in place. Without an alternative consistent with fluid social roles, public care remains bound to the traditions of a parochial dualistic moral logic and female private virtue.

Moral judgments in care ethics also entail a parochialism since reaching these decisions results from everyday engagement with others in relationships from which emanate moral standards of "best" practices. For Sara Ruddick, mothers act as the best judges of the traits necessary for good parenting, since those engaged in a practice are best qualified to judge "the intellectual strength and moral character" required for the practice as a whole.[42] Humility, cheerfulness, proper trust, and attentive love arise from these practices. As virtues, they link individual mothering practices to a broader moral belief system providing standards for the judgments all mothers make. Parochialism, however, confines the creation of moral standards for mothering to mothers. Extended family members, friends, teachers, and even social workers, accordingly, lack the qualifications to judge or provide input into a mother's decision making, although their critical distance from the daily work and subjective experience of mothering can strengthen caring practices. Moral judgments remain localized as a private—parochial—matter limited to those engaged in specific sets of practices such as mothering, teaching, accounting, or nursing. Outsiders to these contexts, much less the broader citizenry, lose sight of how these practices relate to each other in an interconnected web of decisions that shape a political community. Joan Tronto asks, "How are we to guarantee that people, who are enmeshed in their daily rounds of care-giving and care-receiving, will be able to disengage themselves from their own concerns to address broader needs and concerns for care?"[43]

Virtue's conceptual capacity to bridge the finite space of practices and the infinite arena of the common good represents a viable means of resolving the problem of parochialism in care ethics. "Judging with care," Sevenhuijsen asserts, requires "political virtues" that, decoupled from virtue's gendered and sentimental legacy, free care from the domestic sphere and attribute this concept status in public life.[44] Instead of the static moral traditions and value systems that limit care to motherhood, moral standards of judgment derive from fluid relationships and practices. Private values attributed to women's care in the private sphere such as attentiveness, responsiveness, and responsibility become political virtues essential to citizenship and public decision-making processes. Virtue, for Julie Anne White, remains a concept incompatible with her shift from moral character traits and practices to social roles and processes designed to ensure all participants in deliberative processes an equal voice independent of preconceived judgments about caregivers and care receivers.[45] Rejecting virtue to separate morality from social roles, however, avoids addressing how people rely on personal experience and value systems associated with their social roles when engaging in deliberations with others. Political decision making involves moral judgments. Neither Sevenhuijsen nor White interrogates virtue-based ethics and its gendered legacy, opting either to decouple virtue from its conceptual past or to dismiss the concept. In the absence of an alternative framework, the virtue-vice dualism will continue to inform current moral thinking and determine how citizens engage in "judging with care" or deliberative processes.

Feminist care theorists, whether avoiding, rejecting, or revising virtue, struggle with identifying care as a virtue given the concept's gendered legacy, static ideals of moral character, and basis in predetermined traditions. These limitations emanate from a parochialism inherent to virtue that locates moral value in a static conception of an individual's moral character instead of fluid social roles or deliberative processes. Our understanding of the moral subject remains narrowly confined by a dualistic framework limited to identifying people as either virtuous or vice-ridden. This internal parochialism prevents the fluidity of social roles, practices, relationships, and contexts that grounds feminist care ethics. Focusing on practices, a critical element in virtue ethics, generates moral values based on relationships and contexts while insulating its practitioners from the broader community. This insularity prevents a full view of the web of relationships and the integral role of care in forming all societies.

Virtue serves as a conceptual bridge between local parochial spaces and national and global communities by linking specific practices to broader moral understandings through its finite and infinite dimensions. At the same time, virtue anchors a moral tradition premised on ethical standards of excellence that transcend individual experience and allow some to acquire a status above others based on their ability to live according to a predetermined tradition's moral beliefs. Legitimacy in the virtue tradition derives from a moral parochialism, the parameters of which are determined by a set of practitioners insulated from the vice of those deemed less valuable. In this tradition, care, a practice devalued as women's work in the private sphere, lacks this legitimacy. If framed in virtue-vice terms, care will never acquire its full moral authority because of the parochial standards against which it is measured. Derived from moral traditions, cultural beliefs, and practices, virtue, in the absence of a conceptual alternative, logically remains the default mechanism for creating a sense of the common good necessary for national and individual political identity.

The Vice of Omission: Sex and Sexuality in Feminist Care Ethics

Contemporary feminist care ethics, in stark contrast to Mary Wollstonecraft's critique of eighteenth-century morality, essentially omits sex and sexuality from its understanding of basic human needs, practices, and relationships. Victorian society, despite its façade of modesty and chastity, led women in the sentimental family to focus on biological sex as the foundation of their marital relationship rather than friendship and love. Wollstonecraft narrowly confines sex to procreation and sexuality to heterosexuality, positions geared toward granting women moral value for their reason rather than their appearance and manners. Despite strict social constraints, Wollstonecraft addresses sex and sexuality as integral to achieving gender equality, which entails reconfiguring women's role as wives and mothers in the private sphere. Contemporary feminist care theorists cover similar analytic ground by examining personal relationships and practices as critical to considering ethics from a viewpoint inclusive of women. Omitting sex and sexuality from this work illustrates how the dualistic virtue-vice logic frames the options available to feminist care ethics by narrowing its scope and capacity to break with a patriarchal moral legacy.

Sex and sexuality characterize female virtue and vice throughout their conceptual history, either granting women moral excellence for purity, modesty, and chastity or devaluing them for any real or perceived immodesty or impurity measured by their behavior, dress, and manners. Finite or material, visible actions, as Wollstonecraft points out, deflect attention away from cultivating "true" virtue, which remains invisible and unknowable other than through reason. Virtue also deflects attention away from vice, leaving a range of moral assumptions and exercises of political power uncontested. Finite and infinite vice play a critical role in shaping women's moral and political identity that still remains interconnected with their sex and sexuality. Despite its foundation in basic human needs and the practices of human relationships, feminist care ethics avoids sex and sexuality because they carry a deeply embedded association with female finite and infinite vice, which would devalue care as an ethical standard equivalent to virtues such as justice.

This omission, based on a moral and political legacy aligning female sex and sexuality with vice, prevents feminist care ethics from identifying the biological act of sex as a basic human need, capturing the moral subject as fully as possible, and accounting for relationships essential to democratic communities. Dan Engster explicitly omits sex and sexuality from feminist care ethics on the grounds that the biological act of sexual intercourse does not constitute a basic human need. He contends that sexual activity only generates rather than sustains human life and that, "while sexual activity may contribute to a person's pleasure or general well being, it is not immediately necessary to survival in the ways that food, clothing, and medical care are."[46] Such a position negates the relationship of sexual activity to human survival, particularly for women.

Sexual violence, including domestic violence and rape, affects 70 percent of women worldwide.[47] Procreation perpetuates human existence, the fundamental and most basic need from which all others derive. Pregnancy endangers women's lives globally, as approximately 1,000 die in childbirth each day, an indicator of how sexual activity links to procreation as a survival issue for mothers and their children.[48] Medical care inherently involves sexual health issues related to survival, as illustrated by the fact that globally 34 million people have HIV/AIDS.[49] Sexual activity, such statistics only begin to suggest, plays a necessary part in human survival, especially for women, and should not be dismissed as outside the realm of basic human need or the scope of caring.

Sex and sexuality carry a heavy moral weight that aligns them with female vice, which functions to justify dismissing their positive role in healthy human life, self-identity, and relationships. Assumptions of sex and sexuality as vice-ridden negate their role in caring for the self, others, and communities. Importantly, Engster argues for the virtues of caring, which locates his position clearly within this dualistic gendered framework that functions to reestablish moral hierarchies based on predetermined traditions.[50] Caring, when linked to mothering, the most virtuous of female practices, achieves full recognition as a practice essential to basic human needs, whereas the sexual activity that allows mothering to occur falls outside the scope of care ethics. How sexuality shapes care for the self and others also fails to emerge as significant to a fuller understanding of the moral subject and human relationships in care ethics. Intertwined with sexual activity, the range of sexualities from hetero and trans to bi, gay, and lesbian, long associated with vice, also remain overlooked factors. The dualistic logic of virtue functions to negate the possibility of morally valuing behaviors categorized as vices, which, in the case of care ethics, effectively deflects attention away from sex and sexuality as inherent to human relationships, practices, and basic human needs, the very elements on which this moral perspective is built.

Sexual activity also represents an act essential to establishing and maintaining political communities. The sexual contract between a man and a woman that underlies marriage, Carole Pateman notably argues, embeds women's social, political, and economic inequality and subordination in the social contract tradition.[51] Redefining the family from a public care perspective, contends Traci Levy, requires addressing how the biological act of sex plays a foundation role in this social institution.[52] As Pateman and Levy articulate, sexual activity provides the scaffolding for social institutions and, thereby, political communities. Yet sex and sexuality remain absent from feminist care ethics. This omission subordinates an entire realm of human activity central to personal identity and a basic human need crucial to survival, human development, and relationships. Failing to account for sex and sexuality assumes a position of privileged irresponsibility toward vulnerable classes of people, including children, teens, women, gay men, and lesbians, and an entire sphere of caring practices related to sexuality, reproductive health, protection against violence, and human development. A democratic politics attentive to meeting human needs and to care as part of human life entails integrating sex and sexuality into a basic understanding of the moral subject, its relationships, and communities.

Framing care as a virtue locks this concept into the problems of moral perfectionism, parochialism, and inequality that contradict the grounding of feminist care ethics in material contexts, human relationships, practices, and equality. The dualistic logic of virtue and vice negates equality and imports a set of gendered assumptions deeply embedded in Western political thought and the American political script into a feminist ethics oriented toward democratic goals. Care, then, should not be framed as a virtue in feminist ethics. Yet the internal infinite and finite dimensions of virtue and vice indicate the need to seek out a mechanism capable of bridging the gap between material practices and broader ethical contexts.

Without a viable alternative to the virtue-vice framework, this paradigm's moral logic serves as the default option, which maintains a predetermined moral tradition that sustains women's identity as moral guardians but suspect citizens. The omission of sex and sexuality from feminist care ethics speaks to the ongoing suspicion with which society treats behaviors outside the realm associated with female virtue. Indeed, leaving the virtue-vice framework in place sustains women's political identity as suspect. Women's inability to measure up to predetermined standards of moral excellence sets them up for the failure that undermines their legitimacy as citizens. Societal doubt always lingers as the expectation of women's inability to uphold the double burden as moral guardians remains. Moral perfection, as a staple of virtue ethics, becomes an untenable expectation for women as moral guardians, which makes them suspect citizens. This legacy of virtue and vice perpetuates a range of gendered moral assumptions that undermine feminist care ethics and generate backlash politics against such challenges to the moral order.

Conclusion

Beyond Virtue and Vice:
Toward a Democratic Feminist Ethics

The gendered moral logic of the virtue-vice dualism plays out on the stage of American politics through the tension within women's political identity as moral guardians but suspect citizens. Assigning women the double burden of moral responsibility for self, family, and the nation equates any real or perceived failure to fulfill their civic obligations with traitorous behavior and triggers backlash politics. This conceptual history of virtue and vice highlights key junctures in American political development that affected women's relationship to the public sphere to illustrate how this dominant moral dualism limits women to the private sphere as a way to create political stability amid the disorder and chaos of public life. This paradigm maintains women's moral guardianship through their responsibility for protecting virtue against the threat of vice and corruption.

The Puritans, the point of emergence for this conceptual history, took the dramatic step of granting a few daughters of Eve the capacity for the finite and infinite virtue necessary to become daughters of Zion. Puritan women, as Cotton Mather asserts, belong to the collective effort to establish the New World as a heaven on earth, a move that links women's moral guardianship to American exceptionalism. Republican era debates over women's education capture the ongoing tension between female vice and virtue. Opponents viewed granting women greater access to education and expanding its scope as threats to the nation's future. Advocates contended that developing female reason would cultivate women's virtue, making them better mothers and more capable of raising future male citizens. Alexis de Tocqueville observes that America's transition to democracy involved attributing great political significance to women, as the link between religion and the family, by granting them the moral superiority to anchor the nation against waves of political and economic change. Contemporary "back to virtue" theorists, whether social conservatives arguing for abstinence education or those concerned about America's decline (the result of the moral relativism and pluralism caused by identity politics and the Sexual Revolution), continue to envision women as moral guardians over the nation's future, protecting it against the corrupting forces of change.

Virtue and vice also trigger backlashes in debates among women identified by society as suspect citizens, those aligned so closely with vice that they lose the protections of female virtue and moral guardianship. The Lowell mill girls lost their virtuous status simply by walking onto the factory floor. The debate among those loyal to the company and those who wanted certain workers' rights and protections broke down into two camps—the loyalists, who claimed virtue for female workers, and the rebels, who eventually identified Traditional Womanhood as antithetical to their democratic and, at times, socialist goals. Nearly a century later, lesbian feminists similarly existed on America's political margins, where in the late 1960s and early 1970s, they collectively experienced a backlash from the dominant society and the women's movement. Debates among lesbian feminists over S/M also split their community into two camps. Those opposing S/M as a vice-ridden, deviant behavior redeployed the same moral dynamic used against lesbians by the patriarchal society. Anti-S/M lesbian feminists leveraged female virtue to claim moral superiority. Pro-S/M lesbian feminists, in a way reminiscent of the rebels in Lowell, embraced their association with vice and challenged the dominant moral paradigm as inherently oppressive to women and all those who failed to meet its predetermined standards of excellence.

Suspect citizens such as the rebellious Lowell mill girls and pro-S/M lesbian feminists populate this conceptual history of virtue and vice.

For the Puritans, women accused of witchcraft represented the disorder threatening the settlers' tenuous hold on political power as Native Americans attacked their villages, new religious groups arrived in their colonies, and a growing mercantile class threatened their economic control. Focusing on the moral failures of certain women seemingly overtaken by the Devil deflected attention away from structural issues and communicated the consequences for deviating from the virtuous path of God. In the republican era, Judith Sargent Murray stood up for women's right to equal education. Mary Wollstonecraft took on Enlightenment thinkers such as Jean-Jacques Rousseau to make the radical claim that women's capacity for reason and virtue should grant them equality with men. Public exposure of her private sexual behavior led to a dismissal of Wollstonecraft's work based on suspicion of her moral character. In the 1960s and 1970s, Mary Daly challenged established religion and the church as a patriarchal institution including its role in determining moral beliefs. Contemporary feminist care theorists offer a different vision of liberal democracy as inclusive of justice and care. Questioning the moral status quo distances such women from moral guardianship's protections and frames them as potential threats to the nation given their assigned moral responsibility for the common good. Such women, however, only place into stark relief how all women actually exist in the precarious space somewhere between virtue and vice that generates societal doubt about their citizenship and holds their legitimacy as loyal members of the political community under constant suspicion.

Virtue and vice play essential roles in the backlash politics that characterize the American political script. Vice defines female moral character in such a way that women must struggle against patriarchal standards of virtue to try to receive recognition as equal and legitimate members of the political community. Virtue deflects attention away from this political reality in a society that extols the virtues of women's moral guardianship as wives and mothers. The instability arising from suspicion about women's ability to meet their civic obligation as moral guardians shapes women's citizenship in such a way as to leave them vulnerable targets to backlash politics. Such gendered moral dynamics, however, speak to the way in which a backlash against citizenship and active engagement in politics as valued and essential elements of democratic life may put all citizens under suspicion.

The virtue-vice dualism—the default moral logic in American political discourse—polarizes people into opposing positions and lends moral legitimacy to backlashes against those who, by challenging the moral tradition, jeopardize the nation's future. Women, as moral guardians of that tradition, the family, and the common good, represent permanent targets in backlashes that blame them for any sign of the nation's demise. Efforts to confront or change this dynamic, including advancing women's full citizenship, are threats to the moral and political order that generate societal mistrust. In many ways, such direct political engagement challenges a way of American life that devalues such participation in the corrupt, vice-ridden realm of politics and places democracy itself under suspicion. Without an alternative moral framework to the virtue-vice dualism, backlash politics against vulnerable categories of people and democracy will continue, making all Americans suspect citizens.

The Frontiers of Collective Responsibility: Toward a Democratic Feminist Ethics of Belonging

The question then remains: If virtue and vice trigger ongoing backlashes, how might we imagine possible routes for moving beyond virtue and vice and toward a democratic feminist ethics aligned with freedom, equality, and inclusion? Answering this question begins with the difficult task of reimagining how we think about morality and politics. Dualistic thinking shapes engagement with both spheres of life and limits our epistemology to oppositional either/or categories. Morality narrows to virtue and vice, good and evil, right and wrong—normative judgments that track onto political positions limited to Left and Right, liberal and conservative, developed and developing, First and Third World. These boundaries and borders determine the political terrain's moral landscape, parceled into spaces separating the virtuous from the vice-ridden Others. Exploring the territory where virtue and vice intersect with women's relationship to the political sphere reveals the permeability of the boundary separating these two oppositional moral categories. The dominant society actually moves women between virtue and vice in response to changing political, economic, and social contexts instead of permanently locating them in one category or the other.

As moral guardians but suspect citizens, women occupy a space in between the dualistic boundaries of morality and politics. This position makes women particularly vulnerable to backlash politics. At the same time, it affords them the ability to see how dualistic moral frameworks provide a shaky scaffolding on which to build democratic political communities committed to inclusion, equality, and freedom. From this location, women such as the rebels in Lowell, S/M lesbian feminists, and feminist care theorists become innovating ideologists who attempt to resolve the contradictions between two (or more) sets of oppositional belief systems. Imagining an ethical framework more aligned with democratic and feminist views of political life than the virtue-vice dualism begins with the geographic metaphors of boundaries, borders, and frontiers that inform current thinking about morality and politics and ways to rethink their relationship.

Spaces in between boundaries such as those occupied by suspect citizens emerge as women experience their dislocation from the dualistic categories structuring societal institutions. Black women, Katie Cannon explains, create a moral framework outside that established by the dominant white male society where they turn to their experiences to survive and feel valued. Black women, throughout their American political history, Cannon states, "carve out 'living space' within the intricate web of multilayered oppression," where they "have fashioned value patterns and ethical procedures in their own terms, as well as mastering, transcending, radicalizing and sometimes destroying pervasive, negative orientations imposed by the mores of the larger society."[1] Such "living space" exists between their everyday experiences in a society shaped by race and patriarchy and those within the black community, creating what Patricia Hill Collins calls the "outsider-within" stance. The black female domestic worker in a white household exemplifies this standpoint, since these women "have a distinct view of the contradictions between the dominant group's actions and ideologies."[2] Ideological innovation arises in such spaces, as black women live at the intersections of race, class, and gender and move in and out of the dominant society.

Mobility between the center determined by those in power and the margins of society populated by those deemed less valuable captures, in bell hooks's work, the constant movement of those defined by society as Others.[3] Such mobility also grants an ability to see society's intersecting multiple dimensions, giving those pushed to the margins a powerful vantage point from which to challenge systems of oppression. People on the move in this way acquire blurred vision that transforms a lack of clarity into a capacity to see while in motion across conceptual boundaries. Those living at the intersections of dominance and subordination experience the effects of power and see the possibilities of liberation in the in-between spaces of their everyday lives.

The virtues of vice become visible from women's position between the opposing poles of virtue and vice. The moral middle ground occupied by women shapes their political identity as moral guardians but suspect citizens. Backlash politics capitalizes on this tenuous location. Women explicitly affiliated with vice by the dominant society directly experience how morality exercises power, granting them the capacity to see through the veil of gender neutrality around virtue as the standard of moral excellence necessary for the good life. Despite its association with corruption, moral decay, and forces destructive to a community, vice becomes a virtue in the sense of helping those excluded from it to see the way toward the good life. Vice provides a means by which women assume a critical distance from virtue and their moral guardianship. This position clarifies how the moral framework of virtue and vice obstructs women's participation in shaping the institutions, beliefs, and practices in ways that reflect their experiences in and understandings of the world. Aligned with vice, women see how virtue operates to secure inequality, constraint, and exclusion, and generates backlashes against their advances toward full citizenship.

Vice as a standpoint, however powerful for critiquing the dominant moral framework, still traps women in a dualistic moral logic that makes this concept an effective tool for analysis rather than a resolution to the contradiction between women's experience and democratic values. The virtues of vice conveys how this default moral category, generally dismissed from analysis, clarifies how the virtue-vice dualism denies women the moral legitimacy required of full citizenship *and* simultaneously carves out a "living space" for ideological innovation. This middle ground between the shifting terrain of female virtue and vice, made evident to women who deviate from the path of virtue, offers a theoretical standpoint conducive for identifying the oppressive nature of the dominant moral discourse and its potential for radical transformation.

A middle ground connotes the location on the boundary separating a conceptual space into two different categories such as virtue and vice, morality and politics. Boundaries represent sites of political contestation where those excluded from full access to public life because of their race, class, and gender struggle for inclusion and against current ways of thinking about the world.[4] The boundary between morality and politics specifies how attributing greater moral value to certain groups morally justifies unequal distribution of resources and power within a political community. Framing the virtue-vice dualism within these terms underscores the political dimension of these moral concepts by identifying their contested nature. The boundary between virtue as the uncontestable standard of moral excellence and vice initially appears to be impermeable. Yet tracking women's relationship to virtue and vice throughout American political history reveals how easily and frequently the dominant society moves women back and forth across this boundary. American women actually occupy a moral middle ground as virtuous moral guardians but suspect citizens capable of vice that, depending on the political circumstances, enables society to move them from one moral category to the other. Boundaries greatly facilitate conceptualizing the abstract moral categories of virtue and vice while indicating the political dynamics involved in determining their location and placement of people on either side.

Borders share these traits with boundaries while shifting attention to the power exercised on the borderlands, a literal and figurative geographic space marking the beginning of one governing unit's or nation-state's control and the end of another's. Such borders establish who legitimately and legally possesses the rights of membership in a political community. Walls, fences, crossings, and patrols such as those along the border between Mexico and the United States put the political nature of borders across the globe into sharp relief. "The U.S.-Mexican border," Gloria Anzaldúa explains, "*es una herida abierta* [is an open wound] where the Third World grates against the first and bleeds."[5] Borders determine the inclusion of some and the exclusion of all others to establish the physical parameters of citizenship. Citizenship, while embedded in a person's identity as he or she moves across borders, remains associated with a nation-state's geographic territory.

Suspicion characterizes the borderlands as an in-between space filled with moral and political ambiguity. Literally crossing from one nation-state to another requires assessment by a governing authority according to its standards of legality for entry. Standing before U.S. customs agents when entering the country, regardless of whether the person is a legal citizen, typifies the suspicion with which all people are treated while their legality remains in question. This borderland where the individual directly encounters governing authority represents a place where the nation-state protects its identity from invading cultures, traditions, morals, and beliefs. Moral contestation occurs here by identifying immigrants as "illegal," which categorizes them as vice-ridden, corrupt, and dangerous in a dehumanizing way. Backlashes against immigrants resemble those against American women in the sense that, for both, suspicion of their legitimacy characterizes their relationship to the nation-state as potential threats to its core traditions and moral beliefs. Suspicion of American women derives specifically from their failure as moral guardians to stay at their post on the internal borders, protecting America's common good and exceptional future with their virtue; by engaging in the vice of pursuing full citizenship, which involves greater participation in political and public life, they arouse suspicion. This precarious borderland position undermines women's political legitimacy by categorizing them as neither "legal" nor "illegal"—a space fraught with the dangers of moral and political ambiguity.

Virtue makes it difficult for American women to identify their citizenship as suspect given the construction of their political identity as moral guardians—as wives and mothers, they epitomize the purity or perfection inherent to this standard of moral excellence. A veil of gender neutrality makes virtue appear as an innocent or uncontested concept representing the good, which hides from view a range of assumptions about women, morality, and politics. Looking at this concept from a gendered perspective turns attention to vice as operating in tandem with virtue to shape women's political identity in terms of their location on the borderlands. "A borderland is a vague and undetermined place created by the emotional residue of an unnatural boundary," Anzaldúa continues. "It is in a constant state of transition."[6] This space loosens the ties binding its inhabitants to stability and the status quo as instability and change transform epistemological stagnation. People living on the borderlands, such as Anzaldúa, a self-described "border woman" who grew up between Mexican and Anglo cultures, live with the reality of borders where dualistic frameworks fail to help them understand their experiences in the world. "The prohibited and forbidden are its inhabitants. *Los atravesados* [the crossers] live here: the squint-eyed, the perverse, the queer, the troublesome, the mongrel, the mulato, the half-breed, the half dead; in short, those who cross over, pass over, or go through the confines of the 'normal.'"[7] American women as moral guardians but suspect citizens belong to the borderlands as those who, knowingly or not, stand on the boundary between virtue and vice.

Those living on the borderlands—women, gays and lesbians, people of color, and "foreigners," just to name a few—develop *la facultad* [the power of knowledge]. This capacity, Anzaldúa explains, enables border people "to see in surface phenomena the meaning of deeper realities, to see the deep structure below the surface" because of their lack of psychological and physical safety.[8] Unprotected by societal norms and morality, border people are able to escape the "consciousness of duality" and rationality that defines the dominant way people understand the world and are granted the capacity for a fuller awareness of irrational, emotional, and imaginative possibilities. Clearly defined oppositional categories such as the virtue-vice dualism fail to explain life on the borderlands where dividing lines lose their meaning. This space creates the opportunity for its occupants to identify structures of social, political, and economic oppression and, most importantly, as those living in and outside its confines, to imagine a world beyond existing borders and boundaries.

As spatial metaphors, borders and boundaries greatly facilitate thinking about the space between two oppositional categories such as virtue and vice. Yet both metaphors presume a dualistic framework that operates on a dialectic premise of thesis versus antithesis, which synthesizes the two and results in a continuous cycle, separating again into the thesis and antithesis, which become a synthesis. Borders and boundaries, no matter how transitory or permeable, act as barriers that divide nation-states, groups of people, and moral categories. Those located in between these spaces, given their vulnerability, still must think in terms of the places on either side of dividing lines. The problem of distributing resources in political life on the basis of attributing moral value to people underscores the importance of thinking about how morality shapes politics through virtue and vice in different ways that move beyond dualistic confines and toward the horizon of possibility.

The frontier, though entailing certain limitations, represents a metaphor conducive to orienting our vision beyond the borders and boundaries of our identities, consciousness, and lived realities without abandoning the idea that such separations also protect freedoms and privacy. As a spatial metaphor, the frontier entails masculine exercises of violence as men conquered America's wilderness and its indigenous peoples to establish civilization in the New World. The frontier in the American political script sets the stage for telling the story of nation building and taming the Wild West, where settlers and cowboys encountered outlaws and Native Americans in their struggle to establish the farms and ranches that extended U.S. territory from the Atlantic to Pacific Oceans. Manifest destiny merges with American exceptionalism to justify occupying these territories regardless of the cost to human life on the grounds that God granted the United States an abundance of land and resources meant for the nation's development. The frontier often serves the political purpose of deflecting attention away from people's oppression and suffering and toward the greater good of nation building.

With such limitations in mind, the frontier retains a metaphorical means for keeping our sight lines trained on the horizons without losing our footing in the relationships, practices, and contexts that constitute our lived reality. Here, the meaning of the frontier derives from *la frontera*, the Spanish term that Anzaldúa uses to reference the borderlands. People go through the frontier, an in-between space, bringing their belongings, ideas, traditions, and cultural beliefs from their homes to unknown territory. The borderlands between the wilderness and civilization require its settlers to carve out "living spaces" and to navigate the moral middle ground where the boundary identifying virtue from vice begins to fade as fluidity characterizes relationships of people to each other, their contexts, and space itself. Frontiers put people in motion in ways that cultivate the capacity for change and the valuing of difference. Such mobility facilitates escaping the limits of dialectical thinking that synthesizes two opposing categories only to break apart again along similar lines by shifting attention to the process of moral decision making as an ongoing, integral part of political life. This perspective dislodges a reflexive reliance on established moral traditions and definitions inherited from a legacy of virtue and vice that perpetuates inequality, constraint, and exclusion. The dualistic framework that generates cycles of backlash politics loses its epistemological footing as the moral terrain changes in response to people's needs and the demands of differing contexts instead of in efforts to return to idyllic visions of moral tradition.

The frontier also represents unsettled territory just outside government control, creating the possibility for corruption and chaos that, while dangerous, destabilize moral and political frameworks and lead to doubt about previously accepted standards. As moral boundaries and political borders fade, the assumptions behind them come into view. Questioning them opens up a frontier for alternatives and possibilities. The frontier, then, refers to underexplored territory outside moral and political bounds that frees its inhabitants to step into a space of adventure conducive to imagination by casting the gaze toward the horizons. Ideological innovation thrives on this frontier where existing concepts no longer meet the demands of a given political context and resolving this contradiction demands pushing ahead into unknown terrain beyond predetermined borders and boundaries. Moving beyond virtue and vice entails venturing out onto this frontier in order to imagine an ethics consistent with the goals of equality, inclusion, freedom, and full citizenship that anchor democratic and feminist political theory.

Collective responsibility provides an alternative moral groundwork on which to build a democratic feminist ethics of belonging by overcoming women's double burden of moral responsibility and men's privileged irresponsibility. This ethical orientation overcomes the limits of dualisms to establish an inclusive understanding of community based on belonging rather than citizenship. Politics, as a result, becomes a central responsibility of all democratic citizens by equalizing the distribution of moral responsibility among groups of people and across personal, social, and political boundaries.

Hannah Arendt frames collective responsibility in explicitly political terms. Germans who avoided direct participation in Hitler's regime claimed that, as nonparticipants, they remained free from guilt or blame for their government's actions. Nonparticipants, Arendt argues to the contrary, assume responsibility for their government's deeds and misdeeds as members of the political community. Citizenship, then, entails collective responsibility defined as "always political, whether it appears in the older form, when a whole community takes it upon itself to be responsible for whatever one of its members has done, or whether a community is being held responsible for what has been done in its name."[9] The fact that people live in community determines the inherently political nature of collective responsibility. Arendt, while blurring the line between a community and its members in this context, ultimately draws a thick boundary between the self and politics. "In the center of moral considerations of human conduct stands the self," Arendt states. "In the center of political considerations of conduct stands the world."[10] Clearly separating the moral from the political further underscores this boundary by contrasting personal with political or collective responsibility to emphasize that individuals cannot shift blame for their actions to the system under which they live.[11]

The understanding of collective responsibility advanced here builds on Arendt's attention to the way that politics relates to moral judgment while recasting the relationship between the self and politics from an inclusive perspective. This move prevents the dualistic operation of deflection, which transfers responsibility for a government's actions away from the people to politicians and officials. As the boundary between morality and politics becomes less visible, a frontier opens up where responsibility for politics belongs to all the people, including the nonparticipants now denied the privileged irresponsibility of deciding whether to assume responsibility for the government and its actions. Shifting blame for a nation's perceived decline no longer falls to a category of women assigned moral responsibility for the common good.

Collective responsibility facilitates this inclusion of the individual, the social, and the political by moving from a dualistic framework to an inclusive groundwork that conveys a different epistemological perspective reflecting the dynamic and shifting web of relationships actually shaping our lives and communities. This moral geography's weblike character is conveyed in Joan Tronto and Berenice Fisher's definition of care as "a *species activity that includes everything that we do to maintain, continue, and repair our 'world' so that we can live in it as well as possible. That world includes our bodies, our selves, and our environment, all of which we seek to interweave in a complex, life-sustaining web.*"[12] The moral terrain of collective responsibility similarly encompasses these arenas of life and alters in response to changing needs and contexts and the shifting boundaries among people, society, and politics that shape the relationships extending from the individual to the local, national, and global levels. The collective's moral groundwork recasts feminism's relational approach in terms of this weblike geography. Doing so escapes limits placed on this approach by the dualistic framework that channels movement in a unidirectional flow from one oppositional category to the other by allowing for dynamic movement within and across categories and spheres in many directions simultaneously.

The separate threads that make up a web represent the collective's tangible aspect in terms of the relationships and material practices involved in the daily lives of people living in a community. This aspect of the moral groundwork facilitates tracking the distribution of responsibility within the collective in order to ensure relative equality. The equalization of responsibility among all categories of citizens creates the possibility of a collective action problem: if everyone is held responsible for everything, then no one is responsible for anything.[13] To address this issue, collective responsibilities shift and change depending on the different capabilities, needs, and resources of the community's members throughout the course of their lives, which, by eliminating men's privileged irresponsibility, relieves women of the double burden of moral responsibility. Negotiating the assignment of responsibilities becomes a site of collective engagement, since standing moral assumptions behind who assumes responsibility when, how, for what, why, to what degree, and for how long move from a marginal set of inquiries to the center of public deliberation.

Collective responsibility also draws out an imaginative dimension deeply embedded in this concept. The ethical moment of decision making, when we determine the way in which we will assume responsibility for ourselves, others, and even our communities, entails looking beyond a given reality to imagine outcomes and possibilities. People in these moments often reach beyond their perceived capacities and assume responsibility for strangers, family members, and political issues in ways that they never imagined possible. Such exercises of moral imagination involve thinking, based on the immediate contextual reality, what could be possible and how to achieve it, an exercise of power that we engage in on a personal level capable of being harnessed for large-scale political change. Collective responsibility involves the political imagination to consider the possibility of how we all, as democratic citizens, assume responsibility for our politics and the promise of its ongoing transformation toward greater freedom, equality, and inclusion.

Thinking beyond virtue and vice toward frontiers such as collective responsibility invites a consideration of moving beyond citizenship toward belonging. The gendered moral dynamics of virtue and vice tracked throughout this conceptual history specify how their inherent dualistic logic functions to include some in the political community while excluding others and leaving some, such as women, to exist on the borderlands as moral guardians but suspect citizens. Ending the endless cycles of backlash politics requires escaping these dualistic confines, which jeopardize the nation's future by placing all its citizens under suspicion. Citizenship requires boundaries and national identities that grant people membership to specific political communities in ways antithetical to a global understanding of politics. The fluid terrain of contemporary life, in which virtual relationships connect people across the world, climate change affects us all, and external as well as internal migration characterizes the human experience, no longer seems to fit into the narrow confines of traditional citizenship. Belonging to a global community for which we all share collective responsibility may suggest a conceptual point of departure for imagining a democratic feminist ethics beyond virtue and vice.

Notes

INTRODUCTION

1. Firestone 1968.
2. Amatniek 1968.
3. Ibid.
4. Here I rely on Susan Faludi's definition of backlash as cyclical reactions against women's progress toward equality that blame feminism for women's "lesser life" in "an attempt to retract the handful of small and hard-won victories that the feminist movement did manage to win for women" (1991, xviii–xxiii).
5. Himmelfarb 1995, 2001.
6. Glendon 1991.
7. Macedo 1990; Galston 1991, 1995, 2002; Berkowitz 1999.
8. Glendon and Blankenhorn 1995, 1.
9. Shallitt 1999.
10. Guttmacher Institute 2012.
11. Ibid.
12. Plumwood 1993.
13. Throughout this book, I refer to the moral and civic, and infinite and finite, dimensions of virtue and vice as well as their gendered aspects when appropriate to the analysis. When referring to virtue and vice without these identifiers, this particular definition is the one operating.
14. Rawls 1971, 3.
15. Dietz 2002.
16. Etzioni 1996.

17. Sparks 1997.

18. Honig 1993, chap. 1. Following a brief discussion of virtue and *virtù* in the context of Machiavelli, Fortuna, and the virago, she states "aside from occasional ruminations like this one, I do not engage questions of gender and politics in a sustained way in this book" (17). My point is that gender is crucial to understanding the power dynamics inherent to virtue and vice.

19. Sevenhuijsen 1998.

20. Card 1997; Hoagland 1988.

21. Kerber 1980; Norton 1980.

22. Snyder 2004. Others examine the complex role of morality in women's Progressive Era activism for social reform. See Skocpol 1992; and Sarvasy 1992, 1997.

23. Hirschmann and Di Stefano 1996.

24. Gallie 1962. See also Pitkin 1972; Connolly 1993; and Ball, Farr, and Hanson 1989.

25. Hirschmann and Di Stefano 1996, chap. 1.

26. Farr 1989.

27. Ibid., 37.

28. Tocqueville 1988, II:611.

CHAPTER 1

1. Okin 1979, pts. 1–2; Saxonhouse 1991, chaps. 1–2.

2. I am indebted to Professor Sara Brill for informing me on this point about vice as well as various issues related to conceptions of virtue in the ancient Greek context.

3. Elshtain 1981, chap. 1.

4. Pitkin 1999.

5. English and Ehrenreich 1973, 1978.

6. Okin 1982.

7. Wolin 2001; Janara 2002.

8. Hunt-Botting and Carey 2004.

9. Hunt-Botting 2009.

10. Wollstonecraft 1995, 223.

11. Ibid., 270.

12. Ibid., 229.

13. Ibid., 275.

14. Ibid.

15. Boryczka 2009a, 281–304.

16. Tocqueville 1988, II:527.

17. J.G.A. Pocock (1975, chap. 15) alternatively argues that commerce became the new force against which male virtue, though in a different form, must struggle. Pocock's point does not negate that the economic displaces the political, which shifts civic and moral virtue outside the public sphere.

18. Mandeville 1997, 34.

19. Tocqueville 1988, II:603.

20. Ibid., I:292.

21. Ibid., I:287.

22. Tocqueville, often seen as Montesquieu's protégé, however, was undoubtedly influenced by Montesquieu's use of guardianship to discuss women's relationship to the republic. Montesquieu states, for instance, that "the laws that give guardianship to the mother are more attentive to the preservation of the person of the ward; those that give it to the closest heir are more attentive to the preservation of the goods. Among peoples whose mores are corrupt, it is preferable to give the guardianship to the mother" (Montesquieu 1989, 323).

23. Tocqueville 1988, II:603.

24. Ibid., II:590.

25. Phillips 1993; Rowe 2008.

26. Lister 2003, 195.

27. Marshall 1992, 18.

28. Ibid.

29. Joan Tronto's position that "we should think of care as a ground for conferring citizenship" informs this definition (2005, 131).

30. Richardson 2000; Sarvasy 1997; Young 2005; Sparks 1997; Ackelsberg 2010.

31. Tocqueville 1988, I:408.

32. Ibid.

33. Walzer 1989, 218.

CHAPTER 2

1. Winthrop 1992, 12. To facilitate the reader's accessibility to the material from this period, the Puritan's English usage is translated into its contemporary version in this chapter.

2. Abbott 1991, 2.

3. Saxton 2003.

4. Zion generally references Jerusalem in the Old Testament. In Isaiah 3:16–4:16, the daughters of Zion are described as adorned with bracelets, fine clothing, and jewels. Yahweh cleanses the city and daughters of Zion of their sin, as represented by the value placed on appearance and material wealth, and exposes their true virtue and faith. As a result, Zion transforms into a place of refuge and glory in the world, similar to what the Puritans hoped for in the New World.

5. Many feminist theorists dismiss Daly's work because of its essentialism, which narrows difference into a biological understanding of male and female that excludes any other factors such as race or class. Audre Lorde (1984) put forward perhaps the most well-known criticism of Daly's failure to account for black women. Uma Narayan (1997, chap. 2), in a similar vein, challenges Daly for taking a First World perspective on Third World women. Linda Alcoff (1997) locates

Daly within the broader feminist argument against essentialism. Sarah Hoagland, Marilyn Frye, Janice Raymond, and Val Plumwood reclaim Daly's work, despite certain limitations, as significant to feminism's theoretical development (Hoagland and Frye 2000).

6. Farr 1989, 38.
7. Norton 2002.
8. Mather 1705, 23.
9. Mather 1713, 22.
10. Ibid., 23–24.
11. Mather 1691, 10.
12. Mather 1713, 40.
13. Mather 1722, 31.
14. Ibid., 44.
15. Ibid., 48, 50.
16. Mather 1713, 27–28.
17. Mather 1722, 32–33.
18. Mather 1691, 98.
19. Mather 1713, 27.
20. Karlsen 1998, 181.
21. Sprint 1709.
22. Cott 1972.
23. Karlsen 1998.
24. Kamensky 1988.
25. Kramer and Sprenger 1971, 47.
26. Mather (1692) 1974, 110.
27. Ibid., 115.
28. Mather, quoted in Levin 1960, 98.
29. Mather (1692) 1974, 13.
30. Ibid, 67.
31. Daly 1984, 261.
32. Ibid.
33. Ibid., 262.
34. Ibid., 226.
35. Ibid.
36. Ibid., 262.
37. Plumwood 1993, 62.
38. Daly 1984, 263.

CHAPTER 3

1. Norton 1980; Ryan 1983, chap. 2.
2. Norton 1984, 617.
3. Singh and Darroch 2000; Ventura et al. 2006.

4. Badgley and Musselman 2004, n.p.
5. From the mid-1990s to the mid-2000s forty-eight states received nearly $1 billion in federal funding to support abstinence-only programs, and 86 percent of America's public school districts mandated that sex education curricula promote abstinence (Guttmacher Institute 2006). Three federal funding streams supported abstinence-only education: the Adolescent Family Life Act, Section 510(b) of Title V of the Social Security Act, and the Community-Based Abstinence Education Program established in 2001 (Advocates for Youth and SIECUS 2001, 7–11; SIECUS 2009).
6. Boryczka 2009b, 1–26.
7. Tronto 1993, 120–121.
8. Walker 1988.
9. Kann 1998.
10. Bennett 1818, 109.
11. Fordyce 1814, 51.
12. Ibid., 59.
13. Ibid., 62.
14. Rush 1965, 10.
15. Murray 1995, 11.
16. Ibid., 24.
17. Ibid., 42–43.
18. Fordyce 1814, 8.
19. Rush 1965, 27.
20. Ibid., 39–40.
21. Murray 1995, 13–14.
22. Rush 1965, 38.
23. Ibid., 37–38.
24. Ibid., 39.
25. See "Text of Bush's State of the Union Speech" 2006.
26. Generations of Light 2007.
27. LifeWay n.d.
28. Badgley and Musselman 2004, 68.
29. Ibid., 66.
30. Ibid.
31. Martin, Rector, and Pardue 2004, 15.
32. Kempner 2001, 46–47.
33. Frainie 2002, 4.
34. Badgley and Musselman 2004, 66.
35. Ibid., 73.
36. SIECUS 2004, 73.
37. Hunter-Geboy 1995, 266–267.
38. Ibid., 282–284.
39. SEICUS 2004, 29–31.

40. Planned Parenthood Federation of America 2004–2005a.
41. Focus on the Family 1999, ii.
42. True Love Waits 1999–2000, 15.
43. Kempner 2001; S. Rose 2005.
44. Frainie 2002, 11.
45. Benn and Derby 1999, n.p.
46. SIECUS 2004, 43.
47. Planned Parenthood Federation of America 2004–2005b.
48. Finer 2007.
49. Darroch, Frost, Singh et al. 2001, 89–90.
50. Ibid., 7–8.
51. SIECUS 2010.

CHAPTER 4

1. Dublin 1979.
2. Plante 2006.
3. Moser and Kleinplatz 2006, 4.
4. Rubin 2004.
5. Boryczka 2006, 49–68.
6. Farr 1989, 35.
7. Farley 1843, 48.
8. Farley 1845, 263.
9. Ibid., 281.
10. Ibid., 264.
11. Farley 1844.
12. Bagley 1846b.
13. Ibid.
14. Bagley 1846c, 165.
15. Stone, 1846a.
16. Farley 1843, 282, 284.
17. Farley 1845, 284.
18. Stone 1845.
19. Bagley 1845.
20. Bagley 1846a.
21. Farr 1989, 35.
22. Stone 1846b.
23. Martha 1846.
24. Pioneer 1847.
25. Ibid.
26. "Female Influence" 1846.
27. "Correspondence" 1846.
28. "Female Influence" 1846.
29. Ibid.

30. Rian 1982, 49.
31. Davis 1987, 8–9.
32. Hoagland 1982, 154.
33. Ibid., 155.
34. Rubin 1987, 195.
35. Rubin 1984, 278.
36. Rubin 1987, 215.
37. Hoagland 1988, 70.
38. Ibid., 100.
39. Ibid., 51.
40. Rubin 1987, 217.
41. Ibid.
42. Bar On 1982, 80.
43. Butler 1982, 172.
44. Rubin 1987, 223.
45. Rubin 2004.
46. Morgan 1977, 237 (emphasis in original).
47. Ibid.
48. Davis 1987, 11.
49. B. Rose 1987, 14.
50. Bailey 1987, 21.
51. Hopkins 1994, 126.
52. Zerilli 2005, 129.
53. Ibid., 9.
54. Wolin 2004, 18, 19.
55. Rubin 1987, 226–227.

CHAPTER 5

1. Tocqueville 1988, II:585.
2. Ibid., II:589.
3. Ibid., II:603.
4. Etzioni 1996, 60.
5. Ibid., 64.
6. Ibid., 67–68, 71–72.
7. Ibid., 69.
8. MacIntyre 1981, 256.
9. Tocqueville 1988, II:611.
10. Ibid., II:692.
11. Ibid., I:254.
12. Ibid., App. I:732.
13. Ibid., II:593–594.
14. Ibid., II:593.
15. Pierson 1996, 245.

16. Tocqueville 1988, II:622.
17. Ibid., II:603.
18. Ibid., App. I:732.
19. Ibid., II:591.
20. Ibid., II:592.
21. Ibid., II:623.
22. Ibid., II:617.
23. Ibid., II:626.
24. Ibid., I:189.
25. Ibid., I:285.
26. Ibid., II:527.
27. Ibid., I:220–221.
28. Ibid., App. I:733.
29. Ibid., 732.
30. Ibid., I:291.
31. Ibid., I:291, 292.
32. Ibid., I:287.
33. Ibid., I:278, n1.
34. Ibid., II:590.
35. Ibid., II:622.
36. Etzioni 1996, 73.
37. Aristotle 1995, 36.
38. MacIntyre 1981, 32.
39. Ibid.
40. Ibid., 222.
41. Ibid., 187.
42. Elizabeth Frazer and Nicola Lacey (1994, 279–280) echo the need for MacIntyre to address power if his work hopes to correct the deficiencies that he identifies in the liberal tradition.
43. Etzioni 1996, xvii, xviii, xix.
44. Galston 1991, 11.
45. Ibid., 289.
46. Galston 1995, 57.
47. Iris Marion Young (1995) powerfully critiques Galston's narrow view of the family as denying the very liberal pluralism for which he advocates.
48. Tocqueville 1988, II:611.
49. Ibid., 694.
50. Shklar 1984, 249.

CHAPTER 6

1. Heymann 2002.
2. Rosen 2007.

3. Quoted in Tronto 1993, 103 (emphasis in original).

4. Sevenhuijsen 1998, 25.

5. Held 2006, 19.

6. Tronto 1993, 161.

7. Ibid., 127–137.

8. Dan Engster (2001) similarly argues for placing Wollstonecraft in dialogue with care ethics, but for the different purpose of resolving the justice-care debate.

9. Hunt-Botting and Carey 2004, 708.

10. Wollstonecraft 1995, 219.

11. Ibid., 281.

12. Ibid., 281–282.

13. Ibid., 270.

14. Ibid., 229.

15. Ibid., 211.

16. Ibid., 207.

17. Ibid.

18. Ibid., 79.

19. Ibid.

20. Ibid., 82.

21. Ibid., 124.

22. Ibid., 214–215.

23. Noddings 1984, 4.

24. Ibid., 79–80.

25. Ibid., 130.

26. Ibid., 143–44.

27. Okin 1989, 15.

28. Tronto 1993, 138, 167.

29. Kittay 1999.

30. White 2000, especially chap. 4.

31. Held 2006, 71.

32. Noddings 1984, 42. Although in later work Noddings engages with harm and deviance, a systematic analysis of how virtue operates in tandem with vice remains outside the scope of her analysis (2002, chaps. 2 and 13).

33. Tronto 1993; Sevenhuijsen 1998; West 1997.

34. Ruddick 1980, 353.

35. Ruddick 1989, xx.

36. Ibid., 73.

37. Ibid., 74.

38. Ibid., 120.

39. Ibid., 118, 119.

40. White 2000, chap. 1.

41. Ibid., chap. 7.

42. Ruddick 1989, 25.

43. Tronto 1993, 142.
44. Sevenhuijsen 1998, 15.
45. White 2000, chap. 6.
46. Engster 2005, 52.
47. Joint United Nations Programme on HIV/AIDS and World Health Organization 2010.
48. World Health Organization 2010.
49. United Nations Women 2011.
50. Engster 2005, 54–55.
51. Pateman 1988.
52. Levy 2005.

CONCLUSION

1. Cannon 1988, 76.
2. Collins 1991, 11.
3. hooks 1984.
4. Ackelsberg and Shanley 1996, chap. 11.
5. Anzaldúa 2007, 25.
6. Ibid., 25.
7. Ibid., 25.
8. Ibid., 60–61.
9. Arendt (1968) 2003, 149.
10. Ibid., 153.
11. Ibid., 149.
12. Quoted in Tronto 1993, 103 (emphasis in original).
13. Olson 1971.

References

Abbot, Philip. 1991. *Political Thought in America: Conversations and Debates.* Itasca, IL: F. E. Peacock.

Ackelsberg, Martha A. 2010. *Resisting Citizenship: Feminist Essays on Politics, Community, and Democracy.* New York: Routledge.

Ackelsberg, Martha, and Mary Lyndon Shanley. 1996. "Privacy, Publicity, and Power: A Feminist Rethinking of the Public-Private Distinction." In *Revisioning the Political: Feminist Reconstructions of Traditional Concepts in Western Political Theory,* edited by Nancy J. Hirschmann and Christine Di Stefano, 213–234. Boulder, CO: Westview Press.

Advocates for Youth and SIECUS. 2001. *Toward a Sexually Healthy America: Roadblocks Imposed by the Federal Government's Abstinence-Only-Until-Marriage Education Program.* Washington, DC, and New York: Advocates for Youth and SIECUS.

Alcoff, Linda. 1997. "Cultural Feminism versus Post-Structuralism: The Identity Crisis in Feminist Theory." In *The Second Wave: A Reader in Feminist Theory,* edited by Linda Nicholson, 330–355. New York: Routledge.

Amatniek, Kathie. 1968. "Funeral Oration for the Burial of Traditional Womanhood." In *Notes from the First Year.* Documents from the Women's Liberation Movement, Online Archival Collection. Special Collections Library, Duke University, Durham, NC. Available at http://scriptorium.lib.duke.edu/wlm/notes/.

Anzaldúa, Gloria. 2007. *Borderlands/La Frontera: The New Mestiza.* San Francisco: Aunt Lute Books.

Arendt, Hannah. (1968) 2003. "Collective Responsibility." In *Responsibility and Judgment*, edited by Jerome Kohn, 147–158. New York: Schocken Books.

Aristotle. 1995. *The Politics*. Translated by Ernest Barker. New York: Oxford University Press.

Badgley, Anne M., and Carrie Musselman. 2004. *Heritage Keepers: Abstinence Education Teacher Manual I*. Charleston, SC: Heritage Community Services.

Bagley, Sarah. 1845. "Report of Female Labour Reform." *Voice of Industry*, June 12.

———. 1846a. "The Female Department." *Voice of Industry*, January 9.

———. 1846b. "Lowell Offering." *Voice of Industry*, January 2.

———. 1846c. "To the Editor of the Voice, and Ourself." *Voice of Industry*, May 15.

Bailey, Crystal. 1987. "How Many More?" In *Coming to Power: Writings and Graphics on Lesbian S/M*, edited by members of Samois, 21–28. Boston: Alyson.

Ball, Terence, James Farr, and Russell L. Hanson, eds. 1989. *Political Innovation and Conceptual Change*. New York: Cambridge University Press.

Bar On, Bat-Ami. 1982. "Feminism and Sadomasochism: Self-Critical Notes." In *Against Sadomasochism: A Radical Feminist Analysis*, edited by Robin Ruth Linden, Darlene R. Pagano, Diana E. H. Russell, and Susan Leigh Star, 72–82. San Francisco: Frog in the Well.

Benn, LeAnna, and Alfred J. Derby. 1999. *Maturing in Body and Character*. Spokane, WA: Teen-Aid.

Bennett, John. 1818. *Letters to a Young Lady, on a Variety of Useful and Interesting Subjects*. 7th American ed. Philadelphia: William Fry.

Berkowitz, Peter. 1999. *Virtue and the Making of Modern Liberalism*. Princeton, NJ: Princeton University Press.

Boryczka, Jocelyn M. 2009a. "The Separate Spheres Paradox: Habitual Inattention and Democratic Citizenship." In *Feminist Interpretations of Alexis de Tocqueville*, edited by J. Locke and E. Hunt-Botting, 281–304. University Park: Pennsylvania State University Press.

———. 2009b. "Whose Responsibility? The Politics of Sex Education Policy in the United States." *Politics and Gender* 5 (June): 1–26.

———. 2006. "The Virtues of Vice: The Lowell Mill Girl Debate and Contemporary Feminist Ethics." *Feminist Theory: An International Interdisciplinary Journal* 7, no. 1 (April): 49–68.

Cannon, Katie. 1988. *Black Womanist Ethics*. Atlanta, GA: Scholars Press.

Card, Claudia. 1997. "Gender and Moral Luck." In *Feminist Social Thought: A Reader*, edited by Diana Tietjens Meyers, 646–663. New York: Routledge.

Collins, Patricia Hill. 1991. *Black Feminist Thought: Knowledge, Consciousness, and the Politics of Empowerment*. New York: Routledge.

Connolly, William. 1993. *The Terms of Political Discourse*. Princeton, NJ: Princeton University Press.

"Correspondence." 1846. *Voice of Industry*, November 13.

Cott, Nancy, ed. 1972. "Church Trial of Mistress Ann Hibbens." In *Root of Bitterness: Documents of the Social History of American Women*, 47–58. New York: E. P. Dutton.

Daly, Mary. 1968. *The Church and the Second Sex*. Boston: Beacon Press.

———. 1978. *Gyn/Ecology: The Metaethics of Radical Feminism*. Boston: Beacon Press.

———. 1984. *Pure Lust: Elemental Feminist Philosophy*. Boston: Beacon Press.

Darroch, Jacqueline E., Jennifer J. Frost, Susheela Singh, and the Study Team. 2001. *Teenage Sexual and Reproductive Behavior in Developed Countries: Can More Progress Be Made?* Occasional Report No. 3 (November). New York: Alan Guttmacher Institute.

Davis, Katherine. 1987. "Introduction: What We Fear We Try to Keep Contained." In *Coming to Power: Writings and Graphics on Lesbian S/M*, edited by members of Samois, 7–13. Boston: Alyson.

Dietz, Mary. 2002. *Turning Operations: Feminism, Arendt, and Politics*. New York: Routledge.

Dublin, Thomas. 1979. *Women at Work: The Transformation of Work and Community in Lowell, Massachusetts, 1826–1860*. New York: Columbia University Press.

Elshtain, Jean Bethke. 1981. *Public Man, Private Woman: Women in Social and Political Thought*. Princeton, NJ: Princeton University Press.

English, Deirdre, and Barbara Ehrenreich. 1973. *Witches, Midwives, and Nurses: A History of Women Healers*. New York: Feminist Press.

———. 1978. *For Her Own Good: 150 Years of Experts' Advice to Women*. New York: Feminist Press.

Engster, Daniel. 2001. "Mary Wollstonecraft's Nurturing Liberalism: Between an Ethic of Justice and Care." *American Political Science Review* 95, no. 3 (September): 577–588.

———. 2005. "Rethinking Care Theory: The Practice of Caring and the Obligation to Care." *Hypatia* 20, no. 3 (Summer): 50–74.

Etzioni, Amatai. 1996. *The New Golden Rule: Community and Morality in a Democratic Society*. New York: Basic Books.

Faludi, Susan. 1991. *Backlash: The Undeclared War against Women*. New York: Doubleday.

Farley, Harriet. 1843. "Editorial by Harriet Farley." *Lowell Offering and Magazine*, 3rd vol., October 1842–September 1843, 48, 239, 282, 284. Lowell, MA: William Schouler.

———. 1844. "Editorial." *Lowell Offering*, 4th vol., November 1843–October 1844. Lowell, MA: Misses Curtis and Farley.

———. 1845. "Editorial." *Lowell Offering*, 5th vol., 263, 264, 279, 280, 281, 284. Lowell, MA: Misses Curtis and Farley.

Farr, James. 1989. "Understanding Conceptual Change Politically." In *Political Innovation and Conceptual Change*, edited by Terence Ball, James Farr, and Russell L. Hanson, 24–49. New York: Cambridge University Press.

"Female Influence." 1846. *Voice of Industry*, September 11.

Finer, Lawrence. 2007. "Trends in Premarital Sex in the United States, 1954–2003." *Public Health Reports* 122, no. 1 (January/February): 73–78.

Firestone, Shulamith. 1968. "The Jeanette Rankin Brigade: Woman Power?" In *Notes from the First Year*. Documents from the Women's Liberation Movement, Online Archival Collection. Special Collections Library, Duke University, Durham, NC. Available at http://scriptorium.lib.duke.edu/wlm/notes/.

Focus on the Family. 1999. *No Apologies: A Character-Building Abstinence-Based Program*. Colorado Springs, CO: Focus on the Family Educational Resources.

Fordyce, James. 1814. *Sermons to Young Women*. 14th ed. London.

Frainie, Kris. 2002. *Why kNOw? Abstinence Education Programs. Curriculum for Sixth Grade through High School Teacher's Manual*. Chattanooga, TN: Why kNOw? Abstinence Education Programs.

Frazer, Elizabeth, and Nicola Lacey. 1994. "MacIntyre, Feminism, and the Concept of Practice." In *After MacIntyre: Critical Perspectives on the Work of Alasdair MacIntyre*, edited by John Horton and Susan Mendus, 265–282. Notre Dame, IN: University of Notre Dame Press.

Gallie, W. B. 1962. "Essentially Contested Concepts." In *The Importance of Language*, edited by Max Black, 121–146. Englewood, NJ: Prentice Hall.

Galston, William. 1991. *Liberal Purposes: Goods, Virtues, and Diversity in the Liberal State*. New York: Cambridge University Press.

———. 1995. "Liberal Virtues and the Formation of Civic Character." In *Seedbeds of Virtue: Sources of Competence, Character, and Citizenship in American Society*, edited by Mary Ann Glendon and David Blankenhorn, 35–60. New York: Madison Books.

———. 2002. *Liberal Pluralism: The Implications of Value Pluralism for Political Theory and Practice*. New York: Cambridge University Press.

Generations of Light. 2007. "The Pledge." Available at http://www.generationsof light.com/html/thepledge.html.

Gilligan, Carol. 1982. *In a Different Voice: Psychological Theory and Women's Development*. Cambridge, MA: Harvard University Press.

Glendon, Mary Ann. 1991. *Rights Talk: The Impoverishment of Political Discourse*. New York: Free Press.

Glendon, Mary Ann, and David Blankenhorn, eds. 1995. *Seedbeds of Virtue: Sources of Competence, Character, and Citizenship in American Society*. New York: Madison Books.

Guttmacher Institute. 2012. "Facts on American Teens' Sources of Information about Sex." Available at http://www.guttmacher.org/pubs/FB-Teen-Sex-Ed .html.

Held, Virginia. 2006. *The Ethics of Care: Personal, Political, and Global*. New York: Oxford University Press.

Heymann, Jody. 2002. "Can Working Families Ever Win?" *Boston Review* 27, no. 1 (February/March): 4–13.

Himmelfarb, Gertrude. 1995. *The De-moralization of Society: From Victorian Virtues to Modern Values*. London: IEA Health and Welfare Unit.

———. 2001. *One Nation, Two Cultures: A Searching Examination of American Society in the Aftermath of Our Cultural Revolution*. New York: Vintage Books.

Hirschmann, Nancy, and Christine Di Stefano, eds. 1996. *Revisioning the Political: Feminist Reconstructions of Traditional Concepts*. Boulder, CO: Westview Press.

Hoagland, Sarah. 1982. "Sadism, Masochism, and Lesbian-Feminism." In *Against Sadomasochism: A Radical Feminist Analysis*, edited by Robin Ruth Linden, Darlene R. Pagano, Diana E. H. Russell, and Susan Leigh Star, 153–161. San Francisco: Frog in the Well.

———. 1988. *Lesbian Ethics: Toward New Values*. Palo Alto, CA: Institute of Lesbian Studies.

Hoagland, Sarah, and Marilyn Frye, eds. 2000. *Feminist Interpretations of Mary Daly*. University Park: Pennsylvania State University Press.

Honig, Bonnie. 1993. *Political Theory and the Displacement of Politics*. Ithaca, NY: Cornell University Press.

hooks, bell. 1984. *Feminist Theory: From Margin to Center*. Boston: South End Press.

Hopkins, Patrick D. 1994. "Rethinking Sadomasochism: Feminism, Interpretation, and Simulation." *Hypatia* 9, no. 1 (Winter): 116–141.

Hunt-Botting, Eileen. 2009. "A Family Resemblance: Tocqueville and Wollstonecraftian Protofeminism." In *Feminist Interpretations of Alexis de Tocqueville*, edited by Jill Locke and Eileen Hunt-Botting, 99–124. University Park: Pennsylvania State University Press.

Hunt-Botting, Eileen, and Christine Carey. 2004. "Wollstonecraft's Philosophical Impact on Nineteenth-Century American Women's Rights Advocates." *American Journal of Political Science* 48, no. 4 (October): 707–722.

Hunter-Geboy, Carol. 1995. *Life Planning Education Manual: A Youth Development Program*. Washington, DC: Advocates for Youth. Available at http://www.advocatesforyouth.org/publications/lpe/index.htm.

Janara, Laura. 2002. *Democracy Growing Up: Authority, Autonomy, and Passion in Tocqueville's Democracy in America*. Albany: State University of New York Press.

Joint United Nations Programme on HIV/AIDS and World Health Organization. 2010. "Global Report Fact Sheet: The Global AIDS Epidemic." Available at http://www.unaids.org/en/media/unaids/contentassets/documents/factsheet/2010/20101123_FS_Global_em_en.pdf.

Kamensky, Jane. 1998. "Female Speech and Other Demons: Witchcraft and Wordcraft in Early New England." In *Spellbound: Women and Witchcraft in America*, edited by Elizabeth Reis, 25–52. Wilmington, DE: Scholarly Resources.

Kann, Mark. 1998. *A Republic of Men: The American Founders, Gendered Language, and Patriarchal Politics*. New York: New York University Press.

Karlsen, Carol. 1998. *The Devil in the Shape of a Woman: Witchcraft in Colonial New England*. New York: W. W. Norton.

Kempner, Martha E. 2001. *Toward a Sexually Healthy America: Abstinence-Only-Until-Marriage Programs That Try to Keep Our Youth "Scared Chaste."* New York: SIECUS.

Kerber, Linda. 1980. *Women of the Republic: Intellect and Ideology in Revolutionary America.* Chapel Hill: University of North Carolina Press.

Kittay, Eva Feder. 1999. *Love's Labor: Essays on Women, Equality and Dependency.* New York: Routledge.

Kramer, Heinrich, and James Sprenger. 1971. *The Malleus Maleficarum.* New York: Dover.

Levin, David, ed. 1960. *What Happened in Salem?* 2nd ed. New York: Harcourt, Brace.

Levy, Traci. 2005. "At the Intersection of Intimacy and Care: Redefining 'Family' through the Lens of a Public Ethic of Care." *Politics and Gender* 1, no. 1 (March): 65–96.

LifeWay. n.d. "True Love Waits." Available at http://www.lifeway.com/Article/true-love-waits.

Lister, Ruth. 2003. *Citizenship: Feminist Perspectives.* New York: New York University Press.

Lorde, Audre. 1984. "An Open Letter to Mary Daly." In *Sister Outsider: Essays and Speeches,* 66–71. Freedom, CA: Crossing Press.

Macedo, Stephen. 1990. *Liberal Virtues: Citizenship, Virtue, and Community in Liberal Constitutionalism.* New York: Oxford University Press.

MacIntyre, Alasdair. 1981. *After Virtue.* Notre Dame, IN: University of Notre Dame Press.

Mandeville, Bernard. 1997. *The Fable of the Bees and Other Writings.* Edited by E. J. Hundert. Indianapolis, IN: Hackett.

Marshall, T. H. 1992. *Citizenship and Social Class.* London: Pluto Press.

Martha. 1846. "The Rights of Women." *Voice of Industry,* May 8.

Martin, Shannan, Robert Rector, and Melissa G. Pardue. 2004. *Comprehensive Sex Education vs. Authentic Abstinence: A Study of Competing Curricula.* Washington, DC: Heritage Foundation.

Mather, Cotton. 1691. *Ornaments for the Daughters of Zion.* Cambridge, MA: Printed by S. G. and B. G. [Samuel and Bartholomew Green] for Samuel Phillips at Boston.

———. (1692) 1974. *On Witchcraft: Being the Wonders of the Invisible World.* Reprint, New York: Bell.

———. 1705. *Nicetas; Or, Temptations to Sin, and Particularly to the SIN wherewith Youth Is Most Usually and Easily Ensnared; Well Answered and Conquered, in a Sermon, Directing and Engaging Young People to the Resolutions of EARLY PIETY.* Boston: Timothy Green.

———. 1713. *Tabitha Rediviva: An Essay to Describe and Commend the Good Works of a Vertuous Woman; Who Therein Approves Her Self a Real DISCIPLE OF AN Holy SAVIOUR. With Some Justice Done to the MEMORY of That Religious and Honorable*

GENTLEWOMAN, *Mrs. Elizabeth Hutchinson. Who Expired, 3 d. 12 m. 1712, 13.* Boston: J. Allen.

———. 1722. *Bethiah: The Glory Which Adorns the Daughters of God, and the Piety, wherewith ZION Wishes to See His DAUGHTERS Glorious.* Boston: Printed by Franklin for Gerrish.

Montesquieu, Charles de Secondat. 1989. *The Spirit of the Laws.* Edited by Anne M. Cohler, Basia Carolyn Miller, and Harold Samuel Stone. New York: Cambridge University Press.

Morgan, Robin. 1977. *Going Too Far: The Personal Chronicle of a Feminist.* New York: Random House.

Moser, Charles, and Peggy J. Kleinplatz. 2006. "Introduction: The State of Our Knowledge on SM." In *Sadomasochism: Powerful Pleasures,* edited by Peggy J. Kleinplatz and Charles Moser, 7–16. Binghamton, NY: Harrington Park Press.

Murray, Judith Sargent. 1995. *Selected Writings of Judith Sargent Murray.* Edited by Sharon M. Harris. New York: Oxford University Press.

Narayan, Uma. 1997. *Dislocating Cultures: Identities, Traditions, and Third World Feminism.* New York: Routledge.

Noddings, Nel. 1984. *Caring: A Feminine Approach to Ethics and Moral Education.* Berkeley: University of California Press.

———. 2002. *Starting at Home: Caring and Social Policy.* Berkeley: University of California Press.

Norton, Mary Beth. 1980. *Liberty's Daughters: The Revolutionary Experience of American Women, 1750–1800.* Ithaca, NY: Cornell University Press.

———. 1984. "The Evolution of White Women's Experience in Early America." *American Historical Review* 89, no. 3 (June): 593–619.

———. 2002. *In the Devil's Snare: The Salem Witchcraft Crisis of 1692.* New York: Alfred A. Knopf.

Okin, Susan Moller. 1979. *Women in Western Political Thought.* Princeton, NJ: Princeton University Press.

———. 1982. "Women and the Making of the Sentimental Family." *Philosophy and Public Affairs* 11:65–88.

———. 1989. *Justice, Gender, and the Family.* New York: Basic Books.

Olson, Mancur. 1971. *The Logic of Collective Action: Public Goods and the Theory of Groups.* Cambridge, MA: Harvard University Press.

Pateman, Carole. 1988. *The Sexual Contract.* Stanford, CA: Stanford University Press.

Phillips, Anne. 1993. *Democracy and Difference.* Cambridge, UK: Polity.

Pierson, George Wilson. 1996. *Tocqueville in America.* Baltimore: Johns Hopkins University Press.

Pioneer, Lynn. 1847. "Rights of Married Women." *Voice of Industry,* August 14.

Pitkin, Hanna Fenichel. 1972. *Wittgenstein and Justice: On the Significance of Ludwig Wittgenstein for Social and Political Thought.* Berkeley: University of California Press.

———. 1999. *Fortune Is a Woman: Gender and Politics in the Thought of Niccolò Machiavelli.* Chicago: University of Chicago Press.

Planned Parenthood Federation of America. 2004–2005a. "#7: Sexuality Stereotypes."

———. 2004–2005b. "Healthy Sexuality."

Plante, Rebecca F. 2006. "Sexual Spanking, the Self, and the Construction of Deviance." In *Sadomasochism: Powerful Pleasures*, edited by Peggy J. Kleinplatz and Charles Moser, 59–80. Binghamton, NY: Harrington Park Press.

Plumwood, Val. 1993. *Feminism and the Mastery of Nature.* New York: Routledge.

Pocock, J.G.A. 1975. *The Machiavellian Moment: Florentine Political Thought and the Atlantic Republican Tradition.* Princeton, NJ: Princeton University Press.

Rawls, John. 1971. *A Theory of Justice.* Cambridge, MA: Belknap Press.

Rian, Karen. 1982. "Sadomasochism and the Social Construction of Desire." In *Against Sadomasochism: A Radical Feminist Analysis*, edited by Robin Ruth Linden, Darlene R. Pagano, Diana E. H. Russell, and Susan Leigh Star, 45–50. San Francisco: Frog in the Well.

Richardson, Diane. 2000. "Constructing Sexual Citizenship: Theorizing Sexual Rights." *Critical Social Policy* 20 (1): 105–135.

Rose, Barbara. 1987. "Reasons." In *Coming to Power: Writings and Graphics on Lesbian S/M*, edited by members of Samois, 14–16. Boston: Alyson.

Rose, Susan. 2005. "Going Too Far? Sex, Sin, and Social Policy." *Social Forces* 84 (December): 1207–1232.

Rosen, Ruth. 2007. "The Care Crisis." *The Nation*, February 27. Available at http://www.thenation.com/print/article/care-crisis.

Rowe, Aimee Carrillo. 2008. *Power Lines: On the Subject of Feminist Alliances.* Durham, NC: Duke University Press.

Rubin, Gayle. 1987. "The Leather Menace: Comments on Politics and S/M." In *Coming to Power: Writings and Graphics on Lesbian S/M*, edited by members of Samois, 194–229. Boston: Alyson.

———. 1984. "Thinking Sex: Notes for a Radical Theory of the Politics of Sexuality." In *Pleasure and Danger: Exploring Female Sexuality*, edited by Carol S. Vance, 267–319. Boston: Routledge.

———. 2004. "Samois." *Leather Times* (Spring): 3–7. Available at http://www.leatherarchives.org/resources/issue21.pdf.

Ruddick, Sara. 1980. "Maternal Thinking." *Feminist Studies* 6, no. 2 (Summer): 342–367.

———. 1989. *Maternal Thinking: Towards a Politics of Peace.* Boston: Beacon Press.

Rush, Benjamin. 1965. *Essays on Education in the Early Republic.* Edited by Frederick Rudolph. Cambridge, MA: Belknap Press.

Ryan, Mary. 1983. *Womanhood in America: From Colonial Times to the Present.* New York: F. Watts.

Samois. 1987. *Coming to Power: Writings and Graphics on Lesbian S/M.* Boston: Alyson.

Sarvasy, Wendy. 1992. "Beyond the Difference versus Equality Policy Debate: Postsuffrage Feminism, Citizenship, and the Quest for the Feminist Welfare State." *Signs: Journal of Women in Culture and Society* 17 (21): 329–362.

———. 1997. "Social Citizenship from a Feminist Perspective." *Hypatia* 12, no. 4 (Fall): 54–73.

Saxonhouse, Arlene. 1991. "Aristotle: Defective Males, Hierarchy, and the Limits of Politics." In *Feminist Interpretations and Political Theory*, edited by Mary Lyndon Shanley and Carole Pateman, 32–52. University Park: Pennsylvania State University Press.

Saxton, Martha. 2003. *Being Good: Women's Moral Values in Early America*. New York: Hill and Wang.

Sevenhuijsen, Selma. 1998. *Citizenship and the Ethics of Care: Feminist Considerations of Justice, Morality, and Politics*. New York: Routledge.

Shallitt, Wendy. 1999. *A Return to Modesty: Discovering the Lost Virtue*. New York: Simon and Schuster.

Shklar, Judith. 1984. *Ordinary Vices*. Cambridge, MA: Belknap Press.

SIECUS. 2004. *Guidelines for Comprehensive Sexuality Education: Kindergarten through 12th Grade*. 3rd ed. New York: SIECUS.

———. 2009. "The Federal Government and Abstinence-Only-Until Marriage Programs." Available at http://www.communityactionkit.org/index.cfm?page Id=892.

———. 2010. "State by State Decisions: The Personal Responsibility Education Program and Title V Abstinence-Only Program." Available at http://www.siecus.org/index.cfm?fuseaction=Page.ViewPage&PageID=1272.

Singh, S., and J. Darroch. 2000. "Adolescent Pregnancy and Childbearing Levels and Trends in Developed Countries." *Family Planning Perspectives* 32:14–23.

Skocpol, Theda. 1992. *Protecting Soldiers and Mothers: The Political Origins of Social Policy in the United States*. Cambridge, MA: Belknap Press.

Snyder, R. Claire. 2004. "Radical Civic Virtue: Women in 19th-Century Civil Society." *New Political Science* 26, no. 1 (March): 51–69.

Sparks, Holloway. 1997. "Dissident Citizenship: Democratic Theory, Political Courage, and Activist Women." *Hypatia* 12, no. 4 (Fall): 54–110.

Sprint, John. 1709. *The Bride-Woman's Counsellor, Being a Sermon Preached at a Wedding at Sherbourn in Dorsetshire*. Rare Books Division, New York Public Library.

Stone, Huldah J. 1845. "Letter to the Operatives of Manchester." *Voice of Industry*, December 26.

———. 1846a. "Notice." *Voice of Industry*, January 9.

———. 1846b. "Our Cause." *Voice of Industry*, January 30.

"Text of Bush's State of the Union Speech." 2006. CNN, February 1. Available at http://articles.cnn.com/2006-01-31/politics/sotu.transcript_1_union-speech-misguided-idealism-president-bush-s-state?_s=PM:POLITICS.

Tocqueville, Alexis de. 1988. *Democracy in America*. Edited by J. P. Mayer. 2 vols. New York: Harper and Row.

Tronto, Joan. 1993. *Moral Boundaries: A Political Argument for an Ethic of Care.* New York: Routledge.

———. 2005. "Care as the Work of Citizens: A Modest Proposal." In *Women and Citizenship*, edited by Marilyn Friedman, 130–148. New York: Oxford University Press.

True Love Waits. 1999–2000. *Crossing Bridges with Purity.* Nashville, TN: Lifeway Press.

United Nations Women. 2011. "Facts and Figures on Violence against Women." Available at http://www.unifem.org/gender_issues/violence_against_women/facts_figures.php.

Ventura, Stephanie J., Joyce C. Abma, William D. Mosher, and Stanley K. Henshaw. 2006. "NCHS Health E-Stat: Recent Trends in Teenage Pregnancy in the United States, 1990–2002." Centers for Disease Control and Prevention. Available at http://www.cdc.gov/nchs/data/hestat/teenpreg1990-2002/teen preg1990-2002.htm.

Walker, Margaret Urban. 1998. *Moral Understandings: A Feminist Study in Ethics.* New York: Routledge.

Walzer, Michael. 1989. "Citizenship." In *Political Innovation and Conceptual Change*, edited by Terence Ball, James Farr, and Russell L. Hanson, 211–219. New York: Cambridge University Press.

West, Robin. 1997. *Caring for Justice.* New York: New York University Press.

White, Julie Anne. 2000. *Democracy, Justice, and the Welfare State: Reconstructing Public Care.* University Park: Pennsylvania State University Press.

Winthrop, John. 1992. "A Modell of Christian Charity." In *Political Thought in America: An Anthology.* 2nd ed. Edited by Michael B. Levy, 6–14. Prospect Heights, IL: Waveland Press.

Wolin, Sheldon S. 2001. *Tocqueville between Two Worlds: The Making of a Political and Theoretical Life.* Princeton, NJ: Princeton University Press.

———. 2004. *Politics and Vision: Continuity and Vision in Western Political Thought.* Princeton, NJ: Princeton University Press.

Wollstonecraft, Mary. 1995. *A Vindication of the Rights of Woman.* Edited by Sylvana Tomaselli. New York: Cambridge University Press.

World Health Organization. 2010. "Maternal Deaths Worldwide Drop by a Third." Available at http://www.who.int/mediacentre/news/releases/2010/maternal_mortality_20100915/en/index.html.

Young, Iris Marion. 1995. "Mothers, Citizenship, and Independence: A Critique of Pure Family Values." *Ethics* 105 (April): 535–556.

———. 2005. "The Logic of Masculinist Protection: Reflections on the Current Security State." In *Women and Citizenship*, edited by Marilyn Friedman, 15–34. New York: Oxford University Press.

Zerilli, Linda M. G. 2005. *Feminism and the Abyss of Freedom.* Chicago: University of Chicago Press.

Index

Jocelyn M. Boryczka is Associate Professor of Politics at Fairfield University.